ADVENTURES IN
LITHUANIAN GENEALOGY

Adventures in Lithuanian Genealogy

Lutkiewicz and Dowgwillo
Family Stories

Sheriene Saadati

Rev. date: 03/22/2021

To order additional copies of this book, contact:
Xlibris
844-714-8691
www.Xlibris.com
Orders@Xlibris.com
824397

Contents

DEDICATION

This book is dedicated to Grandpa Charles and Grandma Eva Lucas' grandchildren who have joined them in heaven: my mom, Charliene Lucas Saadati (1942-2013), and my cousin, Tom Lucas (1957-2020).

PREFACE

I had nearly thought I was done researching my Lithuanian family when I learned from a fellow genealogist about the possibility of new records in St. Petersburg, Russia. Apparently, when Russia occupied Lithuania and required nobles to "prove" their nobility by submitting legally recognized documents, these records were sent to St. Petersburg for review. Many of the files survived.

Once I requested the records from a researcher in Russia, I received two files—one for the Lutkiewicz (Polish version) or Liutkevičius (Lithuanian version) family, and the other for the Dowgwillo (Polish version) or Daugvila (Lithuanian version) family. I wanted to learn more about both my 2nd great-grandfather's (Antoni/Antanas Lutkiewicz) parents—Adolf Lutkiewicz and Barbara Dowgwillo. While growing up, I heard a lot about Grandpa Kazimierz/Charles' parents, Antoni Lutkiewicz and Barbara Stankiewicz, but not very much about his grandfather, Adolf Lutkiewicz, or grandmother, Barbara Dowgwillo.

The Lutkiewicz file had about 240 documents that included family trees, baptism records from various Roman Catholic churches, census records, and a will. The file also referred to other records, such as receipts for land sales or acquisitions, but these were no longer part of the file. It appears that the last use of this file was so that a Józef Lutkiewicz (born in 1883) could prove he had legitimate noble status and not get conscripted into the Russian military!

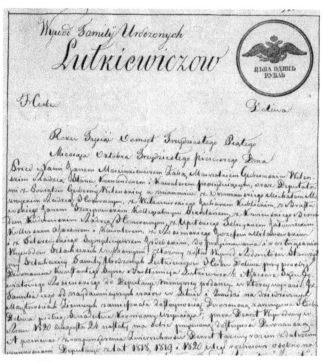

A Fragment of 1835 Lutkiewicz Nobility Document

Although there were records for my direct family line, most of the records were for my extended family. For example, Józef Lutkiewicz was an 8th cousin, four times removed from me. In an interesting coincidence, he left Lithuania and immigrated to Philadelphia, Pennsylvania between 1905 and 1908. This was around the same time my great-grandfather, Kazimierz Lutkiewicz (Charles Lucas), and his sister, Valeria, arrived in Canada.

The Dowgwillo file included about 500 documents—much more complete compared to the Lutkiewicz file. It had family trees and the actual translated wills, gifting documents and sales documents, all in Russian per the Czarist government's requirements.

A Fragment of Dowgwillo Nobility File Cover Sheet

However, it took me a while to know what was actually in the file because most of the records were in pre-revolution handwritten Russian or in handwritten Polish, and I had a hard time finding anyone capable—or who had the time—to translate it.

Fortunately, Roman Sakowicz, a fellow volunteer genealogist helped me to translate most of them. He taught me how to read or at least recognize names in Latin, Russian, and Polish so I could use the documents from St. Petersburg to find the original parish baptism, marriage, and death records myself and then he translated the bulk of the records. Most of the translations are in the Polish version, since that was the language in which the bulk of the records were written, and I wanted to retain linguistic consistency.

To find original parish records, one needs to know the individual's name, date of an event, and parish name; and, depending on the time period corresponding to the record, it's necessary to translate the records from either Latin, Polish, or Russian. None of these records are indexed, so I dedicated hours of my own time going through these extensive files. Throughout this process, I grew cognizant, and incredibly appreciative for:

- Vaccines—I read pages and pages of records of children who died under the age of five from easily preventable diseases like whooping cough and measles. This was very typical of the time.
- Antibiotics—I read through pages of death records of whole families that died from tuberculosis and typhoid. Antibiotics have made these diseases that were once death sentences much more treatable.
- Pre- and post-natal care—I read through pages and pages of records of women that died during or right after childbirth. Grandma Eva's mother, Kotryna, died within six weeks of her last child being born. Grandpa Charles' great-grandmother, Barbara Mieczyńska, and great-great-aunt, Konstancia Dowgwillo, both died in childbirth. This was also very typical of the time.
- Literacy—I read through pages of documents that indicated the person in the record was illiterate. They could not do what I was doing to find them. I also appreciated the fact that so many of my relatives came to the United States not speaking, reading or writing English. I have a hard time reading names and dates on documents in Latin, Polish and Russian. I can't imagine moving to a new country and having to learn how to read, write and speak all over again.

Within a few weeks of receiving and translating a portion of the Lutkiewicz file from St. Petersburg, I was contacted by a Lutkiewicz cousin through a Facebook Lithuanian genealogy site. It turned out that Orinta was the granddaughter of my second great-aunt, Marytė Liutkute, and the sister of my great-grandfather, Kazimierz. Although I knew of Marytė's existence, I had no idea if she was alive. All contact had been lost with her when Valeria, Marytė's sister, and my other second great-aunt passed away in 1985.

Orinta arranged to meet me and my kids in Lithuania, introduce us to family, and see the sites of our ancestors' baptisms, marriages, and burials. This was the trip of a lifetime.

After coming back from Lithuania, I connected with 2 more Lithuanian cousins! First, I was contacted by Darius Kucinkas, who found me through 23andMe. He is the great grandson of Ona Lutkiewicz and Alfonsas Valiuškevičius. This was my 2nd great grandfather's (Antoni/Antanas Lutkiewicz) sister and husband. Then, I found Germante Razanauskaite through Geni.com. She is the great-granddaughter of Konstantinas Duoba, my great-grandmother Eva's half-brother. Without all the records from Lithuania, I would not have known exactly how we were related!

Through my research on my Dowgwillo ancestors, I connected with Zbigniew Dowgwillo, a distant cousin that has a website about the Dowgwillo family history going back to the 16th century. Whenever either of us finds something, he adds it to his website: https://dowgwillo.nl/ Drzewo_1/Linia%20laudanska_tablica.html.

I also had DNA matches with people that were descendants from common ancestors in Lithuania. By using the records from St. Petersburg, Ancestry.com, and https://www.epaveldas.lt— a Lithuanian record site—I have been able to piece together the journeys of several ancestors that left Lithuania in the early 1900s and find out exactly how I'm related to some of my DNA matches.

Through many records and conversations, I became more and more fascinated with how my Lithuanian ancestors came to America, how they transitioned to life in America and how the life they left was so different from those who stayed behind. This book is just a series of stories of ancestors that I could find information about, beyond birth and death records. The first story is of my most direct ancestor, Adolf Lutkiewicz, my 3rd great grandfather. The others are of my more extended Lutkiewicz and Dowgwillo family members.

CHAPTER ONE

Adolf Lutkiewicz

Adolf Mateusz Lutkiewicz was born on September 21, 1820 on the Wolmontowicz Manor Estate in Baisogala Parish to nobles Tomasz Lutkiewicz and Barbara Mieczyniska. He was baptized on the same day in the Pociūnėliai (Lithuanian), or Pacunele (Polish), Parish. His godparents were Jan Dowgwillo and Wiktoria, the spouse of noble Józef Mieczyński. Adolf's family nobility went back to the 16th century, and his family crest was "Doliwa." Adolf was my 3rd great-grandfather.

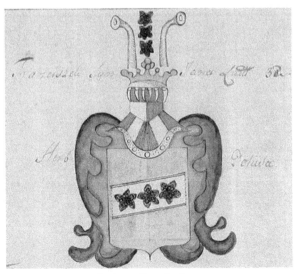

Doliwa Family Crest

The Lutkiewicz nobility status at this time was defined on baptismal records as "Generosus Dominus," or simply GD, which means "well-born lord" and indicates a lower class of gentry. This meant that the noble person did not own a significant size of property, did not hold high office position, and wasn't from a politically influential family. Most nobles at this level had a small estate.

There were three levels of nobility above the GD level:

- PMD or Patronus Magnificus Dominus: had high economic status, family had the same status for several generations, owned significant amount of land, had political, cultural, and economic influence, and may have held high office position. This level influenced the use of the Polish language and European customs as opposed to Russian customs.
- GMD or Generosus Magnificus Dominus: similar to PMD, only status was shared in one generation.
- MD or Magnificus Dominus: middle-class gentry, owned a large estate and land, had some political or economic influence, and culture, or held a state office position.[1]

One could lose noble status in various ways. Lithuanian families left all property to the eldest surviving son. Nobility status required ownership of property, making it possible for the other, younger sons in some families to lose their property, and hence, their nobility title. Although women could own and manage property and be born into a noble family, they could lose their status by marrying someone that was not of noble status. Only men could pass on noble status. After 1795, Czarist Russia took away land and noble status for not being able to prove that status through an expensive bureaucratic process or because someone chose the wrong side of a rebellion against Russia.[2]

Coming from a noble family, Adolf had certain rights and privileges. He did not fear being conscripted into the Russian army. Property was managed by his family and passed down to other family members, rather than managed and owned by the government. Other than that, his life was similar to peasant farmers that owned land. Even with his status as a noble, he was still required to work very hard to sustain a living.

Noble status also conferred a sense of identity: it was how you thought of yourself and how others thought of you and your family. Status was so important that it was noted on every baptism, marriage, and death record prior to the toppling of Czarist Russia. Although Adolf would not have been considered extremely wealthy, his family's long-standing nobility status would have earned him respect throughout his community. It's a hard concept to understand in the modern world.

The estate Adolf grew up on would have been comprised of a manor house, servant quarters, icehouses (a building that stored frozen pond ice collected in the winter and used over the summer before refrigeration), conservatories, cowsheds, stables, warehouses, worker cottages, mills, parks, ponds, distilleries/breweries, a chapel, extensive farmland, etc.

It has been estimated that Lithuania once had thousands of manors. The networks of these manors influenced the development of Lithuanian statehood, agriculture, economy, and spiritual culture in the years to come.

Unfortunately, not much is left of these estates today. When driving across Lithuania, you will see wide open fields, in the middle of which is occasionally a cluster of trees. A manor house previously would have stood in the middle of these trees. In some cases, the remnants of these houses are still there, and in other cases, someone has repurposed the house and maintained it in relatively good shape. Sadly, most of the time, there's nothing left but a few trees.

Adolf had six siblings:

- Konstanty Aleksander Lutkiewicz (1824-?) married Anna Markiewicz (1824-1899).
- Katarzyna Lutkiewicz (1826-?)
- Agniezka Lutkiewicz (1828-?)
- Syzmon Lutkiewicz (1832-?) married Paulina Mackiewicz (1838-1919).
- Elżbieta Lutkiewicz (1834-1840)
- Anna Lutkiewicz (1836-1845)

Unfortunately, his mother, Barbara, died on March 21, 1837 at the age of 35 during childbirth. Sadly, this was a common occurrence.

Adolf's father remarried to Franciszka Piesanko, and he had four half-siblings:

- Rozalia Lutkiewicz (1841-?) married Jan Styczkobier (1840-?).

- Jerzy Lutkiewicz (1844-1845)
- Julian Lutkiewicz (1847-1857)
- Aniela Lutkiewicz (1850-?)

Not much is known about Adolf's childhood. He did speak Russian, Lithuanian, and Polish. And, he must have heard stories about Lithuania's history from his father, Tomasz:

- The Grand Duchy of Lithuania was founded in the 13th century.
- Lithuania became the largest European state in the 15th century. Its borders included modern-day Lithuania, Belarus, Ukraine, and parts of Poland and Russia.
- In 1385, the Grand Duchy of Lithuania combined with Poland in the Union of Krewo. This made Catholicism the national religion, as opposed to Russian Orthodoxy, and created a cultural link to Europe.
- The Union of Lublin in 1569 created the Polish-Lithuanian Commonwealth that lasted until 1795. Writing from this time used Latin letters rather than Cyrillic script. Polish was the language of politics, spoken by nobles and used in church books.
- In 1764, Czarina Catherine the Great placed Stanisław August Poniatowski, on the Polish throne. He was both the King of Poland and the last monarch of the Polish-Lithuanian Commonwealth.
- In 1768, Catherine the Great formally became protector of the Polish-Lithuanian Commonwealth, which provoked an unsuccessful anti-Russian uprising in Poland (1768–72).
- In 1795, Russia, under Catherine the Great, completed the last partitions of the Polish-Lithuanian Commonwealth, erasing both Poland and Lithuania from the map. The Commonwealth became divided among Hapsburg Austria, Russia, and Prussia. Lithuania came under the control of Russia.
- In 1812, Napoleon and his armies marched across Lithuania to get to Moscow. This was during the reign of Alexander I. Lithuanian noblemen joined him to fight the Russians though there were repercussions for those who did.[3]

During 1830-1831, when Adolf was about 10 years old, there was a failed attempt to reestablish the Polish-Lithuanian Commonwealth known as the November Uprising. After that, Lithuania became known as the Northwestern Territory of Russia. Despite repression, Polish language schooling and cultural life were largely able to continue. However, the Czarist Russian Government confiscated many noble estates for their participation in this uprising. [4]

Adolf probably attended his siblings' weddings. His brother, Konstanty, married Anna Markiewicz before 1860. His brother, Syzmon, married Paulina Mackiewiez in 1861, and all three of their surviving children immigrated to the United States.

He would have also grown up around his father's siblings, as well as their spouses and children: Karolina (1798-1886) who married his mother's brother, Karol Mieczyński; Andrzej-Kazimierz (1787-1847); Petronella (1796-1884); Felicjan (1797-1863); and Wiktoria-Rajna (1805-?). He would have known aunts that died in childbirth and many cousins that died of whooping cough, measles, tuberculosis, and diarrhea before the age of five.

Adolf would have also grown up around his grandmother, Elżbieta Zacharzewska Lutkiewicz (born in 1761). She would have told him the story of how she married Szymon Lutkiewicz (born in 1755) around 1780, and how he had inherited Wołmontowicze (Polish) or Valmanciai (Lithuanian) Manor from his father, Andrej-Kazimierz Lutkiewicz, and mother, Rozalia Snarska. She would have shared how the property had been part of a dowry given to Andrew-Kazimierz by his in-laws— nobles Matas Snarskiai and Anna Pergarowska—when he married. She would have told him about life before Russia took complete control of Lithuania in 1795.

As a side note, Wołmontowicze is used as the setting for Henryk Sienkiewicz' historical fiction novel, *The Deluge*. If you want to get an idea of what life was like as a petty, noble family in the Lithuanian Commonwealth in the 16th and 17th centuries, it's worth a read. And, today you can take tours of the Wołmontowicze area and see ruins of the Lutkiewicz estate.

Grandmother Elżbieta and his father, Tomasz, would have shared how the Lutkiewicz family had been granted noble status in ancient times— long before Russian rule. They would have told him how, nine generations before him, Jan Ludkievicz was scribe in the Upytė court in 1586, and how the family was granted the family crest of Doliwa and nobility status for their military service.

They would have shared how the Lutkiewicz family had property in old noble settlements like Roszcze and Raisieniai, and how they had large estates that were passed down through many generations in Taujėnai, Paežeriai, and Jociniai in the Ukmergė region, as well as Pasiliai and Jurodgol in Upytė region. They would have also told him about how many of his ancestors served in the Polish-Lithuanian Commonwealth as attorneys, town notaries, judges, and other roles granting them social importance. They may have even shown him the Lutkiewicz and Dowgwillo family trees and the supporting documentation they had to submit to the Russian government in prior years to prove their noble status. He would have grown up proud to be part of this noble heritage.

Adolf was known for his wonderful singing ability. It's unknown if this helped encourage his future bride, Barbara Dowgwillo, to marry him. Barbara was the 24-year-old daughter of noble Antoni Dowgwillo and Ewa Rukujzo. Adolf and Barbara married on October 26, 1854 in Krekenava (Lithuanian), or Krakinów (Polish), Parish. The witnesses to their married were Heronin Markiewicz, January Wonsowicz, Antoni Dowgwillo (the bride's father), and Kaeton Wolski.

Abdank Family Crest

Barbara Dowgwillo's noble heritage went back to the 1600s and her family crest was "Abdank". Barbara's family had owned land and peasants in Towginajcie (Polish), or Tauginaičiai (Lithuanian), in a subdivision known as Gienie in Veliuona County since 1639. Her extended family had land in Wołmontowicze (Polish), or Valmanciai (Lithuanian), just like the Lutkiewicz family. Her father (Antoni Dowgwillo) participated in the 1830-1831 Uprising against Czarist Russia, and his property was confiscated and his noble status lost forever as a result. However, her uncles—Izydor and Ezachiel Leon Dowgwillo—kept their status. Izydor had grandchildren that immigrated to the United States.

Adolf and Barbara had the following children:

- Ewa Lutkiewicz (1861-?) married Mateusz Lutkiewicz in 1891. They had two children, Wilehmina (1892-?) and Kazimierz (1894-?). It's unclear how Mateusz was related.

- Scholastyka Lutkiewicz (1855-?) married Wincenty Adam Kruszynski on January 24, 1877 in Krekenava (Lithuanian) or Krakinów (Polish) Parish. She was 22, and he was 62. About two months later, they had a daughter, Leontyna, on March 17, 1877. Leontyna married Antoni Orłowski in 1910. Wincenty died before 1886, and Scholastyka remarried to Józef Wojszwiłło on February 23, 1886. He was 67 years old, and she was 31. On September 18, 1886, (about seven months later) they had a son, Tomasz Wojszwiłło. Józef died a few years later in 1892, leaving Scholastyka a widow for the second time at the age of 37.

- Antoni/Antanas Lutkiewicz (1857-1941) married Barbara Stankiewicz on February 23, 1886 in Krakės (Lithuanian), or Kroki (Polish), Parish. This is my 2nd great-grandfather.

- Ona/Anna Lutkiewicz (1871-1939) married Alfonsas Valiuškevičius in 1885 in Krekenava (Lithuanian), or Krakinów (Polish), Parish. He was a soldier that came home for the wedding. Her brother (Antoni Lutkiewicz) and his wife (Barbara) were among the witnesses. They had six children—Antanas, Jonas, Anelina, Juozapas, Pranciskus, Aleksandra, Jan (John) Valiuškevičius (Waleszkiewicz). Jan (John) immigrated to the United States.

- Józefa Lutkiewicz (1872-?) married Józef Lubin (1870-?) on January 21, 1892 in Krekenava (Lithuanian), or Krakinów (Polish) Parish. Józefa had the status of a burgher (middle class) and Józef of a peasant. They had the following children:
  ○ Marijona Lubin (1892-?). She married Władysław Szwiegżda in 1916. They had eight children: six

sons—Kazys, Feliksas, Zigmas, Stasys, Jonas, Vytautas—
and two daughters—Michalina and Vanda. Vytautas
married a woman named Maryte. Adolf's future
granddaughter, Marytė, grew up around these cousins.

o Antonina Lubin (1894-?)
o Michalina Lubin (1896-?)
o Krystyna Lubin (1904-1906)
o Marcin (1908-1911)
o Kazimierz Lubin (1912-1913)
o Anna Lubin (1915-1918)
o Helena Teresa Lubin (1916-1918)

- Joanna Lutkiewicz was born on April 1, 1875 in Józefów in
  Bejsagoła parish. Her godparents were nobles Julian Rymkiewicz
  and Anna, the wife of Konstanty Lutkiewicz (her father's brother's
  wife). Joanna died on May 25, 1877 from weakness. It's hard to
  know what she really died of, but this was common in that day.

In 1863, Adolf participated in the unsuccessful January Uprising (1863-
1864) against the Czarist Russian government that controlled Lithuania.
This was during the reign of Czar Alexander II. According to official
Russian information, 396 persons were executed and 18,672 were exiled
to Siberia. The government confiscated 1,660 estates in Poland and 1,794
in Lithuania. At this time, schools were forced to teach only in Russian. [5]

For his participation, Adolf lost his nobility status and his property.
This meant that his son's, Antoni, schooling was curtailed, and the whole
family adopted a different lifestyle. Antoni became subject to conscription
into the Russian army and had to work to buy his own farm. It is unclear
whether Adolf became an alcoholic before or after the uprising. But, at
some point, he turned to alcohol.

Adolf's wife, Barbara, died on December 15, 1898 in Guty from a
tumor at the age of 69, and Adolf never remarried. He died on April 14,
1916 in Montvidavas Village from old age. He was 86 years old.

Antoni/Antanas Lutkiewicz

Adolf and Barbara's son, Antoni/Antanas Lutkiewicz, was born June
25, 1857 in Bobiniškiai Manor during the reign of Czar Nicholas I and
baptized in Krekenava (Lithuanian), or Krakinów (Polish), Parish by

Reverand Leparski with all rites of the Sacrament. Antoni is the Polish version of his name and Antanas is the Lithuanian version. Since I grew up hearing him called Antoni, I will go with this version. His godparents were nobles Casimir Carženowicz and Mrs. Eufrozina Mieczyńska, the latter probably related to Antoni's grandmother, Barbara Mieczyńska.

Antoni's birth was a few months after the death of his father's younger brother, Julian, who died February 2, 1857 at the age of nine from diarrhea. Adolf and Barbara must have anxiously looked after Antoni, hoping and praying that he would make it to adulthood.

Antoni grew up with lots of aunts, uncles, first and second cousins, as well as extended family cousins. There were several branches of the Lutkiewicz family tree that stayed in relatively the same area over 300 years. The same could be said for his mother's family (Dowgwillo) and grandmother's family (Mieczyńska).

This is quite different than the way we think about family today. Antoni would have known his very distant cousins and the complex relationships within his family because people, for the most part, didn't move very far away from their parents. Antoni also would have heard stories about his family's noble heritage and the cost of participating in uprisings against the Russian government from his parents and his grandparents.

Antoni would have his own memories of a noble life because he would have visited his grandfather's (Tomasz) estate in Wołmontowicze (Polish), or Valmanciai (Lithuanian), his Great Aunt Karolina's estate—Manor Korejwiszki—and his other Great-Aunt Petronella's estate at Gaszczuny. Karolina and Petronella were the sisters of his grandfather, Tomasz. Antoni lived for a brief time on his father's estate in Bobiniškiai.

Antoni experienced living in a large wooden house that had decorative wood carvings on the exterior. It sat on a large parcel of land (over 60 hectares) where he would help servants sow and harvest crops like wheat and flax. He saw the flax spun into thread, made into fabric, and sewn into clothing by his mother and sisters.

He ate vegetables that were grown in a small garden outside his house and saw flowers decorating the house that came from the same garden. He had the opportunity to go to school and was literate.

Antoni would have learned that after Russia took control of Lithuania in 1795, it tried to eliminate noble status and privileges by requiring all nobles to prove their status with each new generation through land, court, church, and records that had to be translated and reviewed by Russian officials in St. Petersburg at the noble's expense. This process could bankrupt a lesser noble. The Polish-Lithuanian Commonwealth had the highest percentage of nobles in Europe, at about 10% of the population, and they were a perceived threat to Czarist Russia.

Antoni would have also heard of the many hopes and dreams of overthrowing Russian control during his grandparents and parents' lifetimes. He would have heard about when Napoleon's troops came through Lithuania in 1812 in an attempt to overthrow the Czar, and the November Uprising in 1830 when Lithuanians and Poles tried to do the same thing.

As Antoni grew up, Czarist Russia tightened control of Lithuania:

- In 1864, Czar Alexander II abolished serfdom abruptly, and nobles lost much of the land they had previously owned.
- In 1865, Russia forbade the use of Latin letters in the publication of Lithuanian books. Books in Cyrillic were allowed but not accepted by the people. Secret book couriers smuggled in Latin-lettered books until 1904.
- Between 1867 and 1868, crop failure, a great famine, and a cholera outbreak resulted in hardship, death, and the beginning of migration to the West.[6]

At the age of 29, Antoni married 28-year-old Barbara Stankiewicz on February 23, 1886 in Krakės (Lithuanian), Kroki (Polish), Parish. Barbara brought a six-year-old daughter, Teresa, to the marriage. It is not clear who the father of Teresa was, but Antoni loved her as his own.

Barbara was born in 1858 and probably baptized in St. Joseph's Church in Kėdainiai, like the rest of her siblings though her record has not been found. Her father was peasant, Benedict Stankiewicz (1822-1906), and her mother was noble woman, Pranciszka Ciolkiewicz (1827-?). Pranciska's family had a "Pomian" family crest, but she lost her official social status by marrying a peasant, as nobility was passed through paternal lineage. However, their social status had little effect on how they lived—they had some affluence in Kėdainiai.

Pomian Family Crest

Barbara's grandparents were Antoni Stankiewicz and Józefata Kowalewska, and nobles Marcin Ciolkiewicz and Ewa Rożynska. Barbara grew up with 7 siblings—Leopold, Casmira, Sophia, Simon, Anastasia, Stanisław and Stanislava. She may have met Antoni through her family's relationship with the Lutkiewicz family. Elżbieta Lutkiewicz was the godmother of her brother, Leopold.

Barbara was a quiet, soft-spoken, and a deeply religious person.

Antoni and Barbara had the following children:

- Jan Lutkiewicz—born June 20, 1887 and died on November 4, 1889 from whooping cough.
- Valeria Lutkiewicz—born March 1, 1888 and died November 25, 1985 in Canada.
- Kazimierz/Charles Lutkiewicz—born March 25, 1891 and died October 6, 1967 in the United States. This is my great grandfather.
- Stanisław Lutkiewicz—born October 25, 1895 and died April 16, 1900 from scarlet fever.
- Michalina Lutkiewicz—born in 1897 and died May 8, 1919 from complications after beating and exposure.
- Romuald Lutkiewicz—born August 1, 1899 and died November 27, 1899 from atrophy.

Antoni and Barbara loved all of their children dearly. It must have been hard to have Valeria born in 1888 and lose two-year-old Jan one year later.

Similarly, they must have been very worried when Kazimierz contracted typhoid in 1894, but fortunately, he survived.

Antoni lost his mother on December 18, 1898 from a tumor. The following year, he and Barbara lost baby Romuald, followed by 4-year-old Stanisław, 6 months later in 1900. They had to care for 11-year-old Valeria, nine-year-old Kazimierz, and two-year-old Michalina while simultaneously grieving the losses of their two children. At 21 years old, Teresa must have been a comfort to grieve with.

Teresa Stankiewicz

Throughout his lifetime, Antoni was highly respected in the community where he lived, and, because of his wisdom and intellect, both wealthy and regular village folk would come to him for advice and consultation. His thinking was much ahead of his time. For example, when questioned why his money was spent on schooling his daughters rather than a dowry, he replied that the best dowry with which he could provide his daughters was an education. Apparently, he was an excellent whistler and would be recognized on the village streets by his familiar whistled tunes even when not in sight.

Barbara, Michalina and Antoni Lutkiewicz

Antoni and Barbara raised Teresa and Michalina to be very reserved, refined and educated. Valeria was also educated but more like her father in character, and she was his favorite child. She was curious and questioned everything, but when she questioned her mother about religious things, Barbara would send her to a corner and only allow her to eat beans. Her father would tell Valeria not to ask her mother so many questions.

Valeria and her sisters attended a Russian-speaking school and lived in Vilnius. They could read, speak and write in Lithuanian, Polish, and Russian.

Two Unidentified People and Valeria Lutkiewicz (seated right)

Their surviving brother, Kazimierz, was favored by Barbara—she gave him special love and attention. He also attended a Russian-speaking school and lived in Vilnius for a time. With an insatiable curiosity and a strong desire to learn, he attended school until eighth grade, graduating as valedictorian of his class. He could also read, speak, and write in Lithuanian, Polish, and Russian.

In 1908, while still teens, Antoni sent Valeria and Kazimierz to a friend in Montreal, Canada to have an opportunity for a better life though it's not clear why he sent Valeria and Kazimierz and not Michalina. His nephew, Jan/John Valiuškevičius (his sister, Ona's, son) went at the same time. Antoni probably wanted his son to avoid the mandatory service in the Czarist army, since the Czar could enforce military service upon an individual indefinitely. By this time, Teresa was probably married to Mr. Sosnauskas.

Unfortunately, about a year after Valeria and Kazimierz left, Teresa died in childbirth in 1909. Her son, Michal/Mykolos Sosnauskas, survived, and Antoni and Barbara raised him.

Around the same time, Valeria went to a dinner and dance sponsored by the Lithuanian Catholic Community in Canada. A fellow Lithuanian immigrant, Victor Masys, asked her to dance. Apparently, it was love at first site, and they were married on February 13, 1909 at St. Casimir's in Montreal. Valeria probably wrote to her family to let them know about her marriage and about her husband's family. Though it's unclear what her parents thought of the marriage, they were probably pleased since Valeria was so happy and the Masys family came from Rukai, which is not far from Mantiviliskis where her parents lived.

Victor Masys' father was also named Antanas. Antanas Masys' wife was Anele Poškutė. In addition to Victor, they had at least five more children:

- Aleksandra Masys (1874-?)
- Mykolas Masys (1877-?)
- Elena Masys (1884-1885)
- Vladislovas/Walter Masys (1886-1917)
- Jonas/John Masys (1880-1968)

Victor Masys served in the Russia Army and was discharged in 1904. In Lithuania, the oldest son would inherit everything, and the younger sons had to find a line of work. In Victor's case, he had an older brother who inherited everything, so he and his younger brother, John, went to Scotland to work in the mines. When they arrived in England, the customs official could not understand their names and wrote them down as "Vic Smith" and "John Smith."

They had a married relative they called "Auntie Bandjus" who lived in Montreal and encouraged them to come to Canada, so Victor and John left Scotland and immigrated there. At some point, their brother, Walter, also immigrated to Canada.

After Victor and Valeria married, Helen Bandjus (Auntie Bandjus' daughter) helped Valeria to assimilate into Canadian life.

By 1912, Valeria and Victor had 2 children: Anthony (February 15, 1910-April 23, 1989) and Victor (July 10, 1911- June 10, 1976). Anthony was named for Valeria's father, and Victor was named after his father.

In 1912, Valeria returned to Lithuania with her first two sons. At the time, Anthony was two years old, and Victor was about six months old. She had intentions of staying since she missed her family so much. Victor was to follow in a few months' time. As Victor's parents were landowners, they agreed to give him a piece of property. Victor and Valeria thought they could live comfortably with such an investment.

Antoni and Barbara were probably very happy to have Valeria and her children come home for a visit and excited about the prospect of her coming back to live there. However, Valeria became disenchanted with life in Lithuania and decided to return to Canada. Victor was pleased about this, since he never had any desire to return to his homeland. However, Antoni and Barbara must have been heartbroken when Valeria left: they had no idea if they would ever see their remaining daughter again.

A booking agent in the village purchased tickets for Valeria and two sons on the Titantic. Fortunately, there was some irregularity in her passport, which prevented her from taking the ship at its scheduled time to leave. The agent had to return these tickets, and new ones were issued on another departing ship. This change of plan was a blessing and saved her life. Antoni and Barbara were probably grateful that their daughter was spared.

Valeria and Victor settled into life in Montreal and had two more children—Adolf (June 17, 1913-1972) and Walter (August 27, 1914-November 28, 1975) between 1913 and 1914. Adolf was named after Valeria's grandfather, but went by "Do" after Hitler came to power.

Victor, Adolf, Anthony, Walter, Vic and Valeria

Meanwhile, Kazmierz had been corresponding with someone in the United States and left Canada with his cousin, Jan/John Valiuškevičius, in search of better life opportunities soon after Valeria married.

Kazimierz, or "Charley" as he came to be known, and John began to work in Canadian lumber camps until Charley slipped over the border into the United States around 1909 and went to Pennsylvania. His cousin John, meanwhile, went to Michigan.

In the Canadian lumber camps, Charley worked as a cook's helper, became a self-taught reader, and somewhat learned how to write English. He learned to play cards, began to drink alcohol, and loved music: he learned how to play a concertina, polkas, waltzes, and mazurkas, and also sung folk songs.

Charley met his future wife, 20-year-old Eva Duobaite, at a dance arranged for a small group of other Lithuanian immigrants in 1914.

Eva was born on March 31, 1892 in Vazniskiai Village to Jonas Duoba and Kotryna Glaubičaitė. She was baptized in Gudeliai Parish. This is in the Suvalkai region of Lithuania—very far from where Charley grew up.

The Suvalkija region had a different history than the rest of Lithuania, and it helps to understand a bit of it to understand Grandma Eva.

The Polish-Lithuanian Commonwealth was partitioned in 1795 when Suvalkija was incorporated into the Province of East Prussia, and German colonists were settled there. This meant that Suvalkija was separated from the rest of Lithuania, which was controlled by the Russian Empire.[7] It also makes a story that Grandma Eva shared about working for a German family as a housekeeper make more sense. She probably understood German.

After Napoleon Bonaparte defeated Prussia in 1807, Suvalkija was briefly part of the Duchy of Warsaw, a small Polish state established by him. The Napoleonic Code was introduced there in 1808-1809 and serfdom was abolished, much earlier than the rest of Lithuania. Peasants learned how to manage their own land in this area long before 1864 when the Czarist Russian government abolished serfdom in the rest of Lithuania and took back control of Suvalkija.

Grandma Eva's parents, great-grandparents, Mykolos Duoba, and Konstancija Zakscheska, and Juozapas Glaubicas, would have benefitted from this. They probably owned their own land and farmed, rather than working on someone else's farm.

Education continued in this area after the 1863 Uprising resulted in the Czarist Russian government closing many educational institutions in other parts of Lithuania. According to the census taken in 1897, the rate of literacy among the peasants of the Suvalkai Province was the highest in the Russian Empire. The people of Suvalkija were also among the first and most numerous emigrants to the United States.[8]

Eva was the sixth child to be born and had the following siblings:

- Mary (Anna/Ona) Duoba (1882-1949) married Lucian (Maciej) Aleknavičius (1876-1945).
- Józef/Juozapas Duoba (1883-1885)
- Jan/Jonas (1885-1887)
- Wincenty/Vincentas (Bill) Duoba (1886-1980) married Sophie Kurtz (1894-1981).
- Anna/Ona Duoba (1989-1915) married Lewis (Julian) Aleknavičius (1879-1927).
- Helena Duoba (1983-1894)
- Petras Duboa (1895-1895)

Eva's mother, Kotryna, died on October 25, 1895 at the age of 35 of a fibrous intra uterine tumor just five days after her newborn son, Petras, died. Eva was just two years old at the time. Her father, Jonas, was left with four young children to provide for. Unfortunately, four children had died before his wife. They all died before reaching the age of two, which was quite common in that day.

Jonas and Kotryna had employed a widowed housekeeper, Ieva Urbonaitė (1870-1930), who Jonas married on November 19, 1895. This was less than a month after his first wife's death. Jonas and Ieva went on to have more children: Rozalija (1896-?), Motiejus (1897-1902), Marijona (1898-?), Teofil (1904-?), Elze (1910-?), Konstanty/Konstantinas (1915-1946), and Anastazija (1920-?). They were born in Daugirdai Village.

Jonas, Ieva, Konstantinas, Teofil and Elze Duoba

From about the time Eva could walk, she was doing chores around the house. From about the age of five, she was working in the fields and herding cows and horses, even during the coldest winters. She was never permitted by her stepmother to receive any schooling whatever, so could never read or write.

While working in the fields, she got her period, but she didn't know what was happening. She thought she was dying. An older woman working in the fields found her crying and explained to her what was happening and helped her with her hygiene.

When Eva was about seven years old, her sister, Mary, married Lucian Maciej Aleknawicz (Liucijonas Motiejus Olechnovičius, born in Laukintukai Village in 1876) in Balbieriškis. She was put up on a table during the dancing that followed the wedding, so she wouldn't be trampled.

Eva left home when she was 13 years old to work as servant for a German family in a part of Lithuania that was then part of Prussia. She was paid at a rate of 10 cents per day, seven days per week, plus room and board.

Over the years, she watched as her siblings left Lithuania, one by one, to go to America. Mary and Lucian left Lithuania around 1901 via Scotland and arrived in Midland Pennsylvania in 1903. Lucian was a foreman in an iron foundry and Mary took care of their two children— Joseph and William.

Bill left in 1907 and worked as a barber at his own shop in Chicago. Bill married Sophie Kurtz in 1914, and they had three daughters – Pearl (1017-2002), Bernice (1919-1984) and Eleanor (1920-1966). Bill also joined Lithuanian organizations that supported Lithuanian Independence.

Bill Duoba and Sophie Kurtz

To give a bit of context, Lithuania was under Russian Czarist rule until 1915. During World War I, Germany occupied Lithuania in 1915. There was hope that Lithuania would become independent with the help of Germany. After World War I ended, and the fate of Lithuania was being fought over by the Soviets and Poland, Lithuanian Americans organized to advocate for the restoration of a free, independent, and democratic Lithuania.

On March 13, 1918, The Third National Congress of Lithuanian Americans met at Madison Square Garden, New York, where both Catholic and national political leaders representing over 700,000 Lithuanians jointly called for the U.S. to recognize Lithuanian independence. This resolution was forwarded to President Wilson and other foreign representatives. Bill Douba was a representative from Chicago at the Congress. Historians would later claim that Lithuanian American support was crucial to the establishment of Lithuanian statehood in 1918.[9]

Eva's sister, Anna, left Lithuania in 1907 to join her sister, Mary, and brother-in-law, Lucian. Anna ended up marrying Lucian's brother, Lewis Halackna (Julian Olechnovičius, born in Liuklingėnai Village in 1879), and they lived in New Castle Pennsylvania with their two children—Anna and Walter.

Anna and Eva Duoba

Even Eva's cousin, Stanley Tamulinas (her Aunt Anna/Ona Duoba Tamulinas' son), left for America in 1904, served in the U.S. Military, and made a living in Chicago as a barber. He married Anna Podzienas and raised three children.

In 1912, Eva went to work with a Jewish family that was planning to move to America. She traveled with them as a servant under the name "Magdalena Schuka." Eva went to live with her sister, Anna, and her family in Pennsylvania.

Eva loved to dance, so she went to the local dance that was arranged for Lithuanian immigrants and met Charley. Charley made a bet with some fellow Lithuanians that he could marry Eva, and he won the bet. They married after a 2-week courtship in New Castle, Pennsylvania on August 24, 1914, about a month after World War I started in Europe. It is not known how Antoni and Barbara felt about their son's marriage to their new daughter-in-law, and it's also not known if Antoni and Barbara ever met Eva's father, Jonas Duoba.

Eva became pregnant soon after their marriage. During her pregnancy, she lost her sister, Anna, to a botched abortion. It is unclear what Charley thought about his sister-in-law's death or about the husband and children she left behind.

Eva gave birth to Charles John, the sixth grandchild for Antoni and Barbara, on September 13, 1915 in Union Township, Pennsylvania. He was baptized on October 17, 1915 in St. Joseph's Parish in New Castle Pennsylvania.

Charles Lucas and Charles (Chuck) John

It is not known when Antoni and Barbara found out about the birth of their second grandchild; they had other things to worry about—Lithuania was in the middle of conflict between Russia and Germany.

In April 1915, the Germans launched an offensive from East Prussia into Lithuania. Among the advancing German forces were thousands of Lithuanians recruited in East Prussia. They were fighting the Russians who also had thousands of Lithuanians fighting on their side. On August 19, 1915, after an 11-day battle, Kaunas fell to the Germans.[10] This is not that far from Mantviliskis, where Antanas, Barbara, Michalina, and little Mykolos were living.

Vilnius fell to the Germans in September 1915, liberating the old borders of the Polish-Lithuanian Commonwealth from Czarist Russia. All of modern-day Lithuania remained in German hands for the rest of the war.

The Germans established a military government and strictly ruled Lithuania during the war. Families and farms were divided, and travel was restricted to such an extent that people could not attend nearby schools or churches. The restrictions frequently prevented farmers from taking their produce to market, destroying commerce and their source of income.[11] It is uncertain how Antanas and Barbara survived this, but they did.

In the middle of this, Antoni lost his father on April 14, 1916. He was 86 years old and was buried in a local Mantviliskis cemetery, probably the same cemetery that his children, Jan and Stanlislaw, were buried in.

In 1917, the Russian Czar Nicholas II was forced to abdicate, and the Communist Party took power. Russia signed a peace agreement with Germany on March 3, 1918 that required them to give up all its provinces west of the Ukraine, including Lithuania. Although the treaty ended Russian-German fighting, it didn't stop the fighting between Red Armies seeking to retain a communist government and the White armies trying to restore the Czar. Some of this fighting affected Lithuania.

On February 16, 1918, a newly formed National Council in Vilnius declared Lithuania an independent state—the first time it had been independent since 1795.[12]

As Valeria was a prolific letter writer, Antoni and Barbara probably kept up with what was happening to their children in Canada and the United States.

Charley and Eva had another child, Anthony Lucas, who was born in Steubenville, Ohio on Wednesday, August 15, 1917 and named after Charley's father. Anthony's birth was not recorded by the city, nor was he baptized in a church - Eva baptized him at home. By October 1918, the "Spanish Influenza" or "Flu Epidemic" hit the Steubenville area and spread rapidly. By the end of October, all public places were closed by the health department – businesses, churches, theaters, bowling alleys and saloons. By December, all schools were closed. To stop the flu from spreading, the local health board and physicians advised: treat all colds as possible influenza, avoid crowds, avoid being coughed and sneezed on and wear masks when caring for the ill. Between 1918 and February 1919, about 208 people died in Steubenville from the flu.[13] It is unknown if Charley, Eva, Chuck or Anthony got sick during this time, but they most certainly knew people that got sick and/or died.

Sam and Mary McLytus

By September 1919, Charley and Eva had moved to Martin's Ferry, Ohio and were living with Eva's sister, Mary, and her husband, Sam McLytus. Eva gave birth to their third child, Agnes Anne, on September 20, 1919 in their home. She was probably named after Eva's grandmother, Agniezka, (who died when Kotryna, her daughter and Eva's mother, was two years old) and her sister, Anna, who had died a few years before.

The Flu Epidemic was still making people sick and Charley and Eva must have feared for the health of their young children. Fortunately, they all survived the flu that claimed three to five percent of the world's population by the time it ended in 1920.

Eva, Agnes, Tony, Chuck and Charley Lucas

Charley supported his family by working at various jobs in Pennsylvania and Ohio along with other Lithuanian immigrants. He tried working in coal mines, but this didn't last long. Instead, he wound up working in the steel and tin mills, where he worked his way up to the job of "heater." Although it paid better than common labor, it wasn't quite as lucrative as the job of the "rollers." He worked 12 hours a day in high heat using long tongs to manipulate the red-hot chunks of steel back and forth through the spinning rolls.

Along with other immigrant farmers, he probably did not expect to be doing this kind of work to support himself and his family. He grew up in open spaces with food to eat and knowledge of farming. He probably also never expected to be treated as poorly as he was in America: locals perceived him as an ignorant immigrant, though, where he came from, he was considered well-educated and from a family that had noble class in its past.

Lithuanian immigrants were discriminated against by Americans, and even by other immigrant groups. Lithuanians lived in their own sections of town, went to Lithuanian (Catholic and Protestant) churches, and spent most of their time with other Lithuanians.

Charley was probably also very lonely. However, most of the Lithuanians he spent time with were from a different region, with a different background. His closest relative, Valeria, was in Canada with her own family. And, his cousin, John Valiuškevičius, who married Anna Budnik, started a family and began a career working on the railroads in Michigan. It's unclear if he shared these things with his parents.

Charles Lucas Declaration of Intention

Charley went through the process to become a United States citizen and filed a Declaration of Intention in 1922 in Pittsburgh, Pennsylvania. Then, he filed a Petition for Naturalization in 1934 in the District Court of Hammond, Indiana. He finally received his Certificate of Naturalization and became a United States citizen on November 8, 1939 in Hammond, Indiana.

Charley and Eva (Duoba) Lucas

Meanwhile, Valeria became a Canadian citizen, raised her boys, learned French and English, and helped other immigrants who arrived in Canada to acclimate to their new country. She wrote articles for a Lithuanian newspaper in Ontario, Canada, became interested in good health, took nutrition classes, and made her own tea. Her husband, Victor, worked at a General Electric Foundry.

Michalina Lutkiewicz

While their children assimilated to life in North America, tragedy struck Antoni and Barbara. Michalina died from influenza caused by exposure on May 8, 1919 at the age of 22 years old. She had been sick but was sent outside to pump water in freezing temperature. Some Russians came by and questioned her (Lithuania had declared its independence but fighting between red and white Russians continued across the former Russian Empire). Whatever they heard displeased them. They beat her with a whip and left her lying on the ground. Someone went out to find out why she was taking so long and brought her back home shortly before she died. Although her death record reports ship fever (as typhoid was known then), her family thought her death was caused by the Russians.

Michalina Lutkiewicz and Unknown Friends

Valeria and Victor had a daughter, Helen, on February 27, 1923, and Charley and his family moved to Gary, Indiana that same year.

Lithuania continued to have instability: in 1926, Nationalist Party leader Antanas Smetona seized power in a military coup after left-wing wins in the national elections. He ran the country as a dictator.

During this time, Barbara's health began to fail. She had a series of strokes that left her bedridden for several years.

Zofia and Mykolos Sosnauskas and Marytė Liutkute

It is not known whether she was aware that Valeria gave birth to her last child, Emilee Irene, on April 12, 1928, whether Valeria had adopted a son, Bernie Mackie, or whether she was aware when her grandson, Mykolos Sosnauskas, left their home, married Zofie, and moved to Basiogala (Lithuanian), or Bejsagoła (Polish).

Emily Masys, Irene Pollard (friend), and Helen Masys

In 1933 or 1934, Barbara died of a massive stroke and was buried at Mantvisliskis cemetery with her other children.

Upon Barbara's death, Antoni became very lonely. He hired a widowed housekeeper, Viktorija Grigytė, to help him. Antoni and Viktorija married on February 12, 1934 in Krakės (Lithuanian), or Kroki (Polish), church. She was in her 30s or 40s, and he was in his 70s. On May 10, 1936, Viktorija gave birth to Marijona Michilina, or Marytė as she was known, at Mantvisliskis.

By this time Antoni was not very healthy—he suffered ulcers on his legs, probably due to complications of diabetes.

Around this time, Charley tried to help his father and Viktorija get a bigger house, sending $80,000 to help them with their purchase. However, the government wouldn't allow Antoni to buy a bigger property, so he sent the money back.

World War II started on September 1, 1939, when Germany invaded

Poland. Soon after, the Soviet Union compelled Lithuania to accept Soviet military bases. On June 15, 1940, the Soviet Union invaded Lithuania and incorporated the county into the USSR. It is not clear how Antoni and Viktorija cared for Marytė during this time.

It also not known how much they knew was going on with Valeria and Kazmierz or about the marriages of their grandchildren:

- Walter Masys married Irina Dudonis around 1932.
- Victor Masys Jr. married Thelma Boomer on September 22, 1940.
- Adolf ("Do") Masys married Marie in the early 1940s.
- Charles John Lucas married Frances Pauline Stone on March 4, 1940.

On February 9, 1941, Antoni died and was buried in the Mantviskiskis cemetery with his father, first and second wives, and children. His life was marked by turmoil: he started life as a noble under Czarist Russian, became a commoner after an uprising, sent two of his children to live in another country and never saw one of them again; he lived through a World War, Lithuanian Independence, saw the beginning of the next World War and Nazi invasion, and outlived his parents, half of his children, and his first wife.

Antoni Lutkiewicz and Family Gravestone

Antoni left behind his second wife, Viktorija, to care for their four-year-old daughter. She would have a very different life than her older siblings.

Marytė Liutkute

From the middle of the 16th Century until the mid-20th Century, Vilnius was the center of Polish (Polish culture that included ethnic Russians, Belarusians, and Lithuanians) and Jewish civilization. It was called "the Jerusalem of the North" by Jews. The Lithuanian language was not spoken there. One third of the homes spoke Yiddish, and Polish was the language of the streets, churches, and schools.[14]

World War II changed Vilnius and what became Lithuania forever: at the beginning of June 1941, thousands of Lithuanians were deported to Siberia by the USSR for being enemies of the people, and by June 22, 1941, the Nazis invaded the USSR and occupied Lithuania. [15]

By the end of June, Nazis and Lithuania collaborators had executed about 207,000 out of 250,000 Jews that lived there. They had made up about 10% of the total population of Lithuania. [16]

Things got worse in Lithuania during the war: Viktorija and Marytė (and other farming families) couldn't sleep in their homes at night. During the day they would go to their homes and feed their livestock, and at night lived in a common house buried in the ground. They would hear troops, both Russian and German, walk over their "house" at night. One day, Viktorija was coming back from feeding the pigs and was caught between gunfire between the Russians and Germans. She survived, and Marytė never forgot the scene.

In 1944, the Red Army returned and over 500,000 Lithuanians were deported, forced into exile, jailed, or shot.[17] Viktorija and Marytė suffered homelessness, as the house they lived in (that had belonged to Antanas, as Marytė called her father) burned down mysteriously. It was rumored to have been burnt by soldiers.

By that time, the USSR didn't allow private ownership, so they were moved to another house that had become available because the owners were sent to Siberia. They shared the house with another family. Many personal items were lost in the fire—like photos and letters.

Between 1945 and 1954, all farms in Lithuania were collectivized, meaning that multiple farmers ran each state-held farm in join enterprises as a type of agricultural production.

Viktorija and Marytė were sent to a collective to live and work. They lived in shared living quarters and ate their meals with others that lived there. They worked in the fields planting and harvesting flax; they knew how to plant, harvest, thresh, and spin flax into thread on a spinning wheel. They couldalso make the thread into cloth, and the cloth into clothing. Additionally, they worked a small plot of land to grow vegetables and herbs for their own use.

The people working on the collectives would take vacations to other places in the USSR. In their time on the collective, Viktorija and Marytė were able to travel to Armenia, Russia, and Georgia.

The USSR had compulsory education, so Marytė did go to a Russian-speaking school, and Lithuanian was only spoken at home.

Marytė had three children- Algimantas, Daiva and Rolandas- as a single parent, and her mother helped to raise them on a collective farm.

Algimantas Liutkus, Neighbor, Daiva Liutkute

Her sons served in the USSR military, like all other young men at the time. After their military service, they both became drivers, and her daughter became a dressmaker. Eventually, Marytė's children had their own families.

Helen Masys, Marytė Liutkute, Valeria (Lutkievic) Masys

Marytė kept in touch with her sister Valeria through many letters over the years, and Valeria came to visit Marytė in Lithuania. During the visit, Valeria asked Marytė what she wanted as a gift, and Marytė said "machina," which can mean "car" or other mechanical things in Lithuanian. Valeria thought she meant car and was puzzled. Valeria knew Marytė didn't drive and asked why she wanted a car. Rather than a car, Marytė meant a mechanized loom, and Valeria bought it for her. In those days, all mechanical things came from Russia. Marytė used it for several decades, sending it to Russia for parts for it until it finally could no longer be fixed or used.

Viktorija, Marytė's mother, died in 1978 in Mantviliskis and was buried with Antanas in the family grave.

Algimantas Liutkus, Vikorija (Grigytė) and Daiva Liutkute

In 1990, Lithuania became an independent nation again. By 1993, the last of the Russian soldiers left the country. During this time, Marytė applied to the government to give her father's land back to her, and they did. She was able to sell the parcel very close to the cemetery that her parents are buried in and buy another property in a village. She lived in her own home for many years and had good neighbors that became friends. Her grandchildren have lots of fond memories of that home.

Eventually, Marytė sold her house and moved into a small apartment where she has lots of photos of loved ones hanging up in her living room. Despite living by herself, she remains close with her remaining children and grandchildren.

Rolandas Liutkus (between two friends)

Marytė makes beautifully knitted socks and shawls. In fact, she gave me several pairs of socks and a red shawl on my visit! She came with us to see where her parents' house used to be, the cemetery they were buried in, and all the other sightseeing during that 10-hour—including to the Hill of Crosses. She was a rather quiet person, always dressed nicely, and ready to go wherever we went. Even though I never met her before, it was like she was my aunt that I had known all my life.

Kazmierz/Charles Lutkiewicz/Lucas

Over the years, Kazmierz, or "Charles Lucas" as he was known to his children, would tell stories about his parents, grandparents, and great-grandparents to his children—Chuck, Tony, and Agnes. However, he never went back to Lithuania and didn't keep in touch with Viktorija or his sister, Marytė.

Tony, Agnes and Chuck Lucas

After Charles and Eva had children, they moved frequently due to Charles' addiction to gambling and drinking and their inability to pay rent. From 1919 to 1923, Charles, Eva, and their family lived in many different towns: the family moved to Gary, Indiana in 1923, travelling from Pittsburg on an overnight Pennsylvania Railroad steam train in a coach car and roomed in a cheap hotel there with only one bed for about 2 weeks before finding a house to rent on Van Buren Street near 15th Avenue (1535 Van Buren Street, to be specific).

Here is a list of places they lived in Gary, Indiana:

- 1535 Van Buren
- 4167 Adams Street
- 2270 15th Avenue
- 1609 Vermont Street
- 4571 Pennsylvania Street
- 409 West 41st Avenue

- 1486 E Ridge Road (now a gas station corner and fast strip market)
- 1642 West 15th Avenue
- 835 Louisiana

In a couple of instances during the Depression years of 1933 to 1936, as banks and loan associations went into bankruptcy, no one knew—or was around long enough—to determine legally what property belonged to whom, so the Lucas family would remain in a formerly owned home until somebody showed up with enough paperwork to prove ownership and the family needed to move. In at least one instance, at the house at 441 West 41st Avenue, at least 3 parties showed up at the door claiming ownership at separate times. None of them came back, as in each case, the legal basis for true home ownership changed. While living in the West 41st Avenue house, the Vasil family, family friends, paid their rent for 3 years!

At some point, Charles and his family were on welfare for 6 months at $11 per month. While living on 41st Avenue they had a large garden and grew vegetables to eat, and the Red Cross gave them a 24-pound sack of flour once a month.

Charles and Eva's children attended seven different schools because of these moves and the instability of the times.

Charles and Eva did have one more child, stillborn and named John, probably in Gary, Indiana in the 1920s. It is unclear whether Antoni and Barbara knew about these parts of their son's life.

Charles was good with his hands: he loved to invent gadgets and worked hard to find investors from all walks of life to fund his ideas. Although he did work in steel and tin mills, he wanted a life in which he could use his intelligence to make a living, not a routine factory or laborious job. He loved good music, good movies, and fine things.

Charles Lucas Social Security Application

Charles's wife, Eva, had to help make ends meet, working various jobs as a school janitor, housecleaner, and even a whiskey and beer-maker in a copper clothes boiler in the midst of Prohibition (1920-1933). There was a pool hall in town where the best customers for the illegal liquor were the doctors, lawyers, priests, sheriffs, mayor and police chief. Charles' disillusionment surrounding politics and religion increased as a result of this.

Charles' gambling problem grew worse over time: he lost Eva's wedding ring in a card game and would often try to get Eva to sign over the papers to their last house so he could gamble with it. Naturally, she refused.

Charles' drinking problem likewise grew worse over time. He would come home drunk and angry wanting to beat his children. Eva would have the children hide and take the brunt of most of the beatings, and, on other occasions, Chuck would take the beatings for everyone.

One of the most harrowing events was when Charles came home drunk with a shotgun, threatening to shoot everyone. His children—Chuck and Tony—and his wife, Eva, were very scared although it's unclear whether Aggie was there or not. Chuck tried to protect Tony and Eva by approaching Charles, who he was able to talk out of shooting anyone.

Charles lost his faith in God and tried to influence his children (when they were young) to believe the same way. He would sit down in a chair and have Chuck climb up into his lap and tell him there was no God. Then, he would put Chuck down and proceed in the same fashion with Tony. When he reached for Aggie, though, she would tell her father she didn't want to get in his lap to hear this—she said she believed in God. He just smiled at her and let her be. Aggie said this caused both her brothers to stop going to church though they eventually both went back to church when they each married women of faith.

Chuck, Tony, and Agnes graduated from Lew Wallace High School in Gary, Indiana—Chuck in 1933, Tony in 1934, and Agnes in 1937.

Charles and his sister, Valeria, remained close. In 1936, Charles took his whole family to visit Aunt or "Tata" Valeria.

In the 1940s, he went to visit Valeria in Canada and met his nieces and nephews and some of their children.

Chuck left home in 1939 and set out be a bush pilot in Alaska when the Roosevelt Recession hit. Instead, he ended up in Burbank, California, working in a plane manufacturing facility at Lockheed where he met Frances Stone. They married on March 1, 1940 and had two children, Charliene Eva and Ronald Charles. During World War II, he was transferred to the Vega Aircraft facility in Fresno, where they ended up living for many years.

Charliene, Fran, Ronnie, Chuck Lucas

When Charliene and Ronald were young, Chuck took them to visit his parents in Gary, Indiana. These were the only grandchildren that Charles ever met.

Eva, Agnes, Charliene, Charles, and Tony Lucas

Although Tony always wanted to go to college, he worked in steel mills and helped support his parents and sister. He was in the Coast Guard during World War II where he spent most of his time welding hulls that had cracked from freezing at the Navy pier in Chicago. He was supposed to get on a Coast guard cutter in the Gulf, but a freeze kept him in Chicago, and the cutter went out and got sunk with all hands by a U boat. After the war, Tony returned to Gary, Indiana and had a partnership in Presson and Lucas—a welded fabrication and welding engineering company. He continued to support his parents through the 1940s.

After graduating high school, Agnes went to work as a nurse's aide at St. Mercy Hospital in Gary in 1938. She graduated from training in 1942 and enlisted in the Army as a registered nurse during World War II (March 1943- December 1945). She spent much of her time at the American base in Blandford, England and was in England during the blitz.

In 1949, Charles Lucas and a friend of his, Swytuk, swindled another friend, 60-year-old Joseph Pazero, out of his $4600 of life's savings. Charles and Paul had convinced Joseph that they had created an "atomic fluid" that would double the number of $10 bills he had, if the fluid were applied to the bills. To demonstrate, Charles and Paul asked Joseph to bring $4600.

They sprinkled water on some of the $10 bills and bolted them between two pieces of plywood. They sent Joseph to get a tool to tighten the bolts to make it work. When Joseph came back, his $4600 was gone, and so were Charles and Paul. Joseph didn't report the swindle right away because he felt foolish. Charles became conscience-stricken and later walked into a Gary police station and put $3100 on the desk of a policeman. He asked to be locked up because he had taken the money from a friend fraudulently, telling the police that he had spent $200 and that Paul had the rest ($1500). The police eventually arrested Paul, Charles was charged with running a confidence game, and Paul was charged with conspiracy to defraud. Paul claimed he was innocent, and both men were sent to Chicago to face the grand jury.[18]

At some point, a policeman beat Charles on the head for trying to swindle an elderly man of his life savings, even though Charles turned himself in. According to his son, Chuck, he sustained some brain trauma.

Charles was given probation and had to pay a fine of $1700 for restitution for his crime. His son, Tony, had to sell his sailboat to pay the fine and took Charles to a mental sanitarium to get help. Charles did leave the sanitarium and came home briefly. Tony and Chuck were making plans to send him to California to be with Chuck to work on a remodel project to build a room for him and Eva to live in.

However, in April of 1950, Charles violated his probation and displayed some mental instability. Tony took him to court and Charles was committed to Kankakee Mental Asylum in Illinois, and he never left until he died.

His daughter, Agnes, was best friends with Claire Massart and introduced her to brother, Tony, after the war. According to the stories, after their first date, Tony told his sister he had met the woman he was going to marry. Tony married Claire in Gary, Indiana on April 7, 1951. Charles was not in attendance. They went on to have eight children—Ray, Cathy, Tom, Greg, George, Eileen, Christine, and Matthew.

Tony, Claire and Ray Lucas

Agnes was working in a hospital when she met Wilson (Bill) Henderson, who was working as an orderly. On January 20, 1951, they married in Orange, California. Charles didn't attend this wedding either. Agnes and Bill had 6 children—John, Eve, Kathy, James, David, and Paul (Eva was not pleased about this name, since Paul Swytuk was a partner in crime with her husband).

Paul, John, Agnes, Bill, James, Eve, Kathy, David Henderson

Charles' wife, Eva, lived with Tony and Claire for a while in Gary, Indiana in the 1950s. She also lived with Chuck and Fran and their children, Ronnie and Charliene, in Fresno, California on Pine Street in the 1950s.

On November 13, 1956, Eva became Charles' guardian by order of the court in Indiana.

During the early 1960s, Tony and Claire decided to move to Fresno, California with their children, to join Chuck and Fran. Chuck and Tony had been writing letters back and forth for years about Tony coming to California to invest in a business together. Business ventures included purchasing real estate off Herndon Avenue and Valley Chrome. These times were very uncertain – children in a new home and new school, Tony and Chuck in new business ventures that put them under financial strain, Charles in a mental institution, etc. Claire and Tony would gather their young children every night to pray.

After being transferred to Little Co. of Mary Hospital, Evergreen Hospital, Charles Lucas died on October 6, 1967 from a massive GI hemorrhage (other conditions included aorta duodenal fistula and abdominal aortic aneurism.) He had a large family funeral attended by his wife, children, grandchildren, and his sister, Valeria and her daughter, Emily. He was buried in St. Peter's Cemetery in Fresno, California. It is not known if Marytė was notified of her brother's death at this time or if Mykolos, his nephew, was informed.

Eva lived in an in-law apartment at the back of Tony and Claire's house for many years. Toward the end of her life, she was moved to a facility that could care for her 24 hours a day. By this time, she wanted to die: she loved her husband, "Charley," saying she just wanted to be with him. Upon waking up in the nursing home, she'd often say, "Oh, doggone it, I'm still here." She died on December 12, 1983 from a cardio-pulmonary aneurism.

Chuck was the first of Charles' children to die. He died on March 21, 1994 in North Bend, Oregon. His packed funeral at North Bend First Presbyterian Church, at which he was a member, was attended by his brother, Tony; sister-in-law, Claire; and his children and grandchildren. His myrtle wood art decorated the building in which he was such a beloved member of the community for years.

Chuck, Fran, and Charliene Lucas

Chuck's daughter, Charliene, was the first grandchild born to Charles and Eva, and the first to die. She was born in 1942 in the San Fernando Valley, grew up in Fresno, and graduated from Clovis High School and Fresno State. She was highly influenced by her Aunt Aggie and Aunt Claire to become a nurse. She got a BS Degree and became a RN (Registered Nurse) and MICN (Medical Intensive Care Nurse). She loved taking classes and reading more about nursing. She married Said Saadati and had two children—me and my brother, Komron. Charliene became an emergency room nurse and a flight nurse on a helicopter that brought trauma patients to St. Agnes. She died on March 19, 2013 at the age of 70 from bladder cancer.

Agnes was the second of Charles and Eva's children to die. She died on June 3, 2003. Her funeral was a testimony to her life: the church was packed with family and friends from the community, all sharing how much she meant to them. And her extended family learned just how involved she was in her community:

- The City of McFarland declared June 5, 1992 as Agnes Henderson Day
- McFarland's Christmas Parade's Grand Marshall in December 1998 was named for her "many, many years of dedication, devotion, and love to her city, school, family, and especially the children of the community."
- She received an Appreciation Award from the Salvation Army for "helping to brighten the lives of others" in 1993.
- She was named Citizen of the Year by the Greater McFarland Chamber of Commerce in 1994

Tony was the last of Charles and Eva's children to pass away. He died on October 24, 2006 after about a 10-year decline in health. Likewise, his funeral was a testimony to his life, the church packed with family, friends, and employees from the company he founded, Valley Chrome. He was remembered for his big heart and generosity to so many.

Chuck, Agnes, Tony Lucas

Valeria Lutkievic

During her lifetime, Valeria was the person who kept the family connected: she kept in contact with her sister Teresa's son, Mykolos, and his wife, Zofie, in Tytuvenai, with her sister, Marytė, in Kėdainiai, and with her brother, Kazimierz, in Gary, Indiana.

Sisters-Marytė and Valeria

Valeria's sons served in World War II—Victor at a weather station in Labrador, Newfoundland and Anthony in the Merchant Marines.

Anthony (Tony) married Gladys Purcell prior to 1942, and they went on to have 3 children - Marie, Earl and Charles. Marie married Valeria's adopted child, Bernie, in 1960.

Vic and Evelyn (Boomer) Masys with Reverend Kitching

Victor married Thelma (Evelyn) Boomer on September 22, 1940, and they went on to have three children - Victoria, Donald and Verna. No one was quite sure what Victor did for a living, but he was an engineer involved with bridge building project and had mines. He made beautiful jade jewelry. His sister, Emily, has keeps some of his handmade pieces to this day.

Adolf (Do) married Marie and had 2 daughters, Patricia and Anita.

Do and Anita Masys

Walter eloped when he was 18 with Irina Dudonis sometime around 1932. In 1942, they had a daughter Sandra. The marriage did not last. Irina and Sandra moved to Chicago, Illinois. Despite being left an inheritance from both her grandmother, Valeria, and her father, Walter, she chose not to be in contact with the Masys family.

Sandra, Walter, and Irina (Dudonis) Masys

Helen was a model for Elizabeth Arden. When she tired of that, she became a secretary working as one in Washing, D.C. during World War II. After the war, she married Joseph Gelleny on September 6, 1947. They had 3 children - Sharon, Lorne and James. Joseph also served in World War II at Camp X, a secret special school for training covert agents on the northwestern shore of Lake Ontario. Basically, he was a spy. He went on to write a book about his experience called *Almost*.

Helen Masys and Joseph Gelleny

At some point, Helen traveled to Lithuania with Valeria to search out her family's ancestry, but she never shared what she found.

Emilie or Emily married Victor Smider on November 15, 1952. They had three children - Cathy, Ted and Lisa. Emily met Vic at her sister, Helen's, wedding. They liked each other but dated others until they were sure they wanted to marry.

Emily, Cathy and Vic Smider

Emily and Vic ran a farm and a marina with a restaurant, store, and even U.S. mail! Their children, cousins (including the Hendersons), and other children spent a great deal of time working on both.

Emily remembers her mom, Valeria, as "the queen"—she did whatever she wanted and her father, Vic, adored her.

Valeria fully immersed herself in Canadian life while keeping close to the Lithuanian community: she left Catholicism to attend Riverside United Church but also belonged to the Lithuanian Club in Toronto and was involved with lots of weddings and bridal showers.

One of the bridal showers Valeria got involved with was between a young, Lithuanian woman engaged to a Chinese man. The bridal shower was going to be thrown for the young woman at the Club, but no one was going to attend because of discrimination towards the young man. Valeria let everyone know that if they did not attend and support the young woman, that she would no longer help them out. Valeria helped them with reading and writing English, getting food rations during the War, and just figuring out how to do day to day things in Canada. Everyone showed up for the bridal shower.

Valeria enjoyed having tea with other ladies and reading their tea leaves for fun. She understood people and seemed to know what they needed, so her reading of the tea leaves gave always gave practical advice.

She got tired of people in that community saying how much better Lithuania was and that they wanted to be buried there, so she organized a trip of 100 Lithuanian-Canadians to take a trip back to Lithuania to visit their families and see where they grew up. They were escorted by a Communist guide the whole trip and could not take a detour from their planned itinerary.

Valeria started talking with the guide and learned that he was actually the nephew of her husband, Vic! She also learned that Vic's brother and sister were still alive and living in Siberia, so she eventually figured out a way to send scraps of clothing to Siberia to help them out.

During this trip she went to visit her sister's (Teresa) son, Mykolos Sousnakas, and his wife, Zofie. They never had any children. Valeria kept in touch with him until his death. She also went to visit her sister, Marytė and her children. Some of the gifts she gave on that trip are still being used by her niece.

When the group returned from the trip, no one ever said a word about moving back to Lithuania or being buried there.

Eva Duoba Lucas, Helen Masys, Charley Lucas and Valeria Masys

Valeria and her daughter, Helen, traveled to the United States to visit Valeria's brother, Kazimierz/Charley and his wife and two kids (Tony and Agnes) in the 1940s. Chuck had moved to California, married Frances Stone, and did not meet with them at that time.

In 1967, Valeria went with her daughter, Emily, to her brother's (Kazimierz) funeral. According to Emily, Chuck, Tony, and Agnes were so happy to see them and did not allow them to drive their rental car—they insisted upon driving them around and hosting them. Emily really enjoyed Chuck's company. Chuck remarked about how much energy Valeria had at the time: she was 78 years old, ran up the steps to his mother (Eva's) apartment, and could still kick her leg up above her head!

Valeria wrote several letters to Marytė during the time period when Helen and Emily had property in Florida in the 1970s and 1980s. She wrote about enjoying the warm weather in Florida when it was so cold in Canada.

Around the age of 95, Valeria got a blood clot. The doctors recommended that she not have surgery, but she decided to do the surgery any way. She took her children with her to see her lawyer to settle her affairs and said goodbye to all her friends. She went in for surgery on November 25, 1985, but doctors said her veins were like paper and would not clot properly. She never regained consciousness from the surgery and died two days later.

Walter, Do, Helen, Valeria, Tony, Emily, Vic Masys

Valeria outlived all of her siblings (except Marytė), as well as her husband Victor (who died in 1960) and three of her children—Victor died in 1976, Adolph (Do) died in 1972, and Walter died in 1975.

Valeria's son, Anthony, died on April 23, 1989. Her daughter, Helen, suffered from osteoporosis and pulmonary problems and died on October 13, 1999.

CHAPTER TWO

Ona/Anna Liutkevičiūtė/Lutkiewicz

Ona/Anna Liutkevičiūtė/Lutkiewicz was born around 1865 to Adolf Lutkiewicz and Barbara Dowgwillo. She was the sister of Antoni/Antanas Lutkiewicz, my 2nd great-grandfather, making Ona/Anna my 3rd great-aunt. She stayed in Lithuania and used the Lithuanian version of her name—Ona Liutkevičiūtė.

Ona married Alfonsas Valiuškevičius on June 16, 1885 in Krakės (Lithuanian), or Kroki (Polish), Parish. Ona was 20 years old and Alfonsas was 38. Alfonsas was the son of Ludwik Valiuškevičius and Marianna Dobkeviciūtė and a soldier on leave. Previously, he had served in the army for the Czar Alexander II in the Russo-Turkish War (1877–78), a conflict between the Ottoman Empire and the Eastern Orthodox coalition led by the Russian Empire and composed of Bulgaria, Romania, Serbia, and Montenegro. Fought in the Balkans and in the Caucasus, it originated in emerging 19th Century Balkan nationalism, as well as Russian goals of recovering territorial losses endured during the Crimean War of 1853–56, Russia re-establishing itself in the Black Sea, and Russia supporting the political movement attempting to free Balkan nations from the Ottoman Empire.[19]

The witnesses to their wedding were Antoni Lutkiewicz (my 2nd great-grandfather), Józef Wojtkiewicz, and Szymon Stankiewicz (Antoni's brother-in-law).

Alfonsas and Ona had the following children:

- Antanas (1887-1953) was born June 13, 1887 in Nowa Wieś and was baptized on June 14 in Pociuneliai. His godparents were Mikołaj Wołczkiewicz and Urszula, the wife of Adam Wołczkiewicz. Antanas/Antoni married Maria Żuperko in Kiejdany on Nov 11, 1912.

- Jan (1889-1980) was born June 21, 1889 in Nowa Wieś and was baptized at Krakės Parish on June 25. His godparents were Bronislovas Dobkevičius and Juzefa/Józefa Liutkevičiūtė/Lutkiewicz (Jan's aunt or his mother's sister).

- Anelina (1892-1960) was born around 1892. She married Jeronimas Blandis on February 12, 1894 in Dotnuva (Lithuanian), or Datnów (Polish), Parish.

- Juozas (1894-1960) was born on March 7, 1894 in Kirkily. He was baptized in Pociūnėliai (Lithuanian), or Pacunele (Polish), Parish on March 12. His godparents were Antanas Dambrauskas and Paulina, the wife of Bogdanas Čeliu. On January 23, 1823 he married Ona Zukauskaie (1904-1966) in Dotnuva (Lithuanian), or Datnów (Polish), Parish.

- Pranas (1899-?) was born on April 14, 1899 and baptized in Dotnuva (Lithuanian), or Datnów (Polish), Parish. He tried to immigrate to America to join his brother, Jan, but got on the wrong ship, ending up instead in Buenos Aires, Argentina on April 8, 1930 after a trip aboard the Lloyd Saubado.

- Aleksandra (1902-?) was born on June 4, 1902 and baptized in Dotnuva (Lithuanian), or Datnów (Polish), Parish. She married Vladislovas Gorodeckas (1883-1963) on September 30, 1930 in Dotnuva (Lithuanian), or Datnów (Polish), Parish.

- Stanislovas (1905-1974) was born around 1904. He married Sofija Valatkaite on February 18, 1930 in Dotnuva (Lithuanian), or Datnów (Polish), Parish.

1st row: Juozas Valiuškevičius, Ona Liutkevičiūtė-
Valiuškevičienė, Alfonsas, Stanislovas
2nd row: (standing) Anelina, Aleksandra, Pranciškus, Antanas

Alfonsas and Ona had one child—Jan/John Valiuškevičius—immigrate to Wisconsin in the United States and one child—Pranas—immigrate to Buenos Argentina. Not much is known about Pranas, other than that he married and had children there. The rest of their children stayed in Lithuania.

Alfonsas was a farmer. He died on January 5, 1931 at the age of 85 and was buried three days later in Gelainai Cemetery. Ona died on March 9, 1931 at the age of 68 and was also buried in Gelainai Cemetery two days after her death.

Jan/John Valiuškevičius (Waleszkiewicz)

Jan was the second child born to Alfonsas and Ona, and he grew up on a farm.

When Jan became 18 years old, Alfonsas gave him a horse and told him he could keep the horse and become a farmer or sell the horse and go to America. Jan sold the horse and sailed for Montreal, Canada in around

1908. He met up with his cousin Kazimierz/Charley Lutkiewiez, and they worked their way down to the United States through the logging camps.

According to their naturalization papers, Charley headed towards Pennsylvania, and John headed towards Wisconsin in 1912.

Jan Valiuškevičius and Anna Budnek

Jan met his future wife, Anna Budnek, in a rooming house. They saw each other a few times and married right away when Jan was about 26 and Anna was 16. They married on October 19, 1914 in Grand Rapids Michigan.

Jan was very good with his hands and had a mechanical mind. He started out in logging, and then became a blacksmith and shoed horses. Eventually he went to work for the C&O Railroad in the machine shops. He was illiterate, so someone would demonstrate how to fix a railroad engine, and he could fix it. Over the years, he gained a reputation for being able to fix anything. He worked there for 40 years—through the Depression—which is quite amazing. He was very strong and large (not tall, just large) and was a happy person not easy to upset.

Jan became John, and John and Anna had five children—Bernice Mary

(1915-2016), Frank (1917-1928), Charles Stanley (1920-?), Dorothy M. (1924-2019), and Alfonso (1927-1928).

John and Anna also helped to raise some of Anna's siblings as well.

John would receive letters regularly from Lithuania from his mother, Ona Lutkiewicz, until her death in 1939, but John couldn't read them. His wife, Anna, would read them and write back to Lithuania. After his mother's death, he still received letters from family.

John also kept in contact with his brother, Pranciskus. Pranciskus was supposed to meet Jan in Michigan in 1930, but he ended up getting on the wrong ship. He ended up in Argentina and got married there.

Pranciskus Valiuškevičius

John and Anna's son, Frank, died in 1928. Their daughter, Bernice, married Chester Boomgaard in 1936. Chester's parents were from Holland. Bernice and Chester had 2 sons.

Their son, Charles, married Magdalen Vogt in 1942. They never had any children.

Unfortunately, John's wife, Anna died young—she got scarlet fever and rheumatic fever and died from heart failure at the age of 47 in 1946. As a sad side story, Anna's father died when he was 31 years old—his horse reared up on a railroad track and a train ran over him! After Anna's death, few letters went back and forth from Lithuania.

John and Anna's daughter, Dorothy, worked during WWII as a secretary and driver for the admirals in the navy. She met her future husband, Gerald Holst, during the war. He was drafted into the military in 1941 right after the bombing of Pearl Harbor when he served as a bomber pilot during WWII. Most of his friends died during the war—they were shot down. He also got shot and lost about 40 percent of his stomach, but he survived and married Dorothy in 1947, about 8 months after her mother's death. They had two sons.

John remarried to Kamila Skorupski and ended up outliving her. She died in 1967. John retired from C & O in 1964. He died on January 25, 1980 at the age of 91 years old, leaving behind 3 children, five grandchildren and five great-grandchildren.

Juozas Valiuškevičius

Juozas Valiuškevičius grew up in Lithuania. During this time, Lithuania was under Russian rule. From 1864 to 1905, all books and periodicals in Polish or Belorussian were banned from entering the country, and books in Lithuanian could be published only in the Cyrillic alphabet. Russian was the only language permitted in the schools, and the Roman Catholic Church was banned.

When Juozas went to the village school for three years, he was taught exclusively in Russian and became quite fluent. He also spoke Polish and Lithuanian, but these he learned exclusively at home.

Juozas worked on farm with his family until 1910 when he was 17 and was taken into the Russian military service. He served for 8 years with his brother, Antanas, both of them fighting for the Russian military in World War I. At one point, Antanas was captured by Germans, but he was later exchanged for a German officer.

All frontline soldiers of the Czarist Russian Army were made up of tall men that could shoot. Juozas was a tall man and could shoot, so he was sent to the front line. Juozas took part in a battle with bayonets in August 1915, during the defense of an Osovec castle or Osowiec, a 19th century fortress located in northeastern Poland that was built by the Russian Empire. It saw heavy fighting during World War I when it was defended for several months by its Russian garrison against German attacks. The Germans knew the Russians did not have any gas masks, so on August 6, 1915, they used chlorine gas. The Russians put wet rags on their faces to filter some of the gas. Most died, but some, like Juozas, survived the attack, though he was poisoned and lost consciousness. After the battle, Russians were looking for live soldiers and called out to them. Juozas heard them and gave a sign he was still alive. This gas attack not only affected the lungs of Juozas: it affected his children as well—all died of cancer (of the blood and kidneys or tumors).

At the end of World War I, the Russian army fell apart, as many soldiers deserted. Juozas also threw away his gun and started walking home, but the Russian army police were out looking for deserters. On his way home, Juozas saw some of them coming from a distance, quickly took off his military coat, and asked a farmer working in a nearby field if he could help plow his land. While they were both plowing in white shirts, the Russian army police came up close on horseback. They did not pay attention to the two farmers plowing their land.

After returning home, Juozas lived with parents and worked on their land. When he was 28, he married Ona Žukauskaitė from Beržytė village. She was 19 years old, 9 years younger than Juozas.

They had met at the village dances—Juozas liked the young, pretty girl who danced the quadrille very well. Ona Žukauskaitė had learned to read and write—she had completed 4 years at the same Russian school Juozas had attended and was able to read and write in Russian and Lithuanian (that she had learned at home) and little Polish. They married on January 23, 1923 in Dotnuva (Lithuanian), or Datnów (Polish), Parish. As a dowry, she received six hectares of land, next to her parents. Her father died in 1919 and her mother decided to move with her relatives in Ąžuolaičiai.

Juozas Valiuškevičius and Ona Žukauskaitė

Juozas and Ona had seven children—four sons and three daughters:

- Petras (1923-1984)
- Apolonija (1925-2014)
- Jonas (1927-1985)
- Bronislovas, or "Bronius" (1928-1971)
- Marijona Veronika, or "Marytė" or "Marija" (1933-1991)
- Danutė Margarita, or "Danutė" (1938-2017)
- Kęstutis Kazimieras (1948-?)

All of them were sent to school, and six of them received higher education. Their oldest daughter, Apolonija, received a PhD in Art history and worked at the Lithuanian Academy of Sciences. It was difficult for Juozas and Ona to send all their children to study during that time, but they saw the value of education and did not pay attention to the ridicule of their neighbors.

Juozas and Ona were a religious couple and went to church each

Sunday, taking turns taking the children. Ona had a nice voice, and she sang in a church choir. The whole family sang many folk songs each evening at home.

Juozas and Ona had a farm that had a horse, a cow, one or two pigs, and many hens. The cow was a Holland and gave 12-14 liters of milk each day, its milk used to make sour cream, curd, butter, and cheese. A lot of this, along with eggs from the hens, were sold in Kėdainiai market.

For additional money, Juozas and his family worked in the Kamarauskas (Komorowski) manor, in Sirutiškis. This was mostly summer work weeding around the sugar beets. The Kamarauskas manor paid 2 Litas (about 20 cents in USD, around 1930) for each person per day.

Juozas and his family grew a lot of beans, and Juozas sold them to a military kitchen in Dotnuva (Lithuanian), or Datnów (Polish), for a good price each year. They had also 40 shrubs of black currants for juice and for drying (for hot drinks in winter). They also had a garden that consisted mainly of apple and pear trees. The largest pear tree had a name—Dulia.

After Soviet occupation in 1945, Juozas' family was on a list of people to send to Siberia. During 1945 and 1946, the Soviets deported a couple hundred-thousand Lithuanians to Siberia, including people who were educated, had nobility in their backgrounds, or resisted any prior occupation.[20]

In 1945, soldiers came to Juozas and Ona's farm and left one young soldier to guard everything before sending the family to Siberia. The other solders went to a neighbor to drink vodka. The young soldier warned Juozas to leave immediately. The whole family successfully moved in with a cousin, Cironka, who lived about 15 kilometers away and escaped going to Siberia.

Sometime later, when the passports of independent Lithuania were changed to Soviet passports, Juozas changed his passport. He was very happy when the inscription indicating nobility status in his old passport was not copied to his new one: if it had, his entire family could have been sent to Siberia immediately.

Juozas kept up correspondence with his brothers in the Americas—Jonas (John) in the United States and Pranciškus (Pranas) in Argentina. They corresponded in Polish, and there are still few letters that survive today, but after the Soviet occupation started, communication stopped.

In 1968, when the relationship between the United States and the Soviet Union had improved, Dorothy, the daughter of John Waleshkiewicz (Juozas brother that had Americanized the last name of Valiuškevičius), visited Lithuania with a tourist group trying to find relatives. Unfortunately, all tourists were prohibited from leaving Vilnius where they stayed for a few hours.

Both Juozas and Ona had died before her visit. Juozas Valiuškevičius died on December 18, 1960 at the Kaunas state hospital from kidney cancer and was buried in Gelainiai Cemetery close to his parents.

His wife, Ona, died in March 1966, in an auto crash: she was sitting as a passenger in a small car and was going to visit her sons living in Kaunas when the driver hit a truck by accident. Ona is buried in Dotnuva (Lithuanian), or Datnów (Polish), cemetery, close to her family.

After Juozas and Ona died, the Soviet government destroyed their house around 1967 as part of a government decision to reclaim many lands and fields in Lithuania and to demolish many houses. In some cases, whole villages were demolished.

All the children of Juozas and Ona lived in different cities—Kaunas, Ukmergė, Vilnius, Pabradė, Kėdainiai. They were educated—teachers and engineers—and respected by their colleagues and the institution leaders where they worked. Many of their grandchildren also received higher education and are working as school and university teachers or researchers and scholars. There are four with PhDs—two assistant professors and two professors.

Chapter Three

Gabriel Bronislaw Lutkiewicz and Weronika Ciechanowicz

Although Gabriel is a very distant cousin to me, a 7th cousin five times removed, he probably did know Adolf Mateusz Lutkiewicz, my 3rd great grandfather. They used a common parish for worship, baptisms, weddings, and funerals—Krakės (Lithuanian), or Kroki (Polish), Parish. These extended families were in the same areas for centuries, and, because of their noble status, were more mobile than you would expect for the time. The stories of two of Gabriel's children—Józef who came to America and Ludwika who did not—demonstrate how families were separated and often never saw each other again. Here is his story.

Jaswojnie (Polish) or Josvainiai (Lithuanian) Parish

Gabriel Bronislaw Lutkiewicz was born on June 28, 1836 in Ongiry to legally married nobles Adam Lutkiewicz and Aniela Juchniewicz. He was baptized on June 29, 1836 in Jaswojnie (Polish) or Josvainiai (Lithuanian) Parish. His godparents were noble Karol Spandowicz and maiden Franciszka Wabikiewicz. Gabriel married twice, the first time at Krakės (Lithuanian), or Kroki (Polish), Parish to Leokadia Mikulski, a 22-year-old widow. He was 28 at the time, and the witnesses were Jan Mikulski, Aleksander Leotkowicz, and Kazimierz Wołtkiewicz. They and had the following children:

- Kazimiera Lutkiewicz (1865-?)
- Adolf Lutkiewicz (before 1867-?)
- Adela Waleria Lutkiewicz (before 1867-?)

Unfortunately, Leokadia died on October 24, 1867 from a fever at the age of only 30.

Gabriel remarried to Weronika Ciechanowicz, and they had the following children:

- Katarzyna Lutkiewicz
- Michalina Lutkiewicz
- Antoni Lutkiewicz
- Jan Lutkiewicz
- Paulina Lutkiewicz (1880-?) who married Teofil Rymkiewicz (1877-1949)
- Józef Lutkiewicz (1883-1927) who married Stefania Stefaniewicz (1888-1970)
- Ludwika Lutkiewicz (1884-1978) who married Kazimierz Dowgwillo (1874-1954)

Józef Lutkiewicz

Józef Lutkiewicz was born on March 14, 1883 in Żwalany. He was baptized on March 20, 1883 in Betygala (Lithuanian) or Betygola (Polish) Parish. His godparents were nobles Cyprian Janczewski and maiden Franciszka Dobkiewicz. Not much is known about Józef's early life, but what is known is that his parents wanted to have his noble status documented and accepted by the Czarist Russian government. On November 25, 1892 a report documenting the Kaunas Nobility Deputation Organization decision to confirm Józef's status was written. On April 3, 1893, there was a report from the Kaunas nobility association that they received and recorded the nobility department decision. This would have given Józef certain rights and privileges, like not being conscripted into the Russian military. However, Józef chose to leave Lithuania. On August 8, 1908, he boarded the ship, Deutschland, in Hamburg and headed to New York. Józef changed his name to Joseph and headed to Philadelphia.

In 1907, he married a fellow Lithuanian immigrant, 19-year-old Jadwiga Stefanawicz, before she changed her name to Ida. Joseph and Ida had four children: Josephine, Leo, Ida, and Joseph Addison. Unfortunately, Leo died from enterocolitis on August 28, 1910. He was only about a year old and was buried at Holy Redeemer in Philadelphia.

In 1913, Joseph bought a home on 2649 Westmoreland Ave. in Philadelphia. Joseph did lots of odd jobs: he was a machinist at Midvale

Steel Works, a barber, and a cigar salesman. On May 11, 1915, Joseph became a naturalized citizen.

Ida was a saleswoman in a candy store. Joseph died on February 21, 1931 in Philadelphia at the age of 47. It's unclear where he was buried. After Joseph died, Ida ran a tavern. Ida died in November of 1970 and was buried in Moreland Memorial Park in Baltimore, Maryland because her daughter, Josephine, lived there at the time.

Joseph and Ida's daughter, Josephine, was born on March 17, 1908. She married William Underland in 1930, and they lived on 1228 Pratt Street in Philadelphia. They had a daughter, Joyce, who died from acute ileocolitis on October 16, 1931 at only seven months of age. They went on to have another son. William was a sales representative for a truck manufacturer that made trucks, tanks, trailers, and petroleum equipment. By 1944, Josephine and William moved to Maryland, and William started his own petroleum services company. Petroleum Services, Inc. supplied petroleum tanks, trucks, pumps, and other equipment to oil companies in Maryland. By 1952, Josephine and William divorced. Josephine died on June 4, 1984 at the age of 76 and was buried at the same location as her mother, Moreland Memorial Park in Maryland. William died on May 28, 1970 in Baltimore and was buried in Druid Ridge Cemetery.

Joseph and Ida's daughter, Ida, was born on March 1, 1912 in Philadelphia. By 1940, she married Edwin Nowicki. Edwin worked as a bartender at Ida's mother's tavern. Unfortunately, he died on February 10, 1951 at the age of 40. On May 21, 1957, Ida remarried to Chester Orzel in Alexandria, Virginia. By 1984, the couple had moved to Florida. Chester died on August 21, 1984 at the age of 74 in Pinellas, Florida and was buried in Calvary Catholic Cemetery and Mausoleum. Ida died on May 8, 2007 in Pinellas, Florida at the age of 95. She was buried with her first husband, Edwin, in Most Holy Redeemer Cemetery in Philadelphia, Pennsylvania.

Joseph and Ida's son, Joseph, was born on June 23, 1917 in Philadelphia. He married Mary T Dzara in 1947, and they lived at 4070 Roosevelt Road in Philadelphia. Joseph died on September 5, 1997 and Mary died on August 24, 2001. They are buried at Our Lady of Grace Cemetery in Langhorne, Pennsylvania.

Ludwika Lutkiewicz

Ludwika Lutkiewicz was born in 1884 and lived in Angiriai. She had quite a different life than her brother, Józef. She never came to America, but she did leave Lithuania.

When she was 22, Ludwika was supposed to marry a bachelor whose heart was taken by another woman—a widow who lived in the area. The widow gave the matchmaker a horse to try to stop the marriage. However, the banns were announced, and a grand wedding reception was prepared. Ludwika was taken to the Jaswojnie (Polish), or Josvianiai (Lithuanian), Parish for the wedding by her father, and the groom was taken to the wedding by the matchmaker. At some point while driving to church, the groom decided not to go through with it and did not show up at the church.

Ludwika and her father, Gabriel Bronislaw, waited 45 minutes for the groom before leaving the alter. However, there was another man standing behind a pillar near the alter hoping such a thing would happen. Kazimierz Dowgwillo wanted to marry Ludwika himself.

Kazimierz Dowgwillo was born in 1874 in Vandžiogala (Lithuanian), or Wędziagoła (Polish), in the Kaunas district. He was one of nine children born to Jan Piotr Dowgwillo and Kazimiera Ibiańska, and he lived about 50 kilometers away from Ludwika.

Kazimierz approached the bride, took her father's place, led her into the sleigh that was waiting, and went to the house where the wedding reception would take place. They celebrated for the customary three days, even though there was no wedding! If Kazimierz had not stepped in to host the party, Ludwika would have been shamed by the invited guests.

Later, Kazimierz and Ludwika had the banns announced for their own wedding and set the date for February 7, 1906 in Krakės (Lithuanian) or Kroki (Polish) Parish.

Krakės (Lithuanian) or Kroki (Polish) Parish

Attempting to get married for a second time, Ludwika was incredulous that this was really happening. At the side of Kazimierz, she crossed the church threshold.

Traditionally, there is a place where female beggars wait for alms by the church known as a "babiniec." On their wedding day, Kazimierz gave alms to each sitting beggar and joked: "Pray for me so that I would not get married..." After the wedding, he went back to the surprised female beggars to take his alms back, shouting: "And how did you pray? ... I did get married." He didn't take the alms back, but he did give the female beggars a serious fright. Kazimierz Dowgwiłło was famous for his pranks, good humor, and great kindness.

Kazimierz and Ludwika had the following children:

- Bronislaw Dowgwillo (1906-1986)
- Otton Dowgwillo (1908-?)
- Antoni Dowgwillo (1909-?)

- Stefan Dowgwillo (1911-1911)
- Katarzyna Dowgwillo (1913-1991)
- Jan Dowgwillo (1914-1914)
- Weronika Dowgwillo (1917-?)
- Kazimierz Dowgwillo (1923-1978)
- Donat Dowgwillo (1926-1989)

Kazimierz and Ludwika had about a 70-acre farm in Radziewiliszki (Polish), or Radviliškiai (Lithuanian), in the Chekiszki district.

During the summer of 1948, Kazimierz and Ludwika were sent to Igarka, a town in the Turukhansky District of Krasnoyarsk Krai, Russia (101 miles north of the Arctic Circle), on Yenisei River in Siberia. Their job was to cut down trees.

To contextualize these happenings, this occurred during the Soviet deportations of 1948-1951. Thousands of civilians were deported from newly occupied territories of USSR, including some 5,000-10,000 Lithuanians who were forcefully deported from their homeland. About 1,000 of them died there from the cold and poor conditions in the winter of 1948-49.[21]

Even in Siberia, Kazimierz did not lose his cheerfulness and kindness towards people. He died in Igarka at the age of 90 in 1954 and was buried there.

Kazimierz and Ludwika's son, Donat, managed to sneak Ludwika away from Igarka and bring her to Kaunas, where she died in 1978. She was buried in Kruwondach. Later, her sons - Kazimierz and Donat- were buried with her. A gravestone was erected for Kazmierz, Ludwika, Kazimierz (son) and Donat. However, Kazimierz's body was never moved from Igarka.

Kazimierz, Ludwika, Kazimierz (son), and Donat Dowgwillo's Gravestone

CHAPTER FOUR

Izydor Dowgwillo and Zofia Brygida Buharewicz

Izydor Dowgwillo was the brother of Antoni Dowgwillo. Antoni Dowgwillo was the father of Barbara Dowgwillo. Barbara Dowgwillo was the wife of Adolf Lutkiewicz and the mother of Antoni Lutkiewicz. Antoni was the father of my Great-Grandfather Charles. So, Izydor was my fourth great-uncle.

Krekenava (Lithuanian), or Krakinów (Polish) Parish

Izydor was born on May 12, 1790 to nobles Andrzej Dowgwillo and Katarzyna Rojcewicz. He was baptized in Krekenava (Lithuanian), or Krakinów (Polish) Parish. His godparents were nobles Laurenty Dowgwillo and Sophia Roykiewicz. Before 1814, he married Zofia Brygida Buharewicz, and they had nine children:

- Stefan Albin Dowgwillo (1814-1870) married Franciszka Butkiewicz.
- Aniela Dowgwillo (1816-1840) married Jan Babiański (1809-?).
- Agnes Dowgwillo (1818-?)
- Karolina Anna Dowgwillo (1819-1819)
- Józef Pawel Dowgwillo (1820-?)
- Anna Kunegunda Dowgwillo (1822-?)
- Benedykt Dowgwillo (1824-?) married Teofila Syryjatowicz (1830-?).
- Dionizy Ignacy Dowgwillo (1826-?) married Irena Łukowicz (1839-bef. 1883) and Irena Michałowska.

- Józef Dowgwillo (1833-?) married Teofila Chodorowicz (1837-1873).

Six of their grandchildren immigrated to the United States—three children of their son, Benedykt, and three children of their son, Józef.

Benedykt Dowgwillo

Izydor and Zofia's seventh child, Benedykt Dowgwillo, was baptized on March 17, 1824 in Krakės (Lithuanian), or Kroki (Polish), Parish and lived in Senkany. On November 16, 1849, 26-year-old Benedykt Dowgwiłło married 19-year-old Teofila Syryjatowicz in Krakės (Lithuanian), or Kroki (Polish), Parish. They were both living in the village of Nowareczka at the time.

Benedykt and Teofila had nine children:

- Jan Dowgwillo (1850-1925) married Stanisława Romaszkiewicz (1870-1938).
- Kazimierz Dowgwillo (1853-1928) married Kazimiera Dolongowska (1858-1928).
- Katarzyna/Katie Dowgwillo (1855-1925) married Kaliskt Witort (1850-1925).
- Victoria Dowgwillo (1857-?) married Julian Lipiniewicz (1862-1891).
- Maria Dowgwillo (1860-1862)
- Wincenta Dowgwillo (1862-?) married Franciszek Piotrowicz (1862-?).
- Bronislaw/Joseph B. Dowgwillo (1865-1958) married Bertha Swartz (1887-1973).
- Teofil Dowgwillo (1867-1923) married Jadwiga Pawlik (1875-?).
- Anna Rozalia Dowgwillo (1870-1939) married Józef Dubinksi (1868-?).

Three children immigrated to the United States in the early 1900s—Jan/John, Katarzyna/Katie, and Bronislaw/Joseph B. There is not much information available about the children who stayed in Lithuania—Kazimieriz, Victoria, Maria, Wincenta, Teofil and Anna. But there is information about their grandson—Józef, son of Kazimierz—that will be included in the end.

Jan Dowgwillo

Benedykt and Teofila's oldest son, Jan Dowgwillo, was born on December 29, 1850 in Lithuania. On Jan 17, 1895, Jan Dowgwillo married Stanisława Romaszkiewicz in Krakės (Lithuanian), or Kroki (Polish), Parish. Jan was 44 and Stanisława was 23. Both were from the village of Guty.

Jan and Stanisława had two children in Lithuania—Kazimierz (Charles Walter) born on March 3, 1895 and Kataryna (Katie) born on October 21, 1896. Both were born in Guty and baptized in Krakės (Lithuanian), or Kroki (Polish), Parish.

Jan, Stanisława, Kazimierz, Katarzyna, and Jan's brother, Bronislaw, left Lithuania and settled in Cedar River, Michigan around 1896. He and his brother, Bronislaw, became naturalized citizens by 1900. Jan had another sibling who came to Michigan—Katarzyna/Katie and her husband, Kaliskt Witort.

Jan changed his first name to John, Stanisława changed her first name to Stella and they changed their last name to Dougovito. They had 5 more children in Cedar River, Michigan:

- Anna Dougovito was born on November 9, 1902.
- Carl Joseph Dougovito was born on November 4, 1904.
- Walter Paul Dougovito was born on December 28, 1908.
- Bronislawa Dougovito was born on January 6, 1910.
- Joseph Dougovito was born on March 8, 1912.

By 1910, the family was living in on the same street as John's sister, Katarzyna/Katie Dowgwillo, and her husband, Kalikst Witort. A couple houses down the street were John Wutkevicz and Vincenta Lutkiewicz. Vincenta was 2nd the cousin of Grandpa Charles and Valeria. A few more houses down the street lived Józef B. Dowgwillo, a brother of John. At this point in time, John was working at a sawmill with his brother-in-law, Kalikst Witort.

By 1920, John was a farmer, and Stella was a homemaker. Their daughter, Bronislawa, died on September 2, 1910 at only eight months old. Their daughter, Kataryna/Katie, died in 1916 from pneumonia at the age of 19 and was buried in Stephenson Township Cemetery in Michigan. John and Stella were still living with some of their children—Charles, Carl, Walter, and Joseph.

John and Stella's daughter, Anna, married a neighbor and fellow Lithuanian immigrant, Anton Atkonkunis, and they moved to Proviso, Illinois. Anton and Anna met in 1910 when they lived on the same block. Prior to getting married, Anton had served as a private in the 161st Depot Brigade during World War I. The role of depot brigades was to receive and organize recruits, provide them with uniforms, equipment, and initial military training, and then send them to France to fight on the front lines. The depot brigades also received soldiers returning home at the end of the war and completed their out processing and discharges. Anton was discharged on January 16, 1919 at Camp Grant.

After marriage, Anton worked for the railroad as a car mechanic and eventually became an inspector for the Chicago & North Western Railroad. By 1937, Anton and Anna moved to Cedar River, and Anton became a farmer.

Anton and Anna had three children—Joseph (1920-1942), Walter (1921-1922) and Charley (1927-2010). Joseph died of insulin shock at the age of 22. Walter died infancy. Only Charley grew into adulthood. He married Mary Van Demark. Charley died on April 29, 2010.

Anton died on October 24, 1963 at the age of 72, and Anna died on December 27, 1993 at the age of 91. Anton, Anna, Joseph, Walter, and Charley are all buried in Stephenson Cemetery in Michigan.[22]

According to the 1920 Census, John and Stella Dougovito continued to live close to John Wutkevicz and Vincenta Lutkiewicz, Kalikst Witort and Scholastyka Lutkiewicz, Joseph B and Bertha Dowgwillo (John's brother and sister-in-law), Joseph and Stella Bardowski, John Wutkevicz and Vincenta Lutkiewicz, and Józef Lutkiewicz and Stefania (Stella). They were all interrelated through marriage and enjoyed close locational proximity in both Lithuania and Michigan for a few centuries.

John Dougovito died after a long bout with cancer on March 28, 1925. His funeral was held at Precious Blood Church, and he was buried in Stephenson Cemetery.

Stella died on March 25, 1938 at the age of 60 in her farm home in Cedarville Township. She died a few days before the 13th anniversary of her husband's death. Her funeral was held at Precious Blood Church, and she was buried in Stephenson Cemetery. The people carrying her casket were Walter Bardowski (grandson of her husband's sister, Katie), Bernard Dowgwillo (son of her brother-in-law, Joseph), Edward Vetort (son of her sister-in-law, Katie), Felix Strell, John Wutkevicz, and Peter Wutkevicz.

John and Stella's son, Carl John graduated from Stephenson High School in 1925. He attended the University of Michigan (1926-1932) and was a champion varsity wrestler. He was one of the all-time wrestling greats at Michigan in 1929, 1930, and 1931 and served as the 1931 team captain. He won two Big Ten titles and one national championship, was 8-2 in three NCAA finals, and was a member of the 1932 U.S. Olympic team that was held in Los Angeles, California.

He was in the Army Reserve and was commandant at Camp Wells, John W. Wells State Park, Cedar River.

Carl married Mary Katherine Scaritski on August 30, 1937 in Gaastra Michigan. A few years later, World War II started. Carl went into the Army and was awarded the Soldier's Medal of the Army. He was cited for volunteering to accompany an attachment of unarmed men to fight its way into occupied territory where an allied plane crashed, and everyone was killed. He went to identify the plane and its occupants. He spent 75 hours on horseback and was out of contact with the outside world for more than three weeks.

Carl was also a communications officer under Major General John N. Greely, on whose orders he was on a diplomatic mission in Kuybyshev, Russia from March 13 to June 1, 1942. He continued his military service in Korea, Germany, and many other places in the United State during his 35 years of marriage to Mary.

Carl and Mary raised seven sons and one daughter. In the 1950s, they moved back to Cedar River. Carl achieved the rank of lieutenant colonel before retiring from active duty on September 30, 1957. For several years following his retirement, he was a civilian employee of the Air Force Bast at K.I. Sawyer, commuting back and forth from Stephenson, Michigan.

Carl was an avid sports fan of Stephenson High School. His sons played sports at the school. Unfortunately, his son Carl Jr., a member of the basketball team, was killed in 1957 in a car accident.

Carl was a church usher at the Precious Blood Church, a 4th degree member of the Knights of Columbus of Menominee, a member of the

Godfrey Anderson Post American Legion, and a member of the North Shore Golf Club of Menominee.

Carl died on January 17, 1973, and Mary died on November 27, 2007. Both were members of the Precious Blood Church in Stephenson, Michigan and were buried in Stephenson Cemetery.[23]

John and Stella's next son, Walter Paul, married Monica Constance Payant around 1940. They had five children.

Walter moved to the Kingsford area of Michigan around 1924. He worked at the Ford Motor Company for a while. In 1927, he joined the Wisconsin Michigan Power Company. His last position was as the assistant to the general manager. Walter was active in many organizations, including serving as the president of the Pine Mountain Ski Club. He was also a member of the following organizations: Pine Grove Country Club, Rotary, United Commercial Travelers, Elks Lodge, Iron Mountain-Kingsford Winter Sports Association, Chippewa Club, National Ski Patrol, the Dickinson County Band, and Fourth Degree Knights of Columbus. Walter died on January 30, 1969 of a heart attack at his home. Monica died on September 18, 2001. Both are buried in Iron Mountain Cemetery in Minnesota.[24]

John and Stella's last son, Joseph, became a farmer. He married Olga Jaunsen on May 12, 1939 in Stephenson Michigan and moved to Pembine, Wisconsin. Olga was a teacher while Joseph worked for the Staso Company Pembine until he started his own company, The Midwest Plastic Company, in Pembine. Joseph died on April 26, 1975 at the age of 63 after having a heart attack while driving in the village of Amberg. Olga died on May 30, 1996 at the age of 86. Both are buried in the Pembine Cemetery in Wisconsin.[25]

Katarzyna Dowgwillo

Benedykt and Teofila's oldest daughter, Katarzyna Dowgwillo, was born on October 21, 1896 in Guty. She was baptized in Krakės (Lithuanian), or Kroki (Polish), Parish. She, then 26 years old, married 30-year-old bachelor Kaliskt Witort on February 22, 1881 in Krakės (Lithuanian), Kroki (Polish), Parish. Kaliskt was the son of Jan Witort and Wiktoria Olecki.

Kaliskt and Katarzyna had eight children in Lithuania:

- Zofia Witort (1881-1887).
- Jan Witort (1883-1962) married Mary Cieska (1892-1978).
- Edward Vetort (1884-1967) married Scholastyka Lutkiewicz (1891-1961).
- Władysław/Walter Witort (1887-1962) married Kataryna Zukowska (1897-1927) & Charlotte Wilson (1898-?).
- Stephen Witort (1888-1925) married Helena Zukowska (1893-1948).
- Stefania Vetort (1892-1962) married Józef Bardowski (1886-1964).
- Anna Witort (1895-1959) married Jan Stravinski (1889-1960).
- Władysława/Charlotte/Lottie Witort (1898-1964) married Stanisław Zalewski (1892-1958).

They lost one child, Zofia, to smallpox in 1887 when she was just six years old. Kaliskt and his daughter, Stefania, went to the United States in 1909. They left Bremen, Germany on the SS Rhein on May 28, 1909 and arrived in Baltimore, Maryland on June 10, 1909. Katarzyna and daughters Anna and Lottie arrived a bit later. They left Bremen on the SS Rhein on September 2, 1909 and arrived on September 16, 1909 in Baltimore, Maryland. Jan and Walter arrived in the United States sometime in 1907. They went from Belgium to Quebec and then came to the United States. Stephen arrived in 1907, but it's unclear how he got there.

Kaliskt and Katarzyna's son, Jan, was probably the first to the United States in 1907. By 1910, he changed his name to John and lived in Cedar River, Michigan with parents and siblings where he worked as a laborer in a sawmill. On December 3, 1912, he married 20-year-old Mary Cieska in Menominee County at the age of 29. They moved to Proviso, Illinois soon after that and went on to have four children—Walter, Wanda, Helen, and Bernice. John became a naturalized citizen of the United States on January 24, 1919. In 1920, John was a repairman for railway cars, in 1930, he was a laborer for a steel mill, and by 1940, he owned his own tavern and lived in Melrose Park, Illinois, a popular area for Lithuanians. John died on February 28, 1962. His wife, Mary, died September 7, 1978. They are buried in Chicago, Illinois.

Kaliskt and Katarzyna's son, Edward, married Scholastyka Lutkiewicz on June 30, 1910 in Stephenson, Michigan. Their story is told in another section.

Kaliskt and Katarzyna's son, Władysław, changed his name to Walter.

In 1910, he was working as a laborer in a sawmill in Michigan and living with his parents and siblings. On June 17, 1919, he married Katarzyna Zukowska. By 1920, Walter was employed as a barber and was living in Chicago with his wife. He became a US citizen on April 11, 1924 in Cook County Superior Court. Walter and Kataryna had 3 children. Unfortunately, Katarzyna died on June 20, 1927 at the age of 30. Walter remarried to Charlotte Wilson and had one more child—Ronald. Walter died December 18, 1962 in Franklin Park Illinois. Charlotte died on January 7, 1984 in Merced, California.

Kaliskt and Katarzyna's son, Stefan, changed his name to Steve. In 1910, he was living with his parents and siblings. He, like John, also worked as a laborer in a sawmill in Michigan. On February 26, 1916 he married Helena Zukowska, sister of Katarzyna (the first wife of his brother, Walter). They had three children. By 1920, they moved to Proviso, Illinois where Steve worked as an inspector for the railroads. Unfortunately, Steve died on August 24, 1925 at the age of 36 after being run over by a freight car. Helena remarried to Vincent Mieczynski and raised her children. Helena died on April 21, 1982 in Florida.

Kaliskt and Katarzyna's daughter, Stefania, changed her name to Stella and was living with her parents and siblings in 1910. On June 4, 1911 she married Joseph Bardowski in the Church of the Precious Blood in Stephenson Michigan. She was 19 years old, and Joseph was 25. They stayed in the Cedarville area for their entire lives working on their farm. They had nine children in 16 years. Stella died unexpectedly on February 7, 1962 in St. Joseph Lloyd Hospital in Menominee at the age of 69. Joseph died at the age of 74 in the Roubal Nursing Home in Talbot, Michigan on October 23, 1964.

Kaliskt and Katarzyna's daughter, Anna, lived with her parents and siblings in 1910. On August 1, 1915, she married John Leo Stravinski in Cedar River, Michigan. She was 20, and he was 26 years old. They moved to Melrose Park and had one child. By 1917, they settled in Milwaukee, Wisconsin and had three more children before 1920. In 1920, John was an inspector for the railroad in Milwaukee. He was naturalized on January 12, 1926. In 1930, John was a foreman on the steam railway and by 1940, he was a railway car inspector in Milwaukee. Anna became a naturalized citizen on June 12, 1952. Anna died on March 25, 1959 at the age of 62 after being hospitalized for two weeks. John died on May 3, 1960 from drowning. When he had failed to come home on Sunday, May 3, a search began for him. His body was found behind his home in the Little Cedar River. It was believed he slipped and fell over the steep bank into the river, which was very high from flood waters.[26] Both Anna and John were buried in Stephenson Township Cemetery in Michigan.

Kaliskt and Katarzyna's daughter, Władysława, changed her name to Charlotte or Lottie. In 1910, she was living with her parents and siblings in Cedar River, Michigan. On January 2, 1915 she married Stanisław, or Stanley, Zalewski, a 25-year-old fellow Lithuanian immigrant in Stephenson, Michigan. Lottie was about 17 years old. They went on to have five children in 12 years. By 1920, they were living in Proviso, Illinois where Stanley was a railroad car repairman. Stanley was naturalized on September 25, 1925. By 1930, they were living in Chicago where Stanley continued to make a living by repairing railroad cars. By 1940, he became a self-employed carpenter. Lottie became a US citizen on March 25, 1943. Stanley died on April 29, 1973 in Michigan, and Lottie died in 1989. Both were buried in Queen of Heaven Catholic Cemetery in Hillside, Illinois.

Bronislaw/Joseph J Dowgwillo

Bronislaw was born on January 27, 1865 and baptized on February 1, 1865 in Krakės (Lithuanian), or Kroki (Polish), Parish. He came to the United States in 1896 with his brother, John, and his family. By 1900, both John and Bronislaw were naturalized citizens who had settled in Cedarville, Michigan. Bronislaw changed his name to Joseph B, and married Bertha Swartz on August 27, 1905 in Stephenson, Michigan. He was 40 years old, and Bertha was 18. They had six children in 11 years— Victoria, Matilda, Theodore, Benny, Bernard, and Mary.

By 1910, they had lost one son, Theodore. Staring around 1920, Joseph ran his own farm in Menominee, Michigan and continued to run the farm throughout the 30s with his two remaining sons.

Joseph and Bertha's daughter, Matilda, married William Nash and had two children.

By 1941, Joseph and Bertha's daughter, Mary, married Lawrence Hupy in Stephenson, Michigan. Mary was a graduate of Stephenson High School and Northern Michigan University and taught school in Menominee County and in the Gwinn School system. Unfortunately, Mary died at the age of 50 on January 1, 1969 in Marquette.[27]

Bronislaw Joseph died on October 14, 1958 in Stephenson, Michigan. Bertha died on January 28, 1973 in Stephenson, Michigan. They are both buried in the Stephenson Cemetery in Michigan.

Kazimierz Dowgwillo

Benedykt and Teofia's second child, Kazimierz, was born March 4, 1843. He never left Lithuania. He married Kazimiera Dolongowska in Krakės (Lithuanian), or Kroki (Polish), Parish on February 27, 1878. He was 38, and she was 20 years old. They went on to have six children—Kazimierz, Anna, Stefania, Constance, Józef, and Antoni. Kazimierz was part of the 1863 uprising against the Russian occupation of Lithuania.

Kazimierz died on May 18, 1928 in Vilnius and his wife, Kazimiera, died on the same day.

Dotnuva (Lithuanian), or Datnów (Polish)

Their son, Józef Dowgwillo, was born in Pilnów on November 17, 1892. He was confirmed in Dotnuva (Lithuanian), or Datnów (Polish),

Parish and attended elementary school in Montwidów. He went to a municipal school in Vilnius in 1909 before deciding in 1910 that he wanted to become a priest. In 1914, after graduating from a four-class municipal school, he entered the Vilnius Seminary. He graduated and was ordained a priest in 1919.

He first worked as a vicar in Bialystok, Poland where he was appointed to be the full-time prefect of elementary schools after only a few months. He took prefect courses in Bialystok, as well as courses for prefects at high schools in Poznań (1920) and Lublin (1924). On April 27 and 28, 1925, he passed the official examination before the ministerial and episcopal commission for the prefect of high schools in Warsaw. He was also a member of the Association of Catholic Workers founded in 1908.

In 1920, he moved to Slonim to replace the local priest, who had been taken to Russia. After the return of the priest from Siberia, Józef remained in this city until 1924 to serve as the prefect of high schools.

In 1924, he was appointed prefect of the State Secondary School in Żyrowice near Słonim.

In the spring of 1926, he was appointed by the Vilnius Ordinariate of Archbishops as a pastor of the Roman Catholic parish of St. Teresa of the Infant Jesus in Białowieża, Poland. This parish was erected on August 15, 1926.

Due to the lack of a church building, the first mass was celebrated in a chapel arranged in the former dining room of the tsarist palace. Józef headed the Church Construction Committee and actively raised funds for its construction. Building began in 1927, and the church was consecrated on October 16, 1934.

Along with managing the construction of the church building, Father Józef cared for reviving the religious spirit of his parishioners. He initiated the Eucharistic Crusade, the Living Rosary, Four Columns of the Catholic Action, the Catholic Association of Husbands and Women, and the Third Order of St. Francis. The Polish Youth Association also became very active during the time. A parish library was established, and subscriptions to religious magazines were organized and distributed. Readings, meetings, and various events were organized.

Father Józef taught religion at the State School for Foresters. He damaged his health by excessive work and left his successors an organized religious life but an unfinished church (it did not have the main tower and plaster, but it was already provisionally arranged). On May 15, 1935, he handed over the parish to his successor, Father Władysław Paczkowski.

Father Józef went pastor in Mońki, Poland where he found a newly completed church. Unfortunately, the retreating Germans blew up this church on July 11, 1944 during World War II.

After World War II ended, Father Józef taught religion in the neighboring primary schools: Dzików, Potoczyzna, and Hornostaje. He was also part of the Reconstruction Committee to rebuild the church that was destroyed at Mońki. The church was eventually reconstructed, but it took many years due to the political situation in Poland. It was completed in 1960, but by then, Father Józef had been retired for 2 years.

Father Józef died on September 8, 1964 in Suraż, Poland and is buried at the Suraż Parish Cemetery.

Józef Dowgwillo

Izydor Dowgwillo and Zofia Brygida's ninth child, Józef Dowgwillo, was born in about 1833 although his baptism record has not been found. He grew up in Senkany.

Józef married twice. The first time was to Teofila Chodorowicz, around 1855. They had eight children: Anna, Aleksander, Zygmunt, Stefan, Elwira, Felicjanna, Benedykt, and Józef. One of their children, Zygmunt, died at a few months old in 1868. Unfortunately, a 36-year-old Teofila died on April 18, 1873 from "weakness." Józef married a second time to a 20-year-old Ewa Gosztowt on November 25, 1873 in Krakės (Lithuanian), or Kroki (Polish), Parish. Józef was 40 years old at the time.

Józef and Ewa had five children:

- Felix Dowgwillo (1874-?)
- Hipolit Paul Dowgwillo (1877-1959) married Marjanna Zaworska.
- Katarzyna Katie Dowgwillo (1880-1917) married Władysław Walter Staniewicz (1877-1915).
- Teresa Dowgwillo (1883-1884)
- Teresa Catherine Dowgwillo (1890-1961) married Michael Szwagżdis (1883-1947).

Three children immigrated to the United States in the early 1900s—
Hipolit/Paul, Katarzyna/Katie and Teresa Catherine.

Hipolit Paul Dowgwillo

Hipolit was born on August 13, 1877 in the village of Guty. He
was baptized a day later in Krakės (Lithuanian), or Kroki (Polish),
Parish. He arrived in the port of New York on board the SS Bremen on
March 20, 1899 with plans to meet his uncle at 3242 Thompson Street
in Philadelphia. He married Marjanna Zarwoska on May 23, 1905 in
Philadelphia. Hipolit worked as a machinist and a brakeman on street cars
for the Philadelphia Transit Company. They rented various homes around
the city in neighborhoods filled with other immigrants from Lithuania.
They eventually bought their own home on 2704 Ontario Avenue. Hipolit
became a US citizen on April 23, 1924. He was a member of the Lithuanian
Music Hall Association and the Lithuanian Republican Beneficial Club.

Hipolit and Mary had the following children:

- John Dowgwillo (1906-1964) married Pauline Helen Pawlak
  (1912-1999).
- Andrew Henry Dockwell (1908-2008) married Mildred
  Maskauskas/Mitchell (1911-2004).
- Peter Dockwell (1910-1985)
- Joseph Dowgurl (1912-2002) married Marion Dolores Wargo
  (1908-1988).
- Michael Edwin Dowgwil (1914-1990)
- Alexander Raymond Dowgwillo (1917-1982) married Joanne Gies
  (1930-?).
- Jean Mary Grace Dowgwillo (1924-2004) married Michael Koper
  (1921-2002).

Mary died on December 17, 1953 at the age of 64, and Hipolit died
on November 22, 1959 at the age of 84 from coronary thrombosis. Both
Mary and Hipolit were buried in Holy Redeemer Cemetery.

Hipolit and Mary's son, John, worked as a spinner in a cotton mill, a
dyer in the textile industry, and as a general laborer. He married Pauline
Helen Pawlak in January 1951 in Camden, New Jersey where Pauline's

family lived. John and Pauline had one daughter. John died on May 16, 1964 from a massive acute myocardial infarction and Pauline died on December 4, 1999 in Pennsylvania. They are buried in St. Dominic's cemetery in Pennsylvania.

Hipolit and Mary's son, Andrew Henry, was born November 30, 1908 in Philadelphia. He changed his last name to Dockwell. Andrew worked as a taxi driver and as a truck driver for Moran Transportation. He married Mildred Maskauskas (Mitchell) in 1931 in Camden, New Jersey where she was from. However, they made their home in Philadelphia where they raised three children. Andrew died on March 11, 2008, and Mildred died on June 26, 2004. Both are buried in Resurrection Cemetery.

Hipolit and Mary's son, Peter, was born on February 17, 1910 in Philadelphia. He, like Andrew, changed his last name to Dockwell. Before World War II, Peter was a candy maker though he joined the Army on November 12, 1942 and served until after the war ended. He was discharged on January 1, 1946 and went back to Philadelphia. He died on December 4, 1985 at the age of 75. He was buried in Holy Redeemer Cemetery with his parents.

Hipolit and Mary's son, Joseph, was born on June 12, 1912 in Philadelphia. He changed his last name to Dowgurl. Joseph worked at a grocery store and was a truck driver. He was a member of the International Brotherhood of Teamsters. He married Marion Dolores Wargo in 1956. Joseph died on September 11, 2002 at the age of 90. His sister-in-law, Joanne Gies Dowgwillo, took care of him in the last eight weeks of his life in Maryland. Marion died on March 10, 1988 at the age of 79. Both are buried in Resurrection Cemetery.

Hipolit and Mary's son, Michael Edwin, was born on October 30, 1914 in Philadelphia. Before World War II, he worked as a laborer in a machine shop but enlisted in the Army on February 4, 1943. He was discharged on December 13, 1945, leaving as a private, and he went back to Pennsylvania. Michael died on February 19, 1990 in Pennsylvania. He was buried in Indiantown Gap National Cemetery in Annville, Pennsylvania under the name Michael E Dowgwil.

Hipolit and Mary's son, Alexander Raymond, was born July 24, 1917 in Philadelphia. He enlisted in the Army on August 5, 1937 and saw action in both the Atlantic and the Pacific. On October 15, 1951, he married Joanne Gies in St. Mary's Catholic Church in Annapolis, Maryland. He retired from the military as a major but continued to work as a civilian at

Fort Mead. He volunteered for the Boy Scouts, and in 1963, he was the treasurer for the Grand Jurors Association for the Anne Arundel County, Maryland. In 1965, he was an officer for the Anne Arundel Citizens Committee. In 1966, he ran for school board for the Anne Arundel County School District. Joanne was a clerk for State Board of Law Examiners. Alexander and Joanne had two children. Alexander died on November 14, 1982 in Millersville, Maryland. He was buried in Our Lady of the Field Cemetery. Joanne took care of her brother-in-law, Joseph Dowgurl, during the last eight weeks of his life in 2002.

Hipolit and Mary's daughter, Jean Marie Grace, was born on October 6, 1924 in Philadelphia. She married Michael Koper in 1945 in Philadelphia. Michael joined the Air Corps on August 2, 1939 and served in the military through World War II before being discharged on July 14, 1945. After the war, Michael joined the Air Force and served as a procurement officer for four more years, from August 20, 1954 through August 19, 1958. Then he became a regional property and procurement officer of the Mid-Atlantic Region for the National Park Service. Jean and Michael had three children. Jean was a long-time volunteer at the Frankford Hospital-Torresdale in Philadelphia. Michael died July 2, 2002, and Jean died on November 28, 2004. They are buried in Resurrection Cemetery in Philadelphia.

Katarzyna Katie Dowgwillo

Katarzyna Dowgwillo was born in Guty on March 6, 1880 and baptized in Krakės (Lithuanian), or Kroki (Polish), Parish on March 7. Her godparents were Antoni Niwiński and Izabela Dowgwiłło, maiden. Around 1902, she arrived in Philadelphia, probably to meet her brother, Hipolit. She changed her name to Katie. On April 26, 1902, she married fellow Lithuanian immigrant Władysław, or Walter, Staniewicz in Detroit, Michigan. Walter had arrived in Philadelphia in 1896 on board the Nederland from Belgium. He had other siblings that came to join him—Joseph, Vincent, and Sophia.

Walter worked as a laborer for the railroad and spoke English though Katie only spoke Polish.

Katie and Walter had one child, John, on September 3, 1903 in Michigan before moving to Philadelphia to have six more children: Helen, Czesława/Gessie, Walter, Christina, Willie, and William.

Three children died of the same illness, acute gastroenteritis, between 1910 and 1911, and one child died of malformed bowels in 1913. All of these children were buried at Holy Redeemer Cemetery:

- Czesława/Gessie was born on October 8, 1905 and died on April 3, 1911 at the age of five of acute gastroenteritis.
- Walter was born on April 8, 1907 and died on July 25, 1910 at the age of three of acute gastro enteritis.
- Christina was born on August 30, 1910 and died on September 29, 1910 at the age of one month from acute gastroenteritis.
- Willie was born on June 3, 1913 and died on August 10, 1913 from malformed bowels.

On September 15, 1914, Władysław/William died from gas poisoning in his home. He was also buried at Holy Redeemer Cemetery. On March 22, 1917, Katie was shot in the stomach by her brother-in-law, Anthony Walush, the husband of Sophie Staniewicz. Sophie was Władysław's sister. Katie was taken to Episcopal Hospital where she died on April 7, 1917. Anthony stood trial and was found guilty of second-degree homicide on November 2, 1917.[28] He sentenced to a minimum of 16 years and was sent to Eastern State Penitentiary. He was pardoned on March 30, 1928 and went back to his wife and six children.

It's unclear what happened to John, Helen, and William immediately after the trial. John Staniewicz grew up to be a weaver in the textile industry. He never married and died of carcinoma of the rectum on June 14, 1951 at the age of 48. It's unknown what happened to Helen.

William Staniewicz went to go live with his mother's cousin, Feliks Dowgwillo, in Bristol, Pennsylvania for a while. William married Jean Antczak in Philadelphia in 1940, and they had two children. One died as an infant: Patricia Ann died at the age of nine months on April 18, 1944 and was buried in Holy Redeemer Cemetery.

William joined the Navy on April 13, 1944 and served until February 5, 1946. After his service, William and Jean moved to West Virginia. William died on March 10, 1989 and was buried in the Roseville Cemetery in Martinsburg, West Virginia.

Teresa Dowgwillo

Teresa Dowgwillo was born on February 15, 1890 in Guty. She was baptized on February 18 in Krakės (Lithuanian), or Kroki (Polish), Parish. Her godparents were Kalikst Chrzanowicz and Natalia Juchniewicz, maiden. She immigrated to the United States in 1906 at the age of 16. She married Michael Szwagżdis, a fellow Lithuanian immigrant, on July 22, 1907 in Philadelphia. Michael and Teresa moved to Bristol where Michael owned a restaurant. Teresa and Michael had four children: Helen, Adolf, Stephanie, and Victor. Michael died on October 13, 1947 in Trenton New Jersey, shortly before tragedy struck his daughter, Helen.

Helen Swagzdis was born on December 5, 1908. She married Anthony Gestite in 1928, and they lived in Camden, New Jersey. In 1926, Anthony was employed as a mechanical engineer at the Samuel M Langston Company, a paper box and machinery manufacturer. Anthony and Helen had two children, Dorothy and Thomas. At 7:30 a.m. on November 19, 1947, 18-year-old Dorothy heard her mother screaming from downstairs. Her 12-year-old brother, Thomas, was sleeping and never heard a thing.

Dorothy went down to the living room to find her mother bleeding from her head. Her father, Anthony, had beat her mother in the kitchen with a baseball bat. By this time, her father was nowhere in sight. Her mother told her to get her father from the basement, but Dorothy took care of her mother first. Dorothy tried to call the doctor for help, but the phone was disconnected. She went to a neighbor's house and called their family doctor and the police. When the doctor came to the house, he sent Helen to the hospital. When the police arrived, they went to the basement. They found Anthony hanging in from the joists. The doctor pronounced him dead at the scene.[29] Helen recovered and lived to be 89 years old. She died on April 21, 1998 in Penndel, Philadelphia. She was buried in Resurrection Cemetery in Bensalem, Pennsylvania.

Teresa and Michael's son, Adolf Edward Swagzdis, was born August 27, 1910 in Philadelphia. In 1930, he worked in a grocery store as a salesman. In 1933, he married Katherine Campbell in Philadelphia, and they had five children. By 1940, Adolf was going by his middle name, Edward, and was a machinist in the steel industry. Edward died on June 30, 1976 at the age of 65. Katherine died on May 16, 1999 at the age of 87. They are both buried in Resurrection Cemetery in Bensalem.

Teresa and Michael's daughter, Stephanie Swagzdis, was born on

March 5, 1913 in Philadelphia. On September 3, 1933 she married Anthony Bonikowski in Philadelphia with whom she had one daughter. Anthony was an expediter for Rohm and Hass, a manufacturer of specialty chemicals. Stephanie divorced Anthony and remarried to Alfred Day in 1946. Alfred had four children from a previous marriage to Julia Shisler before she died from cancer. Alfred died on June 20, 1988 at the age of 76. Stephanie died March 14, 2003 at the age of 90. Anthony died on February 22, 1980 at the age of 68.

Teresa and Michael's son, Victor Swagzdis, was born on April 16, 1920 in Philadelphia. In 1940, he was a grinder in a steel mill before enlisting in the US Marine Corps on August 25, 1941 just before Pearl Harbor was attacked on December 7, 1941 and the United States entered World War II. By 1942, Victor was trained as a light machine gunman at the Training Center, Fleet Marine Force Parachute School. By September 1943, he was a lance corporal in the 1st Marine Parachute Regiment and went to Guadalcanal. In December 1943, he was in combat against the Japanese around Bougainville Island in a battle known as the Battle of Hellzapoppin Ridge and Hill 600A. This series of battles was the last significant action undertaken by the 3rd Marine Division on the island before they were replaced by US Army soldiers from XIV Corps. It resulted in the capture of the two positions by the Marines with the support of artillery and aircraft and the withdrawal of the Japanese forces.[30]

By February 19, 1945, Victor had been promoted to Sergeant and was part of the first wave landing of B Company, 1st BN, 28th Marines, on Green Beach in Iwo Jima. He was a machine gun section leader. B Company's mission was to drive across the island at its narrowest point to prevent enemy reinforcements to Mount Suribachi from the island's western shore.

On that first day, 15 men were killed, and six others fatally wounded; 44 more men were wounded and were evacuated from the front lines. B Company lost its Company Commander, Executive Officer, and two Platoon Leaders, and 23 non-commissioned officers were wounded or killed. The leadership was devastated.

Victor assumed the Machine Gun Command on February 24 after the previous commander was wounded, and he remained in command until March 2, 1945 when he was wounded and evacuated. He was sent back to the United States where he recovered and was discharged from active duty in September 1945.[31]

On May 24, 1947, Victor married Elline Hearn in Philadelphia, Pennsylvania, and they had one son and one daughter together. They later divorced, and Victor married Lynn Stephens Nowicki in December 1980 in Medford Township, New Jersey. Victor died on May 19, 2000 at the age of 80 in his hometown of Philadelphia. But he was buried in Riverside Cemetery in New Jersey.

CHAPTER FIVE

Józef Dowgwillo and Antonina Urniasz

Although Józef is not in my direct line—he was my fourth cousin, four times removed—he and his children were close to Izydor Dowgwillo. He and Izydor had children baptized in the same parish, and some of these children stayed connected even after immigrating to the United States.

Józef Dowgwillo was born to on September 29, 1863 to nobles Aleksander Dowgwillo and Petronela Pernerowski. He was baptized in Krakės (Lithuanian), or Kroki (Polish), Parish. He married Antonina Urniasz before 1890. They had four children:

- Feliks Dowgwillo (1890-1956) married Kathryn Mikulis (1892-1984).
- Michal Dowgwllo (1892-1930) married Anna Ruciejska (1897-?).
- Adolf Dowgwillo (1895-1987) married Veronika Marie Adent (1900-1969) & Helen Adent (1904-1979).
- Stefania Dowgwillo (1899-?)

Three of their children immigrated to the United States: Feliks, Michal, and Adolf.

Feliks/Felix Dowgwillo

Feliks Dowgwillo was born on July 7, 1890 in Nowa Wieś Lithuania. He was baptized on July 9 in Krakės (Lithuanian) Kroki (Polish) Parish. His godparents were Mikołaj Babiański and Antonina, wife of Jan Sienkiewicz. Feliks arrived in Baltimore, Maryland on May 30, 1905 from Finland and changed his name to Felix. Felix was a carpet weaver by trade. He married fellow Lithuanian immigrant Catherine Mikulis in 1911 in Philadelphia and became a citizen on May 14, 1922. Felix and Catherine had two children, Adela (1913-2004) and Leon (1916-1918). Unfortunately, Leon died in the influenza epidemic in 1918. Adela went on to marry Edward Babula.

Felix and Catherine cared for Felix's cousin, William Staniewicz, when William's mother, Katarzyna Dowgwillo Staniewicz, was murdered by her brother-in-law in 1917.

By 1930, Felix owned his own business—The General Store in Newport, Pennsylvania. He died at the age of 65 from a coronary occlusion on April 21, 1961, and he was buried in Our Lady of Grace Cemetery in Philadelphia.[32] His wife, Catherine, died in 1984 in Ocean Gate, New Jersey.

Michal Dowgwillo

Michal Dowgwillo was born on August 7, 1892 in Nowa Wieś, Lithuania. He was baptized in Krakės (Lithuanian), or Kroki (Polish), Parish on September 3. His godparents were Bartłomiej Cholak and Barbara Szirmul, or Sirmulis, maiden. He and his brother, Adolf, left Lithuania together. They arrived in Baltimore, Maryland on July 6, 1911 on board the ship Main from Bremen Germany. They listed their brother, Felix's, address as their destination. Michal changed his name to Michael Dongvilla.

Michael married Annie Ruciejska on December 2, 1916. She was an immigrant from Austria. They had 4 children, but none of them survived childhood: Michael (1914-bef. 1930), Józef (1916-bef. 1930), Stanley (1917-1917), and Anna (1818-1818). It's not clear from what the children died.

In 1921, Michael and his brother, Adolf, bought a farm on Washington Avenue in St. Joseph, Michigan. Michael and his wife, Anna, and Adolph worked the property. Michael and Adolf had other farm holdings in the Scottdale area of Berrien County.

On December 27, 1930, Joseph was found dead in the barn by his wife. Joseph was 32. The police were summoned, and they concluded that Michael took his own life with a .22 caliber gun. Anna claimed that Michael had suffered a nervous breakdown over his work and that he took his own life because he feared that someone was trying to kill him.[33] Michael was buried in Resurrection Cemetery in St. Joseph Michigan.

Adolf Edward Dowgwillo

Adolf was born on August 12, 1892 in Nowa Wieś, Lithauna. He was baptized in Krakės (Lithuanian), or Kroki (Polish), Parish on August 20. His godparents were Józef Lubin and Katarzyna Romaszkiewicz, maiden. Józef was the husband of Józefa Lutkiewicz, my 2nd great aunt. Adolf left Lithuania with his brother, Michael. On May 22, 1917, Adolf married Veronica Adent in Chicago, Illinois. Adolf and Veronica had one child in Chicago—Felix (1918-2004) —and three more in Michigan— Henry (1921-2013), Theodore (1924-1927), and Adolph (1931-2019). Unfortunately, Theodore died in 1927.

Adolf became a prominent fruit farmer in southwest Michigan. He was known as the Raspberry King because of his expertise with berries and was a member of the Berrien County Farm Bureau until his retirement. He was also a member of St. Bernard's Catholic Church in Benton Harbor, Michigan. Adolf and Veronika celebrated their 50th Wedding Anniversary on May 22, 1967.

By this time, their surviving sons had married and had successful careers of their own: Felix married Regina Nowicki, had three children and was running the fruit farming center with his brother, Adolph Jr.; Adolph Jr. married Doris Schram, and they had five children; Henry married Margaret Shearer, had eight children, and was an attorney.

Unfortunately, Veronika died at the age of 69 as a result of a car crash on August 28, 1969. Veronika was driving along a canal and struck both a car on the road and a parked car along the road. The impact caused her car to plunge into the 30-feet-deep canal where Veronika drowned. She was buried in North Shore Memorial Gardens. [34]

Adolf remarried to Helen Adent, Veronika's sister, in 1969, shortly after Veronika's death. Helen died on October 31,1979. Adolf lived to be 91 years old. He died on May 29, 1987 and was buried in North Shore Memorial Gardens.[35]

CHAPTER SIX

Szymon Lutkiewicz and Paulina Mackiewicz

Szymon Lutkiewicz was the fifth child of Tomasz Lutkiewicz and Barbara Mieczyńska. He was born on October 15, 1832 in Wołmontowicze (Polish), or Valmanciai (Lithuanian), and baptized on October 17, 1832 in Pociūnėliai (Lithuanian), or Pacunele (Polish), Parish. His godparents were nobles Tadeusz Paszkiewicz and Karolina Lutkiewicz (his aunt, sister of his father Tomasz, spouse of Karol Mieczyński). He was two years younger than Adolf and was Antanas/Antoni's and Ona's uncle. This would make him my Great-Grandpa-Charles' great-uncle.

Szymon was a farmer who lived in Bobiniske manor. He married Paulina Mackiewicz on January 29, 1861 in Krekenava (Lithuanian), or Krakinów (Polish), Parish when he was 27 years old, and Paulina was 23. The witnesses to their marriage were nobles Kazimierz Solohub, Nicodem Ejdrigiewicz, Joseph Mackiewicz (Paulina's brother), and Adolf Lutkiewicz (Szymon's brother).

Szymon and Paulina had at least four children—Józef/Juozas, Ewa/Eva, Anna/Ona, and Wincenta/Vincenta. Józef, Ewa, Anna, and Wincenta are the Polish versions of the name. Juozas, Eva, Ona, and Vincenta are the Lithuanian versions of the name. Baptism, marriage and death records used the Polish version of the names at that time.

It's unknown what happened to Ona, but Józef, Ewa and Wincenta immigrated to the United States. It's unknown when Szymon died, but it had to be before 1919, as Paulina died a widow on October 3, 1919 in Wołmontowicze (Polish), or Valmanciai (Lithuanian). She left behind three children—Józef, Ewa, and Wincenta.

Józef Lutkiewicz

Józef Lutkiewicz was born on August 12, 1868 and was baptized in Pociūnėliai (Lithuanian), or Pacunele (Polish), Parish. His godparents were nobles Jerzy Markiewicz and Anna, wife of Konstanty Lutkiewicz. (Anna would have been Józef's aunt by marriage. Konstanty was Szymon and Adolf's brother.) Józef married Stefania Chodorowicz on February 12, 1890 in Krekenava (Lithuanian), or Krakinów (Polish), Parish. Stefania was also from a noble family. They had the following children in Lithuania:

- Scholastyka Lutkiewicz (1891-1961) married Edward Vetort (1884-1967).
- Zofia Lutkiewicz (1895-1985)
- Jadwiga (Ida) Lutkiewicz (1898-1986) married Joseph Schulz (1887-1924) and Max Naidenovich (1896-1984).
- Veronica Lutkiewicz (1902-1982) married Antoni Petrowicz (1888-1971).
- Michael Carl Lutkiewicz (1904-1979)

Józef arrived in Michigan before 1908 and was a farmer in Cedarville Township, Michigan. Scholastyka came to meet him from Šiauliai, Lithuania. She traveled to the port of Libau (probably by horse and wagon) and traveled to New York on the S.S. Kherson on February 3, 1908 in steerage. She worked as a domestic laborer or maid.

Scholastyka's mother, Stefania, and her siblings—Sophia, Jadwiga (Ida), Veronica, and Michael—departed Hamburg in steerage on October 19, 1911 and arrived in New York on October 28, 1911.

Józef Lutkiewicz changed his name to Joseph Lutkevich. He and Stefania ran a farm in Cedarville Township for over 30 years. Stefania died at the age of 64 in her home on the farm on February 15, 1936. Joseph died on June 17, 1954 in the Menominee Convalescent Home at the age of 85. Both Stefania and Joseph were members of the Church of the Precious Blood and were buried in the Stephenson Cemetery.

Gravestone Stefania Chodorowicz Lutkevich

Scholastyka Lutkiewicz

On June 30, 1910, 19-year-old Scholastyka Lutkiewicz married Edward Witort in Stephenson, Michigan. Scholastyka's father, Józef, was the only one there from her immediate family for the wedding.

Edward Vetort was one of eight children born to Katarzyna Dowgwillo (1855-1927) and Kalikst Witort (1850-1925). He was born on October 13, 1884 in Lithuania. Around 1907 or 1908, Edward immigrated with his parents and siblings—Zofia, John, Władysław/Walter, Stefania/Stella, Anna, and Władysława/Charlotte—to Menominee County, Michigan. According to the 1910 census, he worked as a laborer in a sawmill and lived with his parents and siblings. His neighbors included John Dowgovito and Joseph Dongaille—very misspelled versions of Dowgwillo. These were his mother's brothers. Interestingly enough, one of his neighbors was Charles Kulwic, and one of Charles' daughters, Helen, would marry one of Edward's sons, Edward Jr., in the future.

Scholastyka and Edward had four children before 1920:

- Ida Vetort was born July 18, 1911.
- Edward Vetort was born January 15, 1915.
- Mary (Marie) Vetort was born January 13, 1913.
- Francis (Frank) Vetort was born August 12, 1916.

According to the 1920 census, Edward and Scholastyka lived with their four children—Ida, Edward, Mary, and Frank—in Cedarville, Michigan. Edward was working as a farmer at the time. Edward and Scholastyka lived next door to Edward's parents, Katarzyna (Katie) and Kalikst Witort, and Scholastyka's parents lived down the street with her youngest brother, Michael.

Between 1920 and 1925, Edward's parents moved to Illinois. They probably moved with their children—John and his wife Mary, Walter and his wife Katarzyna, and Władysława (Charlotte) and her husband, Stanley Zalewski.

Edward's father, Kalikst, died on January 29, 1925 in Chicago, and his mother, Katie, died a couple months later on November 22, 1925 in Melrose, Illinois.

In the late 1920s, Edward and Scholastyka had one more son—Herman.

According to the 1930 census, Edward and Scholastyka lived with their five children—Ida, Edward, Mary (Marie) and Francis and Herman—and niece, Valeria Schultz, in Cedarville, Michigan. Valeria was the daughter of Edward's sister, Jadwiga or Ida, and her husband, Joseph Schultz.

Unfortunately, Joseph Schultz died in 1924, leaving behind his wife, Ida, and two children—Valeria, aged four, and Joseph Jr., about 1 month old. Edward and Scholastyka took care of Valeria until Ida remarried to Max Naraenovich. Edward and Scholastyka lived three doors down from Scholastyka's parents—Józef and Stefania Lutkiewicz—and four doors down from John and Vincenta (Wincenta) Wutkevicz. Vincenta was Scholastyka's aunt.

Scholastyka Lutkiewicz Vetort died on March 20, 1961, and Edward died on March 9, 1967. Both were buried in Stephenson Township Cemetery in Menominee, Michigan.

Edward and Scholastyka's daughter, Ida, married Linzey Kupsh on January 23, 1932 in Michigan. Linzey was a navigable lock master. They went on to have four children. Linzey died at the age of 91 on May 11, 1999 in California. Ida died at the age of 88 on February 11, 2000 in Irvine, California. I am a DNA match to one of their descendants.

Edward and Scholastyka's daughter, Marie, married James Marritt on June 19, 1940 in Nevada. They had two daughters. James was an active member St. Eugene's Cathedral of Santa Rosa, a member of the Knights of Columbus, and a World War I veteran (US Army). He died at the age of 85 on November 15, 1985 in Santa Rosa, California. Marie was a very active member of St. Eugene's Cathedral for many years. She was Chairwoman of the Marian Visitors for many years, as well as Ladies Aid and the Legion of Mary. She moved to Rohnert Park in 1995 and became a parishioner at St. Joseph's Catholic Church in Cotati. Mary died on December 8, 2005 in Rohnert Park, California.

Edward and Scholastyka's son, Edward, married their neighbor's daughter Helen Kulwich on June 24, 1939 in Menominee, Michigan. At the time, Edward worked as a truck driver. In the 1940s, Edward worked for Michigan's Conservation Department as a Towerman. He retired from the Michigan Department of Natural Resources after 37 years of service.

Edward was a member of the Church of the Precious Blood and belonged to the Cedarville Township Volunteer Fire Department, the Stephenson's Lions Club, and the County and Township Officers' Association. He served as the Cedarville Township supervisor at the time of his death. He died on March 14, 1993, and Helen died on June 18, 2009. They are both buried in the Stephenson Township Cemetery in Menominee, Michigan. [36]

Edward and Scholastyka's son, Francis, attended Stephenson High School and played football. He later attended Northern Michigan College in Michigan where he lettered in football and became a semi-pro boxer.[37]

Francis graduated from Northern Michigan and joined the Air Force on November 3, 1941, becoming an aviation cadet. In December 1942, during his first tour in the Pacific theater in World War II, he downed a Japanese aircraft over New Guinea and recorded two enemy kills, for which he received the Silver Star for gallantry. Most of his World War II experience was flying air support for ground troops. He participated in 3 major battles and flew in 252 missions. He was one of the pilots that escorted the Enola Gay, the bomber that dropped the first atomic bomb over Hiroshima to end the war in the Pacific. [38]

Francis Vetort WWII Registration Card

After World War II ended, he married Doris Aldrich on September 14, 1947 in New York, and they had four children. After marriage, Francis continued his career in the military. During the Korean War, he downed two MIG-15s with the fourth Tactical Fighter Wing of which he was the director of operations. Later in the war, he took command of the 47th Fighter Bomber Group flying F-84 Thunder Jets in support of allied ground troops. He had checked out in 50 different Air Force aircrafts and accumulated over 8000 hours of flying time. He ended his 30-year career as Commander of the Tactical Air Commands Tactical Air Control Group, an assignment in which he earned the Legion of Merit.[39]

Doris died May 16, 1997, and Francis died on April 18, 2009 at the age of 92. They are both buried in the Stephenson Township Cemetery in Menominee, Michigan.

Edward and Scholastyka's son, Herman Joseph Vetort, received a Bachelor of Science in Engineering from Northern Michigan University in 1947. He went to the U.S. Military Academy and was commissioned as a Second Lieutenant in the U.S. Army in 1951. Herman was also a competitive handball player while in the military and played in State Tournaments.[40]

He advanced through the ranks, eventually becoming a Colonel and retiring in 1981. He served in both Korea (Summer-Fall 52 Campaign and 3rd Korean Winter) and Vietnam (Nov 66- Nov 67). He was awarded the Bronze Star Medal[41], the Legion of Merit, the Army Commendation Medal, and the Republic of Vietnam Armed Forces Honor Medal.[42]

The Bronze Star was awarded when Herman was a 1st Lt. in the Armor, Tank Company, 65th Infantry Regiment, 3d Infantry Division in the US Army. On June 10, 1953, the 65th Infantry Regiment raided Hill "412" near Sagimak, Korea. In support of the raid, Herman directed a task force of two General Patton tanks through a valley to a deep position in enemy territory. After being deployed to firing positions by Herman, they began firing into enemy fortifications on the reverse slope of the hill. The enemy countered, subjecting the tanks to a bombardment of mortar fire. Herman exposed himself to the bursting mortar shells and commanded fire on vital points of the heavily fortified enemy outpost. After observing three seriously wounded friendly soldiers being evacuated, he dismounted from the tank and went through heavy fire to direct the medical aidmen to the tank position where they took cover beneath the tank hulls. He then summoned a personnel carrier and directed its movement to the tanks, directing an orderly evacuation despite the intense shell fire. As friendly troops moved back from the hill, he maneuvered his task force to support their movement.[43]

Herman went on to work as a program manager at Textron Inc. and has been listed as a noteworthy defense company manager/military officer by Marquis Who's Who.[44]

He married Alice Marie Lesperance on June 8, 1957 and had four children. I am a DNA match to their descendants.

Zofia/Sophia Lutkiewicz

Józef and Stefania Lutkiewicz's daughter, Zofia (Sophia), married Stanley (Stanisław) Olecki on May 18, 1913 in Cedar River, Michigan. (Stanisław was probably related to Kalikst Witort's mother Wiktoria Olecki. This would have been Zofia's brother-in-law's grandmother.) They moved to Melrose Park, Illinois and had four children. Sophia died on October 20, 1985, and Stanley died on September 16, 1979. They were both buried in the Queen of Heaven Catholic Cemetery in Chicago.

Jadwiga/Ida Lutkiewicz

Józef and Stefania Lutkiewicz's daughter, Jadwiga (Ida), married Joseph Schultz on August 5, 1919 in Melrose Park, Illinois. They lived with Ida's sister, Sophia, and her husband, Stanley, in 1920. Ida and Joseph had two children—Valeria and Joseph. Unfortunately, Joseph Sr. died of carcinoma of the stomach on May 16, 1924. He was buried on May 24 in Mount Carmel Cemetery in Hillside, Illinois. Ida and her daughter, Valeria, went to live with Ida's parents after his death. It's unclear where her son went at this time. Ida remarried to Max Naidenovich after 1930. Ida and Max raised Valeria and Joseph. Unfortunately, Joseph Jr. died of endocarditis on April 13, 1943 at the age of 19 and was buried in Mount Carmel Cemetery. Max died in July of 1984 and was buried at Elmwood Cemetery. Ida died on April 12, 1986 and was buried in Mount Carmel Cemetery with her son and husband.

Veronica Lutkiewicz

Józef and Stefania Lutkiewicz's daughter, Veronica, married Antoni Petrowicz on November 5, 1919 in Menominee, Michigan. They had one son—Boleslaw (Bill) on April 17, 1921 in Michigan. By 1930, the family had moved to Burns, Oregon where Antoni worked in a sawmill. Antoni died on February 20, 1971 from cancer. Veronica died on January 30, 1982 from a stroke. Both Antoni and Veronica are buried at the Burns Cemetery in Oregon.

Their son, Bill graduated from Burns High School in 1939. He served in the Army in World War II from 1943 to 1945 as a B-17 co-pilot in the 731st Bomb Squadron of the 452nd Bomb Group, which was stationed in England. He received the Air Medal with cluster, the Distinguished Unit Badge, and the European African Middle Eastern Campaign Ribbon. After the war, he married Eunice Higgs on October 18, 1948, and they had two children. Following his military service, Bill worked as an accountant for U.S. Plywood/Champion International. He belonged to the Elks Lodge and enjoyed painting, photography, and bowling. He also volunteered at the Oregon Air and Space Museum. He died of renal failure on March 6, 2006 at the age of 84.

Eunice had graduated from Burns Union High School and attended

Oregon State University. She worked at the Oregon Agricultural Experiment Station, Shascade Realty, and as a court reporter. She died of a stroke on November 18, 2009 at the age of 83.

Michael Carl Lutkiewicz

Józef and Stefania Lutkiewicz's son, Michael Carl, lived on the family farm and worked in local mines in Pennsylvania. At the time, Lithuanian immigrants were recruited for work in the coal mines of Pennsylvania and heavy industries such as steel mills, iron foundries, slaughterhouses, and oil refineries of the Northeastern United States.

Michael Carl was injured twice: on January 21, 1925 in the Milford Mine, a chunk of rock fell from the top of the room and cut the back of his right thumb, and he lost six days of work as a result; in 1928, he slipped and fell off a ladder and lacerated his first, second, and third fingers on his right hand and lost five days of work. After leaving this line of work, he went to Chicago where he did a little professional boxing. He briefly moved back to the family farm in Michigan. By 1936, he had moved to Hines, Oregon. Michael joined the US Army on July 20, 1942. He became a US citizen on July 30, 1943. During World War II, he was injured by an artillery shell and was hospitalized for a fracture and deafness. He was awarded the Purple Heart and was honorably discharged in August of 1944. Not much else is known about his post-military life other than that he moved back to Oregon and worked for Edward Hines until his retirement in 1964. He died on May 9, 1979 and is buried at the Burns Cemetery in Oregon.

Wincenta/Vincenta Lutkiewicz

Szymon and Paulina Lutkiewicz's daughter, Wincenta, was born around 1876. When she came to the United States, she went by Vincenta.

Vincenta married Jan (John) Wutkevicz around 1898 in Lithuania. They had one son, John Leo Wutkevicz, born in Lithuania on April 24, 1907.

The family immigrated to the United States around 1908 and settled in Cedarville Michigan. In fact, they lived next door to Vincenta's brother, Józef, and his wife, Stefania. John started out as a laborer in a sawmill and later operated a farm in Cedar River while Vincenta was a housewife. John died at the age of 74 on November 3, 1945, and Vincenta died in 1960. John Leo was a farmer and died at the age of 88 on July 12, 1995. All three are buried in the Stephenson Township Cemetery in Menominee Michigan.

Gravestone John and Vincenta (Lutkiewicz) Wutkevicz

Ewa/Eva Lutkiewicz (Lutkevic)

Szymon and Paulina Lutkiewicz's daughter, Ewa/Eva Lutkiewicz was born on December 27, 1861 in Bobinske Manor and baptized in Vadaktai Parish. Her godparents were noble Józef Mackiewicz and Antonina Jurewicz, maiden. Her name was documented as Ewa, the Polish version of her name, in Lithuania. However, when she immigrated to the United States, she used Eva, the Lithuanian version of her name.

Eva never married, but she had four children.

- Franciszka Lutkiewicz was born in 1884. She died on October 15, 1888 at the age of four from whooping cough in the village Noworeczka.
- Witold Lutkiewicz was born on June 15, 1887 in Wodokty (now Vadaktai), Lithuania. He immigrated to the United States in 1910. He married Magdalena Zaltowski in Minnesota in 1915. Witold died in 1975 in Duluth Minnesota.

- John Lutkiewicz was born on February 16, 1891 in Lithuania, and he died on December 16, 1971 in Virginia, Minnesota.
- Michalina Anna Lutkiewicz was born on July 9, 1894. She married Kazimierz (Charles) Grigaliunas (Grigal) in Lithuania around 1912 and immigrated to Virginia, Minnesota around 1914 with her mother, Eva. She died on February 25, 1969 in Virginia, Minnesota.

To contextualize, marital status was important enough that it was included on all baptism and marriage records. Eva was documented as a maiden, rather than as a legitimately married woman on each of her children's baptism records, and her children were documented as illegitimate. The god-parents marital status was included on the baptism records as well. Michalina's marriage record to Kazimierz Grigaliunas also stated that she was the illegitimate daughter of Eva Lutkiewicz, while he was the son of legitimately married Dominik Grigaliunas and his wife, Agata Raubus.

Eva having four children without marriage was very unusual for the time. According to *The Lithuanian Family in its European Context, 1800-1914: Marriage, Divorce and Flexible Communities* by Dalia Leinarte, Lithuanian culture was one in which marriage was the norm. Even widows remarried quickly because it was not culturally acceptable to be single once one became a grown adult.

Babies born to unmarried women often died as a result of neglect or infanticide. In the Russian Empire from 1845 until the early 1900s, infanticide was treated as a crime committed out of fear and shame and, as such, was handled leniently by law enforcement. The stigma placed on a single mother raising an illegitimate infant was much greater than the stigma placed on a woman that had given birth and disposed of her infant.

In addition, there really weren't jobs for single mothers raising children, so Eva must have had the help of her parents to raise her children. When they grew into adults, they immigrated to the United States: Eva arrived in the United States in 1914 with her daughter, Michalina, and granddaughter, Stanisława.

Eva seemed to have reinvented parts of her life when she came to Minnesota: she changed the spelling of her last name to Lutkevic, claimed she was a widow on some paperwork, and, on other paperwork, claimed that her husband and son had already applied for citizenship. She also claimed she was older than she really was. She was a member of St. John Baptist Church and of the Rosary Mother's Society. She was very active around her house until she had surgery at the age of 92, after which she was confined to a wheelchair. Her eyesight was poor, but she was mentally sharp until her death on June 5, 1957.

Upon her death, the local paper ran an obituary that stated she lived to be 101 and was the oldest living resident in Virginia Minnesota at the time. She was actually 96 years old. Eva was buried in Calvary Cemetery in Virginia, Minnesota.

On December 29, 1909, Eva's son, Witold, arrived in Pennsylvania on the S.S. Friesland from Liverpool. He was going to meet his Uncle Józef Lutkiewicz in Cedar River, Michigan. He changed the spelling of his last name to Lutkevich. By 1915, he was working in a mine in Virginia Minnesota.

On January 18, 1915, Witold married Magdalena Zaltowski, another immigrant from Lithuania. They went on to have the following children:

- Anne Marie Lutkevich was born on November 10, 1915.
- Charles Anthony Lutkevich was born on August 10, 1917.
- Agnes Adelia Lutkevich was born on February 25, 1919.
- Alexander Lutkevich was born on July 16, 1921.

Witold worked as a miner in the Alpena Mine in Virginia, Minnesota in 1918 and continued working in mines until the 1930s. He became a US citizen on March 18, 1924. By 1940, he was working as a janitor at City Hall. Magdalena was a member of St. John the Baptist Catholic Church, St. John's Society #1047, and was a charter member of Rosary Mothers. Magdalena died on March 16, 1965 at the age of 76. Witold died on December 28, 1975 at the age of 88. Both are buried in Calvary Cemetery in a family plot.

Witold and Magdalena's daughter, Anne Marie, graduated Salutatorian of Roosevelt High School in Virginia, Minnesota and moved to Duluth to attend Young and Hursh Business College. She married Arthur C. Munson on August 16, 1941, and they had one daughter.

Anne was employed as a receptionist for Mutual Insurance. She was a member of St. Benedict's Catholic Church, Daughters of Isabella. She was active in Girl Scouts, Kenwood Garden Club, and Kenwood Young at Heart. She died on January 26, 2004 in St. Mary's Medical Hospital. Arthur died many years before her in 1973.

Witold and Magdalena's son, Charles Anthony, married Lucille Mae Longair on January 13, 1941, and they had four children. He went into the US Army during World War II—he enlisted on October 15, 1942 and was discharged on November 16, 1945. Prior to her marriage, Lucille went to Virginia High School and Virginia Junior College. After her marriage, she worked as a nurse's aide at the Virginia Municipal Hospital for 20 years. She was a member of St. John the Baptist Church and its Rosary society. Charles died on April 16, 1996 in St. Louis Minnesota at the age of 78. Lucille died on October 20, 2004 at the age of 84 and is buried in Greenwood Cemetery in Virginia Minnesota.

Witold and Magdalena's daughter, Agnes, graduated from Roosevelt High School in 1937. She went to Virginia Junior College and graduated in 1939. She was a member of St. John the Baptist Catholic Church in Virginia, Minnesota. She died at the age of 80 on August 20, 1999.

Witold and Magdalena's son, Alexander (Alex), graduated from Virginia High School and enlisted in the US Army in 1939. Natheline Ohmann, Alex's future wife, graduated from St. Francis High School in Little Falls in 1939. During the war, she, like many women in wartime manufacturing, served as a sort of "Rosie the Riveter" at the Douglas Aircraft Plant in Santa Monica. She met Alex in 1939 at a friend's wedding. They reconnected after the war in 1946. Alex and Natheline married on June 1, 1946 in Virginia, Minnesota and had five children.

Alex served in the US Army Air Corps and later in the US Air Force for more than 30 years. He was stationed at bases all over the world until his retirement at Duluth Air Base in 1970. During his time in the service, he was a crew chief for the Berlin Air Lift, worked on the successful development of aerial refuelling in Bournemouth, England, did cold weather flight testing in Alaska, and was crew chief in the early days of jet development at Wright-Patterson AFB and Edwards AFB. He later served as Federal Deputy Marshall at the Federal Building in Duluth, Minnesota. At the age of 87, he died in his home in Duluth, Minnesota on February 10, 2009 after a six-year bout of illness.

His wife, Natheline, raised all their children on those various bases. She enjoyed knitting, sewing, cooking and quilting, as well as gardening and being outdoors. She continued to fish and pick blueberries well into her 90s.

She died on November 24, 2018 in Minneapolis, Minnesota at Catholic Eldercare. She was 96 years old and had suffered from Alzheimer's.

Eva's son, Jan (John), arrived on the June 15, 1911 at Ellis Island, New York from Hamburg, Germany aboard the ship President Lincoln. In 1917, he was working as a miner in the Lincoln Mining Company in Virginia, Minnesota. By 1920, he was self-employed as a carpenter. He never married. He died at the age of 81 years old at the Virginia Municipal Hospital after a brief illness on December 16, 1971. He was buried in Calvary Cemetery in Virginia, Minnesota.

Eva's daughter, Michalina, married before coming to the United States. On January 18, 1911, 17-year-old Michalina Lutkiewicz married Kazimierz Grigaliunas, a 27-year-old bachelor from Skiemie, in Basiogala (Lithuanian), or Bejsagoła (Polish), Parish. Michalina had burgher (middle class) status, and her husband had peasant status, but, at the time of their marriage, they were both living at the Połotkancie estate. They had one child—Stanisława (Stache)—on October 29, 1911 in Lithuania.

Kazimierz left Lithuania and came to the United States around 1912. He went to Cedar River, Michigan where his brother-in-law, Józef Lutkiewicz, was living but continued on to Virginia, Minnesota where he got a job in a mine in 1914. While in the United States, he changed his last name to Grigal.

On May 15, 1914, Michalina Anna Grigal arrived in the port of Baltimore from Bremen on the S.S. Barbarossa with her two-year-old daughter, Stanisława. Her mother, Eva, also travelled with her. They went on to Virginia, Minnesota to where Kazimierz and Witold were living.

Her daughter, Michalina, and son-in-law, Kazimierz, went on to have three more children:

- Charles Edward Grigal was born on February 16, 1915.
- Valentine Grigal was born on February 14, 1916.
- Stanley Walter Grigal was born on April 13, 1917.

Michalina went by the name Anna. She was a member of Sacred Heart Catholic Church. She died at the age of 74 in the Virginia Municipal Hospital after a lingering illness on February 25, 1969. Kazimierz went by the name Charles. He died on November 30, 1970.

Gravestone Charles and Michalina (Lutkavic) Grigal

Kazimeriz and Anna's daughter, Stache Grigal, resided in Virginia, Minnesota for 66 years and was a member of Sacred Heart Catholic Church. She died on January 27, 1980 at the age of 68. Stache and her parents were buried in Calvary Cemetery in Virginia, Minnesota.

Kazimeriz and Anna's son, Charles Edward, served during World War II in the US Army. After the war he married Frances Skerjanc on June 22, 1947 in Virginia, Minnesota, and they had two children. Charles Edward worked at the US Steel Corporation for 31 years and retired in 1977. He, like his mother, was a member of Sacred Heart Catholic Church. He died on May 26, 1986 at the age of 71. Frances died on December 15, 1987.

Kazimeriz and Anna's son, Valentine, married Yvette (Eva) Ohmann on June 24, 1939 in Virginia, Minnesota, and they had three children. Valentine served in World War II and, like Charles Edward, worked for the US Steel Corporation. He was also a member of Sacred Heart Catholic Church, Knights of Columbus, and served as treasurer for Boy Scout troop #115. He died at the age of 59 on December 23, 1975. Eva died on September 24, 2006.

Kazimeriz and Anna's son, Stanley Walter, served in World War II in the US Army. He was part of the 744th Railway Operating Battalion Company B, serving in France and Belgium. After the War, he worked for US Steel as a locomotive repairman. He was a member of Sacred Heart

Catholic Church and Veterans of the 744th Railway Battalion. On July 20, 1940, Stanley married Ann Peterka. Ann graduated from Aurora High School, Duluth Teachers College, and University of Minnesota Duluth. She taught elementary education in the St. Louis County Schools. She loved music, played the piano, and was a talented seamstress. They had two daughters. Stanley died on March 17, 1987. Ann died on December 6, 2004. Both are buried at Calvary Cemetery in Minnesota.[45]

CHAPTER SEVEN

Ignacy Lastowski and Petronela Lutkiewicz

Petronela Lutkiewicz was born around 1796 in Lithuania. She was the daughter of Szymon Lutkiewicz and Elżbieta Zacharzewska. She was the sister of Tomasz Lutkiewicz, my 4th great-grandfather. She was my 5th great-aunt. On January 17, 1812, she married Ignacy Lastowski in Krekenava (Lithuanian), or Krakinów (Polish), Parish. For context, Lithuania had disappeared from the map in 1795 and became part of the Russian Empire. In 1812, Napoleon came through Lithuania on his way to Russia. There was a lot of instability in the country at the time in which Petronela and Ignacy lived. Petronela and Ignacy had the following children:

- Elżbieta Lastowski was born around 1812. She died in infancy on December 9, 1813 in Goszczuny Territory.
- Marianna Madgalena Lastowski was born on November 28, 1814 in Goszczuny Territory. She was baptized in Pociūnėliai (Lithuanian), or Pacunele (Polish), Parish. Her godparents were Kazimierz Lutkiewicz and Barbara Downorwicz, Deorota Audroska, Marianna Lastowska and Catherine Lutkiewicz.
- Petronela Lastowski was born on May 15, 1815 in Goszczuny Territory. She was baptized in Pociūnėliai (Lithuanian), or Pacunele (Polish), Parish. Her godparents were Michał Gosciewicz and

116

Rozalia Iłgowska. She married Nikodem Borowski on September 28, 1841 in Krekenava (Lithuanian), or Krakinów (Polish), Parish.

- Konstancia Lastowski was born around 1818. She married Dionizy Adam Gosztowt on October 22, 1835 in Krekenava (Lithuanian), or Krakinów (Polish), Parish. More about them in the next section.
- Nikolaj Lastowski was born on April 8, 1821 in Goszczuny Territory and was baptized in Pociūnėliai (Lithuanian), or Pacunele (Polish), Parish. His godparents were Józef Jodkiewicz and (the first letter of the first name is missing on the document) ?osina Gosciewicz.
- Jerzy Wincenty Lastowski was born on April 22, 1825 in Goszczuny Territory and baptized in Pociūnėliai (Lithuanian), or Pacunele (Polish), Parish. His godparents were Jacob Januszkiewicz and Gloria Nawlika.
- Wincenta Agata Lastowski was born on January 21, 1828 in Goszczuny Territory and baptized in Pociūnėliai (Lithuanian), or Pacunele (Polish), Parish. Her godparents were Michael (last name not readable on the record) and Zofia Downarwicz. On January 27, 1848, Wincenta married Józef Borowski in Krekenava (Lithuanian), or Krakinów (Polish), Parish. More about them in the next section.

Their daughters, Konstancia and Wincenta, had grandchildren that immigrated to the United States in the early 1900s.

Ignacy Lastowski died on February 12, 1939 at the age of 70. Petronela died on December 16, 1884 at the age of 88. Both of them were buried in Pociūnėliai (Lithuanian), or Pacunele (Polish), Cemetery.

Konstancia Lastowska

Konstancia Lastowska was the 4th child born to Ignacy Lastowski and Petronela Lutkiewicz around 1818. Lastowska was the female ending of her father's last name of Lastowski. In Lithuania, there was a female and male ending for all last names.

Konstancia, at 20 years old, married Dionizy Adam Gosztowt on October 22, 1835 when Dionizy was 25. Dionizy's parents were Tadeusz Gowsztowt and Elżbieta Gosztowtowna. Dionizy was the first of nine children—Paul (1812-?), Jan (1815-?), Aleksander (1817-?), Antoni (1819-?), Ewa (1821-?), Józef (1824-1845), Teofila (1826-?), and Eustachy (1830-?).

The Gosztowt (Polish) or Goštautai (Lithuanian) family was a Lithuanian-Polish noble family and one of the most influential magnate families in the 15th and 16th centuries. Dionizy was probably directly descended from Jonas Goštautas (1408–1458), voivod (kind of a governor during Medieval Times) of Vilnius and Trakai. He led Council of Lords which elected 13-year-old Casimir IV Jagiellon as Grand Duke of Lithuania.

When Dionizy was born on April 12, 1811, his parents lived at Aula manor in Užpurwie and held the MD or Magnificus Dominus nobility status: middle-class gentry, owned a large estate and land, had some political or economic influence, and/or held a state office position.

By the time his brother, Aleksander, was born in 1817, his parents lived in "territorio (noble settlement) Užpurwie" and held the lower GD nobility status, which is a level down from MD. This was during a very turbulent time in Europe, including for Lithuania: it was during the Napoleonic War Years (1803-1815). Many Lithuanians fought with Napoleon against Czarist Russia. Upon Napoleon's retreat, many Gosztowts fled to France with Napoleon and their descendants live there today. Those that stayed in Lithuania lost status, property, and in some cases, their lives.

The 1811 and 1817 Russian Census of Lithuania shows that the nation lost one-third of its inhabitants during that period. Of the approximately 20,000 Lithuanians that joined Napoleon in 1812 to conquer Czarist Russia, only about 8,000 survived the retreat. [46]

I have been unable to make a direct link between Tadeusz Gosztowt (Dionizy's father) and Napoleon's entrance into Lithuania on his march to Russia, but there is documentation of Jan Gosztowt (and Ignacy Lutkiewicz) fighting under Constantin Herbowicz with Napoleon against Czarist Russia.

By the time Dionizy Adam Gosztowt married Konstancia Lastowska, his family's power and influence had been lost. Dionizy and Konstancia went on to have the following children:

- Hiacenta Gosztowt (1836-1846)
- Konstanty Gosztowt (1839-?) married Emilia Paskiewicz (1846-?).
- Julia Gosztowt (1847-?)
- Kazimiera Gosztowt (1848-1898) married Józef Zdanowicz.

- Michal Gosztowt (1850-?) married Veronika Baveraite (1855-?).
- Paulina Gosztowt (1853-?) married Jan Kulikauskas (1856-?).
- Józef Gosztowt (1858-?)
- Ignacy Gosztowt (1848-1908) married Konstanica Rajunc (1854-1914).

Konstancia died on August 13, 1868 in Poniekompie from a common cold at the age of 50. She left behind her husband, Dionizy Gosztowt, four sons—Konstanty, Ignacy, Michał, and Józef— and three daughters—Kazimiera, Julia, and Paulina. She was buried on August 15 in Pacunele (Pociūnėliai) cemetery.

Later that year on September 5, 1868 in village Poniekielpie, Dionizy Gosztowt died from a tumor. He received Holy Sacrament and his body was buried on September 8 by priest Leon Smilgiewicz in the Pacunele (Pociūnėliai) cemetery.

Their son, Konstanty Gosztowt, was born on April 6, 1839 in Užpurviai, Basiogala (Lithuanian), or Bejsagoła (Polish), Parish and was baptized two days later. His godparents were Karol Tamulewicz and Roza Gosztowtowna.

Konstanty married Emilia Paskiewicz in Krekenava (Lithuanian), or Krakinów (Polish), Parish on February 15, 1865. Konstanty was 25 and Emilia was 19. They went on to have seven children:

- Adolf Gosztowt (1865-?)
- Ksawera Gosztowt (1868-?)
- Teodor Gosztowt (1871-?)
- Aleksander Gosztowt (1874-?) married Maksimilijona Juchniewicz.
- Zofia Gosztowt (1878-1880)
- Michalina Gosztowt (1880-?)
- Józef Gosztowt (1884-1885)
- Stanisława Gosztowt (1886-?) married Stanisław Domaszewicz.

Only Aleksander immigrated to the United States. Aleksander was born on March 1, 1874 in Terespolis and was baptized on March 10, 1874 in Pociūnėliai (Lithuanian), or Pacunele (Polish), Parish. His godparents were nobles Karolis Lučickis and Juzefa, wife of Bronislovas Vavžnickis. He married Maksimilijona Juchniewicz around 1902.

At some point they moved to Tbilisi, what is now in the country of

Georgia. During this time period, things were changing: the traditional ways of gaining income and receiving sustenance from farming the land were disappearing. Instead, people were moving to take jobs as clerks and/or administrators, and a professional class was developing. The southern part of the Russian Empire, of which Georgia was a part at the time, was quite an economic hub.

Aleksander and Maksimilijona had a daughter, Regina, on July 17, 1903 in Tbilisi, and she was baptized in St. Peter and St. Paul's church. In 1907, Aleksander, Maksimilijona, and Regina went to Belgium, and proceeded from there to Canada aboard the SS Moutrose on September 25, 1907. They arrived in Quebec on October 7, 1907. The family made their home in Haute, Indiana, and Aleksander and Maksimilijona became Alex and Amelia. On April 6, 1908, the had another daughter, Emilia Mildred, in Seelyville, Indiana.

Aleksander, Alfred, Regina and Maksimilijona Gosztowt/Gostow

By 1909, the family moved and settled in Kenosha. On July 19, 1913, they had a son, Alfred. Alex made his living at West Side Sheet Metal Works. Alex became a US citizen of February 15,1915. Alex died after several months in the hospital on May 17, 1927. Amelia died at the age of 59 in Kenosha Hospital on September 27, 1936. They were both buried in a family plot at the Green Ridge Cemetery in Kenosha.

Regina Gostow

Alex and Amelia's daughter, Regina, went to Kenosha High School and graduated in 1919. She married Lennard Berg on September 20, 1921. Lennard was an immigrant from Sweden. They had two children—Lennard, Jr. and Gloria. Regina was involved with the PTA and Girl Scouts while her children were young. She worked for the Kenosha Labor Paper from 1948-1968 and was active with the Kenosha labor movement. She was the recording secretary for the Kenosha CIO before it merged with the Kenosha AFL. She continued as council secretary for the AFL-CIO and was also a member of the Newspaper Guild Local 159.

She divorced Lennard and married George Poreden on March 25, 1961. They probably met while she was working for the Kenosha Labor Paper. George was a sportswriter, editor, and eventually, the publisher of the Kenosha Labor Paper. On November 20, 1978, Regina died at the age of 75 at Kenosha Memorial Hospital. On July 17, 2006, George died at the age of 95 in the Kenosha Medical Center. Regina's first husband, Lennard, died on November 25, 1968 in Wisconsin.

Gloria and Lennard's daughter, Gloria, was born on January 25, 1927 in Kenosha. She went to Kenosha High School and graduated in 1945. After high school, she went to work at the Great Lakes Naval Base and met her first husband, Robert Gardner. They married on September 8, 1950 in St. John's Chapel in Tallahassee, Florida. Robert was from Florida. They settled there for a while and had two children.

Gloria divorced Robert and went back to Kenosha to attend the University of Wisconsin. She married for the second time to Elmer Ungemach on July 28, 1968 at Frieden's Evangelical Lutheran Church in Kenosha. Elmer was an attorney and partner in the firm Lucarelli, Newman, and Ungemach. He was also very active in his church. Through his work as an attorney and at church, he became aware of people with needs not being addressed by the community and was inspired to help draft documents to set up the Kenosha Achievement Center.

Gloria and Elmer moved to Chatfield, Minnesota in 2005. Gloria was an active member of Resurrection Lutheran Church in Rochester, Minnesota, a member of the Wisconsin Extension of Homemakers, and a member of the League of Women's Voters. She enjoyed reading, art, and being in nature. On January 5, 2014, Gloria died at the age of 81 at the Mayo Clinic. She was cremated and buried in Sunset Ridge Memorial

Park in Kenosha, Wisconsin. Elmer died on March 3, 2011 in Rochester Hospital. Gloria's first husband, Robert, died on June 11, 2016 at the age of 88 in Seminole, Florida.

Emilia Mildred Gostow

Alex and Amelia's daughter, Emilia Mildred Gostow, was born in Indiana, but by the time she turned two, she was living in Kenosha, Wisconsin. She was known as Millie. On January 18, 1936, she married Raymond Saunders in Crown Point, Indiana. They made their home in Chicago and had two children—Steven and Jill. Raymond served as a first lieutenant in the Army during World War II—from October 17, 1942 to January 30, 1946.

In 1949, the family took a trip to Arkansas and fell in love with the Ozarks. In 1951, they moved with another family to Arkansas and purchased the Flippin Telephone Company, which eventually became Northern Arkansas Telephone Company (NATCO). Ray and Millie worked hard to make the company successful in the 1950s. Millie ran the company switchboards at all hours of the day at two offices. She continued to work for the company for many years and was on the board of directors. She also enjoyed traveling around the world. In addition to founding NATCO, Ray founded Citizens Bank and Trust in Summit and Flippin. He was also a charter member of Veterans of Foreign War Post 1341 in Hoevell-Barnett in Bull Shoals. Raymond died on October 13, 1982 at the age of 73.[47] Millie died at the age of 97 at Baxter Regional Medical Center on September 8, 2005. [48] Both are buried at Newton Flat Cemetery in Bull Shoals, Arkansas.

Alfred Gostow

Alex and Amelia's son, Alfred, was born in Kenosha, Wisconsin and went to Kenosha High School. By 1935, he was living in Chicago. On October 12, 1935, he married Evelyn Louise Klein. He and Evelyn lived in Chicago where Alfred made a living as a chief inspector in the steel manufacturing industry. In 1942, Alfred joined Chrysler as a general superintendent of the forging division at the Chicago plant. In 1945, he was transferred to Detroit, Michigan as an assistant manager of the Dodge Forge Plant. This is probably about the time Alfred divorced Evelyn and married Helen McDonough. Evelyn spent her entire life in Chicago.

Alfred and Helen had two daughters. In 1950, Alfred was promoted to plant manager at the Dodge Forge Plant. Alfred joined the Gross Point Yacht Club in Michigan. By 1964 Alfred was a general manager for the power train group of Chrysler and attended a ground breaking ceremony for a new castings plant in Kokomo, Indiana along with Lt. Governor Richard Ristine and Mayor John Miller. [49] Helen died in Grosse Point Woods, Michigan on September 2, 1986 at the age of 74. Alfred died in Phoenix, Arizona on April 15, 1995 at the age of 81. Alfred's first wife, Evelyn, remarried to Thomas Driskell in 1951. She died on December 19, 2003 in Chicago at the age of 90.[50]

Wincenta Lastowska

Wincenta was the the 7th and last child born to Petronela and Ignacy Lastowski in 1828. She married Józef Borowski on January 27, 1848 in Krekenava (Lithuanian), or Krakinów (Polish), Parish. They were both 25 years old. Józef Borowski was the son of Michal Borowski and Barbara Danillowicz. They had the following children:

- Władysław/Walter Borowski was born around 1849. He married Aniela Raicewicz on February 21, 1878 in Krekenava (Lithuanian), or Krakinów (Polish), Parish. The had the following children:
    - Bronislaw/Bruno Borowski (1879-1947) married Stefania Wojtewicz (1889-?).
    - Waclaw/Walter Borowski (1880-1961) married Joanna Liniewicz (1889-1969).
    - Helena Borowski (1886-1947) married Michael Dowgwillo (Doigwillo) (1878-1947).
    - Mary Borowski (1887-1975) married Anthony Snesko (1878-1931).
    - Jan/John Borowski (1886-1954) married Maryanna Lipska (1891-1979).
    - Wincenta Borowski (1891-1919) married Peter Leiliko (1891-?).

- ○ Agota/Agatha Borowski (1893-1988) married Antoni Rymkiewicz (1888-1951).
- ○ Teodora Borowski (1896-1965) married Wincenty Jermolawicz.
- ○ Veronica Borowski (1897-1964) married Władysław Skowronski (1894-1964).
- ○ Annie Borowski (1897-1951) married Bronislaw Jurewicz (1886-1946).
- Adam Borowski was born on March 3, 1857. He was baptized on March 6 in Pociūnėliai (Lithuanian), or Pacunele (Polish), Parish.
- Ksaverij Borowski was born on November 13, 1859 and baptized on November 16 in Pociūnėliai (Lithuanian), or Pacunele (Polish), Parish. He died at the age three of on May 19, 1862.
- Ewa Borowski was born on May 12, 1865. She was baptized on May 16 in Pociūnėliai (Lithuanian), or Pacunele (Polish), Parish.

Józef died on April 27, 1886 at the age of 60. He left behind his wife Wincenta, son Władysław, and daughter Ewa. Wincenta died on December 28, 1893 at the age of 67. Their son, Władysław, had eight children immigrate to the United States: Waclaw/Walter, Bronislaw/Bruno, Helena, Mary, Jan/John, Agata, Veronica, and Annie.

Bronislaw/Bruno Borowski

Bronislaw left for the United States on August 19, 1903 on the SS Switzerland from Antwerp, Belgium. He traveled with his cousin, Michael Stejgwillo, but they parted ways for a while in the United States. Bronislaw changed his name to Bruno and married Stefania Wojtewicz in 1905 in Philadelphia. They had four children: Boleslaw/William John (1907-1993), Bronislawa/Bertha (1909-?), Stanisław/Stanley (1911-2003), and Florence (1921-2004).

Bruno made his living as a chef and sometimes worked with his brother, Waclaw, in a hospital. Bruno also had a meat market with his brother-in-law, Michael Doigwillo/Dowgwillo. Michael was the husband of Bruno's sister, Helena.

Bruno W Borowski WWI Registration Card

Bruno became a US citizen on July 17, 1914 in Philadelphia. In 1940, Michael Stejgwillo moved back in with Bruno while Stefania was the owner of a taproom. Bruno was working as a chef in the Lorraine Hotel at the time. Bruno and Stefania moved to Granada Hills California and Bruno worked as a chef at the Ritz Carlton Hotel. When he was 83 years old, Bruno's shirt caught fire from a pipe ember that resulted in second and third degree burns on his chest. He was moved into a convalescent hospital and died a few months later from atherosclerosis cardiovascular disease on November 29, 1963. Bruno was buried in Glen Haven Memorial Park in Sylmar California. It's unknown when Stefania died.

Bruno and Stefania's son, Stanley, was a baker before serving in the Army during World War II—from April 4, 1942 to January 20, 1946. He was a sergeant when discharged. He died on April 13, 2003 and was buried in Rosedale Memorial Park in Oak Park, Pennsylvania. Not much is known about Bruno and Stefania's other children.

Waclaw/Walter Borowski

Waclaw traveled with his sister, Wincenta, from Bremen to Baltimore on the SS. Brandenburg on March 3, 1910. They were going to meet Bronislaw in Philadelphia. Waclaw married Joanna Liniewicz around 1919. They had one daughter—Leokadia, or "Lea," on May 23, 1920. In 1920, he and Joanna were living with Waclaw's brother, Bruno, and his sister, Annie, at 3131 Salmon Street in Philadelphia. Bruno was a chef, and Walter was a cook in a hospital. Annie was doing winding in a knitting factory.

Waclaw became a US citizen on March 25, 1930. By this time, he owned a grocery store. Waclaw died on April 5, 1961 from congestive heart failure in Perkasie, Pennsylvania. He had moved there with his wife to be close to their daughter. Lea married William Winitsky, and they ran the Fireside Inn Tavern. After being ill for about a year, Joanna died at the Grandview Hospital on January 13, 1969. Waclaw and Joanna were buried at Our Lady of Grace Cemetery, Langhorne.

Helena Borowski

Helen Borowski arrived in the United States between 1903 and 1911. She married Michael Dowgwillo (Doigwillo) before 1920. Michael was born on September 28, 1878 in Lithuania. He immigrated to the United States in 1894 or 1895 probably with his cousin, Henry Lackner. It's unclear how Michael was connected to the Dowgwillo family tree. Michael and Helen had one son, John, around 1924. It's unclear what happened to John. Michael supported his family as a cook, and he also had a meat market with Helen's brother, Bruno, in the 1920s. Helen died on February 24, 1947 from hypertension and cardio-vascular disease at the age of 60. Michael died on October 11, 1947 from coronary artery sclerosis at the age of 69. Both Helen and Michael are buried in Holy Cross Cemetery in Yeadon, Pennsylvania. They are also buried with Helena's brother, Jan/John Borowski, and his family.

Helen & Michael Dowgwillo, John, Maryanna,
Mary & Adolph Borowski Gravestone

Mary Borowski

Mary Borowski arrived in the United States around 1905. She married fellow Lithuanian immigrant, Anthony Snesko, on April 7, 1907 in Baltimore, Maryland. Anthony had immigrated in 1904. They had six children: Michael (1907-1953), Walter (1909-1992), Sophia (1911-1989), Helen (1917-2012), Anna (1919-1999), and John (1923-1991). Anthony worked as an operator in a clothing factory. Unfortunately, Anthony died on April 8, 1937 in Maryland at the age of 53. Mary died on May 5, 1975 in Towson, Maryland at the age of 88. She was buried at Holy Rosary Cemetery in Maryland.

Mary and Anthony's daughter, Sophia, married Lealon Newman in 1934, and they had five children. I had a DNA match with one of their descendants.

Jan/John Borowski

Jan Borowski arrived in New York on July 6, 1906 from Antwerp on the SS Vaderland. He married Maryanna Lipska, an immigrant from Poland, in 1911 in Philadelphia. He became a US citizen on April 12, 1916 and changed his name to John. He made his living as a bartender and as a cook. John and Maryanna had two children: Adolph (1912-1995) and Mary (1915-1979). John died on May 22, 1954 in Colwyn, Pennsylvania of carcinoma of the spine and larynx at the age of 66. Mary died on February 14, 1979 in Warren, Michigan at the age of 87. They were both buried at Holy Cross Cemetery in Yeadon, Pennsylvania along with John's sister, Helena, and her husband, Michael Dowgwillo.

Agota Borowski

Agota arrived in on the SS Neckar from Bremen, Germany on June 19, 1913 in the port of Baltimore. She was going to meet her brother-in-law, Michael Dowgwillo. Michael opened an account at Rosenbaum Bank in 1913 for her. In 1915, she married Antoni/Anthony Rymkiewicz. Anthony was the son of Albinas Rymkiewicz and Tekla Dowgwillo. I am also related to Tekla from a different Dowgwillo line—Tekla is my 3rd cousin four times removed.

No. 4930437

Name RYMKIEWICZ, AGATA

residing at 3166 E. Thompson St., Phila., Pa.

Age 47 years. Date of order of admission 8/21/40

Date certificate issued 8/21/40 by the

U. S. District Court at Philadelphia, Pa.

Petition No. 143543

(Complete and true signature of holder)

Agota Rymkiewicz U.S. Naturalization Index Card

Anthony Rymkiewicz was a fellow Lithuanian immigrant who arrived on March 21, 1912 in the port of Philadelphia. Anthony became a US citizen on January 14, 1926 and Agota became a citizen on August 21, 1940. Anthony and Agota had four children: Hedwig/Hedwick (1916-1986), Anna (1918-1931), Pawel/Paul (1920-1983), and Anthony Jr. (1923-1937). Anthony Sr. supported his family working as a chef.

Unfortunately, Anthony and Agota lost two children tragically within six years of each other. Their daughter, Anna, died at the age of 12 from chronic myocarditis in Germantown Hospital in 1931. Their son, Anthony, died from multiple fractures after accidently falling of Wheaton Railroad Bridge in 1937. He was only 14 years old. Their son, Paul, served in the Army in World War II from January 16, 1942 until July 22, 1944. Their daughter, Hedwig, married Leon Cerankowski in 1934, and they had four children.

Anthony died on August 7, 1951 at the age of 63, and Agota died on March 5, 1988 in Marlboro, Massachusetts. Anthony and Agota were buried in Holy Redeemer Cemetery in Philadelphia Pennsylvania along with their children: Anna, Anthony, and Paul. Paul died at the age of 63 on February 7, 1983. Hedwig and her husband, Leon Cerankowski, are also buried in Holy Redeemer Cemetery.

Veronika Borowski

Veronika Borowski arrived in the United States in 1911. She married fellow Lithuanian immigrant Władysław Skowronski in 1919 in Philadelphia.

Władysław arrived in the United States in 1913 and joined the US Army on November 2, 1917. He served as a private in Company B, 30th Infantry, Third Division in France during World War I. From June 1 to July 30, 1918, he served on the Aisne Marne Front during the Second Battle of the Marne in which the Germans were defeated.[51]

From October 1 to October 11, 1918, Władysław went on to fight on the front in the Meuse-Argonne Offensive, the largest U.S. military offensive in history, involving 1.2 million soldiers. The battle raged until November 11, 1918 and resulted in Armistice or the end of the war. [52]

Władysław was severely wounded with shrapnel to his left knee. He was hospitalized for three months and came back to the United States on

April 2, 1919 with the 338th Infantry, 85th Division. He was honorably discharged on April 10, 1919.

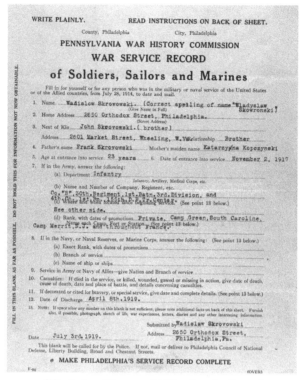

Władysław Skowronski War Service Record

Władysław and Veronika had five children: Stillborn (1920-1920), Wanda (1922-2018), Eleanor (1924-?), Irene (1929-?), and Romaulda (1936-?). Władysław supported his family as a cabinet maker. He died on June 2, 1964 at the age of 70 and was buried in Arlington Cemetery. Veronika died on December 16, 1984 at the age of 87 in Philadelphia. She was buried at Saint Dominic Church Cemetery in Torresdale, Pennsylvania.

Annie Borowski

Annie arrived in the United States in 1912. She married Bronislaw Jurewicz in 1914 in Philadelphia. He was a fellow Lithuanian immigrant who had arrived in Baltimore, Maryland in 1906 from Bremen, Germany. Bronislaw and Annie had four children: Wanda (1917-2007), Bernard

(1918-?), Alfreda (1920-?), and Edwin (1922-2001). Bronislaw supported his family by refinishing furniture and running his own novelty store. Annie also helped support the family by running her own dressmaking shop. Bronislaw died on June 3, 1946 at the age of 59. Annie died September 25, 1951 at the age of 53. They were buried at the Holy Sepulchre in Philadelphia.

CHAPTER EIGHT

Lutkiewicz Extended Family Tree

The Nobility Confirmation documents from the archives in St. Petersburg provided information about the Lutkiewicz family tree going back to the late 1500s. From a modern genealogy perspective, it was fortunate that the Czarist Russia required this information. Most records in Lithuania created before the late 1700s have been lost due to various uprisings and wars.

Most Lithuanian genealogical documentation provides information primarily about males, since noble status passed through them; however, there were a few records that listed wives or daughters. The documentation may list the same people with different names because of what language was used at the time. For example, John would be:

- From the 1700s to the early 1800s, Latin was used (Joannem).
- From the early 1800s to mid-1800s, Polish was used (Jan).
- From the mid-1800s to 1900s, Russian was used (Джон).
- After 1920, Lithuanian was used (Jonas).

I've tried to use the same version of the name for the same person, but some historical factors make documentation less exacting than desirable: some of the places in which individuals were born, married, or died have changed names, and some don't even exist anymore. If I could find them,

I put the current names in. If I couldn't, I just used the name of the village that was on the documentation I reviewed.

I spent countless hours going through thousands of records in various Lithuania churches written in Latin, Polish, and Russian. Although I had someone checking my work, I may have missed something.

Records in Lithuania are not indexed and not everything is available online, so I spent a lot of time going through records to find ancestors. You need to know where someone was born and the date of an event to find records. I saw lots of the same last names in a particular parish—it gave me a sense of the community during certain time periods.

A sobering part of my research was just how many babies and children died between birth and five years old due to whooping cough, measles, diarrhea, smallpox, and "weakness." These children didn't have the benefit of such modern medical advents as vaccines, IVs, or antibiotics.

In addition, I found "death by childbirth" very common on death: women gave birth at home without the benefit and comforts of a hospital setting, nor proper hygiene.

One interesting part of going through so many records was just how common it was that children were born out of wedlock or were born within a few months of their parents getting married—I was under the impression this was a modern phenomenon, but this was quite common even in the 1600s!

To make it easier, I will break the family tree down in two lines, in three sections. The first section will go from Jan Ludkievicz to Baltrejmus to his first son, Stanisław. The second will go from Jan Ludkievicz to Baltrejmus to his second son, Wojciech.

The last section will be from Szymon to Antoni/Antanas Lutkiewicz, because so many more of their baptism, marriage, and death records were available, and these are people my Grandpa Charles would have heard about or known growing up. If information is available about where they were baptized, married, had property, or died, it will be included. My direct ancestors will be in bold font.

Jan Ludkievicz/Baltrejmus/Stanisław

Jan Ludkievicz was born around 1556 and died around 1601. He was a descendant of Lutko Lutkiewicz. Jan Lutko was granted a noble crest "Doliwa," according to historians Dlugosz, Paprocki, and others, for capturing a castle of the town Liwa. He settled in the noble settlement Ruosciai in the Veliuona region, which would have been part of Samogitia (also known as Žemaitija). He was considered Samogitian nobility.

For more than two hundred years, Samogitia played a central role in Lithuania's wars against the crusading order of the Teutonic Knights. In the 15th century, Samogitia was the last region in Europe to be Christianized.

Throughout the period from the 15th to the 18th century, it was known as the Duchy or Eldership of Žemaitija, which included some territories of what is now considered Aukštaitija (where Antoni Lutkiewicz was from) and Suvalkija (where Eva Dobaite was from). The Duchy of Žemaitija was an autonomous administrative unit in the Grand Duchy of Lithuania.

Jan was a nobleman and a scribe in the Upytė Castle court. Upytė had a wooden castle built on an island that was an important northern defense post against numerous incursions of the Livonian Order (Teutonic Knights). Upytė was a capital of the Upytė region in the Grand Duchy of Lithuania. (It still exists today and is one of the longest surviving regional capitals from earlier times.)

Jan had a son, Bartlomiej Lutkiewicz, who inherited an estate in Ruosciai from his parents. He later bought land in Kisuskes. At one time, there was a purchase certificate from Noble Adam Wenclawowicz Semaszkievicz dated May 16, 1596 in the file from St. Petersburg. However, it has been lost.

Bartlomiej had two sons—Wojciech and Stanisław. They inherited an estate in Ruosciai, in the Upytė province. They also controlled an estate in Puslovis in the Upytė province, as well as the Taujenai, Jociniai, and Paezeriai estates in the Ukmergė province.

These properties were eventually divided and inherited by Wojciech and Stanisław's sons.

Wojciech Lutkiewicz had three sons:

- Stanisław Lutkiewicz
- Jerzy Lutkiewicz
- Samuel Sr. Lutkiewicz

Stanisław Lutkiewicz had two sons:

- Jan Lutkiewicz
- Józef Lutkiewicz

A certificate of the division of these estates was issued in April 1670. A copy of the certificate was provided from the Upytė Land Court Books that was dated August 10, 1797 as part of the documentation for the Nobility Confirmation documents sent to St. Petersburg in 1820 and 1835.

In addition to his inheritance, Józef Lutkiewicz bought Liutkiskiai and Milkoniskes estates in Ruosciai. There was a purchase certificate dated March 22, 1678 between Józef Lutkiewicz, Stanisław's son, and Bartlomiej and Scensnas Lickoniai that was in the file from St. Petersburg Russia, but it has since been lost. Unfortunately, the original in Lithuania has also been lost or destroyed.

Józef Lutkiewicz had 2 sons—Krzysztof and Samuel Sr.

Krzysztof Lutkiewicz married twice. First, he married Barbara Koreywowa, and they had two children—Dorothea born in 1700 and Katarzyna born in 1701. They were both baptized in Dotnuva (Lithuanian), or Datnów (Polish), Parish. His second wife was Dorothea Koreywowa, and had they had a son named Józef in 1704 who was baptized in Dotnuva (Lithuanian), or Datnów (Polish), Parish. Between the two marriages, no male heir was alive by 1820.

Samuel Sr. Lutkiewicz had two sons, by two wives:

- Samuel Jr. Lutkiewicz (his mother was Anna Ilaszewicz).
- Kazimierz Lutkiewicz (born on Jan 23, 1689 in Kedaniai; his mother was Marianna Bortkiewicz).

Samuel Sr. Lutkiewicz mortgaged half of his paternal estate in Ruosciai to his wife Anna, née Ilaszewicz, according to a legal document prepared on April 23, 1683 and approved in the Land Court of Raseiniai (Lithuanian), or Rosienie (Polish), on January 18, 1686. They had a son named Samuel Jr, Lutkiewicz.

After Anna died, Samuel Sr. Lutkiewicz married Noble Marianna Bortkiewicz, and they had a son named Kazimierz Lutkiewicz.

Samuel Sr.'s son, Samuel Jr. Lutkiewicz, was born on January 23, 1689 in Kediniai. The file in St. Petersburg used to contain his baptismal record that listed both his father and his mother, Anna Ilazewicz. This was no longer in the file, and the original in Lithuania was lost.

Samuel Jr. Lutkiewicz married a woman named Anna Godwoysz. There was a mortgage document dated April 23, 1711 and notarized by the Raseiniai (Lithuanian), or Rosienie (Polish), Land Court on September 25, 1797 that indicated Samuel Jr. Lutkiewicz gave his wife Anna Godwoysz, half of his paternal estate in Ruosciai. This document states that this land was received from his father Samuel Sr. Lutkiewicz and his paternal uncle Krzysztof Lutkiewicz.

Samuel Jr. Lutkiewicz had three sons and two daughters with Anna Godwoysz, all of whom were baptized in Dotnuva (Lithuanian), or Datnów (Polish), Parish:

- Józef Lutkiewicz (1713-1783)
- Anna Lutkiewicz (1715-?)
- Stefan Lutkiewicz (1719-1792)
- Mateusz Lutkiewicz (1722-?)
- Martianna Lutkiewicz (1725-?)

Józef, Stefan, Mateusz, and their mother, Anna, bought Enckieniszki estate in the Ruosciai neighborhood. There used to be a sales document listing Noble Anna, née Godwoysz, and her sons, Józef, Stefan, and Mateusz as buyers and the Noble Jan Kazimierz Iliaszewicz and Teodora, née Kulesza, as sellers. They were somehow related to Samuel Jr.'s mother. The document was issued on November 10, 1743 and recorded December 3, 1761 in the Land Court of Samogitia. Unfortunately, this document was no longer in the file, and the original in Lithuania was lost or destroyed.

The oldest son of Samuel Jr., Józef Lutkiewicz, married Roza Iawgielanka, and they had four children:

- Jan Lutkiewicz (1755-?)
- Tadeusz Lutkiewicz (1749-?)
- Anna Lutkiewicz
- Katrzyna Lutkiewicz

His children were listed in his last will and testament dated May 22, 1783 and recorded on June 28, 1835 in the County Court of Raseiniai (Lithuanian), or Rosienie (Polish). He left his paternal estate in Ruosciai to his daughters, Anna and Katarzyna Lutkiewicz. The only condition was that if his sons, Jan and Tadeusz, came back, the ownership of the estate should be returned to them. There was also a note that the sons of his brother, Stefan—Wiktor, Tomasz, Michał, and Marcin—had no rights to this land since their father renounced his rights.

Józef's son, Tadeusz Lutkiewicz, settled in Volhynia, a region in modern-day Ukraine, where he had four sons:

- Antoni Lutkiewicz
- Józef Lutkiewicz
- Ksawery Lutkiewicz
- Wojciech Lutkiewicz

However, there is no further information known about them. They must have stayed in the Ukraine.

Józef's son, Jan, with his wife Ludwika Rojcewicz (born about 1770), had the following children:

- Franciska Lutkiewicz (abt. 1788-?)
- Adam Lutkiewicz (born 1790 in Kėdainiai, baptized in Dotnuva (Lithuanian), or Datnów (Polish) Parish.
- Anna Lutkiewicz (born 1792 in Kėdainiai, baptized in Dotnuva (Lithuanian), or Datnów (Polish) Parish.
- Józef Lutkiewicz (born 1794 in Kėdainiai, baptized in Dotnuva (Lithuanian), or Datnów (Polish) Parish. He married Antonina Podhajska. They had one son—Wincenty Lutkiewicz. He was born on January 28, 1817 and baptized in Ariogala Parish.
- Stanisław Lutkiewicz was baptized on April 17, 1800 in Dotnuva (Lithuanian), or Datnów (Polish) Parish. His godparents were Jacob Rymkieiwcz and Anna Szytanska.

     Stanisław Lutkiewicz married twice. He married Elenora Rogalska first, and they had the following children:

  ○ Antonina Lutkiewicz was baptized on April 3, 1823 in Pociūnėliai (Lithuanian), or Pacunele (Polish), Church. Her godparents were Karol Juchniewicz and Barbara Rogalska.
  ○ Józef Lutkiewicz was born on July 2, 1828 in noble settlement of Babiniszki of the Krakinów (Polish), or

Krekenava (Lithuanian), Parish. He was baptized on July 3, 1828 in Vadaktai (Lithuanian), or Wodokty (Polish), Church. His godparents were Jan Grochowski and Anna, daughter of Jakub Jurkiewicz.

o Aleksander-Jan Lutkiewicz was born on October 29, 1831 in the noble settlement Micuny in Krakinów (Polish), or Krekenava (Lithuanian), Parish. He baptized on October 31, 1831 in Pacunele (Pociūnėliai) church. His godparents were Aleksander Jotkiewicz and Ewa, wife of Jan Grochowski.

o Antoni Lutkiewicz was born on July 28, 1834 in Bortkuny. He was baptized on July 30, 1834 in Krakinów (Polish), or Krekenava (Lithuanian), Parish. His godparents were Bernard Downarowicz and Joanna Rogalska, maiden. He married Emilia Kuszdejko in Krekenava (Lithuanian), or Krakinów (Polish), parish in 1858. They had a daughter named Wincenta that was baptized on May 9, 1871 in Krakės (Lithuanian), or Kroki (Polish), Parish.

o Frances Lutkiewicz

o Anna Lutkiewicz

o Petra Lutkiewicz

o Euphrosyne Lutkiewicz.

Stanisław married for the second time to Barbara Mieszkowski (probably around 1844) and they had the following children:

o Jan Lutkiewicz was born on April 27, 1845 in Świle. He was baptized on May 27, 1845 in Jaswojnie (Josvainiai) Parish. His godparents were Kazimierz Juszkiewicz and Koleta Lutkiewicz, maiden. Jan married Konstanja Markiewicz, and they had seven children:

    o Paulina Lutkiewicz was baptized on March 25, 1877 in Krakės (Lithuanian), or Kroki (Polish), Parish. She was born in Jaugiliai (Lithuanian) Jawgiele (Polish) on March 22. Her godparents were Noble Damazy Lutkiewicz and Anna Sypowicz, maiden. She married Jarosław Gulecki in Krakės (Lithuanian), or Kroki (Polish), Parish on April 23, 1896.

o Szymon Lutkiewicz was baptized on January 30, 1880 in Krakės (Lithuanian), or Kroki (Polish), Parish. He was born in Jaugiliai (Lithuanian), or Jawgiele (Polish). His godparents were Noble Bronisław Malinowski and Karolina, wife of Aleksander Markiewicz.

o Albina Lutkiewicz was born on March 4, 1882 in Jaugiliai (Lithuanian), or Jawgiele (Polish), and baptized that same day in Krakės (Lithuanian), or Kroki (Polish), Parish. Her godparents were Noble Jan Malinowski and Bogumiła, wife of Antoni Baniewicz. She died on January 8, 1883 from measles at the age of ten months.

o Pawel Lutkiewicz was born on February 1, 1884 in Jaugiliai (Lithuanian), or Jawgiele (Polish). Four days later, he was baptized in Krakės (Lithuanian), or Kroki (Polish), Parish. His godparents were Adam Borowski and Antonina Sokowicz, maiden. He married Emilia Obolewicz on March 3, 1919 in Pacunele (Pociūnėliai) Parish. Emilia died nine months later of typhus on January 20, 1920. She was only 20 years old.

o Helena Lutkiewicz was born on March 2, 1888 in Jaugiliai (Lithuanian), or Jawgiele (Polish). She was baptized in Krakės (Lithuanian), or Kroki (Polish), Parish seven days after her birth. Her godparents were Dominik Markiewicz and Aniela Majski, maiden. On February 9, 1910, she married Józef Narwid (1882-?). But, Józef must have died because she married Franciszek Kairis on February 6, 1921 in Wasiliszki, Belarus.

o Józef Lutkiewicz was born on January 2, 1891 in noble settlement Jaugiliai (Lithuanian), or Jawgiele (Polish). A day later, he was baptized at Krakės (Lithuanian), or Kroki (Polish), Parish by the vicar priest Malinowski. His godparents were Benedykt Lutkiewicz and Adela Sieklucki (unmarried). He married Elena Gineitaite in 1925.

- ◦ Jan Lutkiewicz was born on June 9, 1893 in Jankuny. He was baptized on June 11, 1893 in Krakės (Lithuanian), or Kroki (Polish), Parish. His godparents were Bronisław Dabkowicz and Anna Jawgiel (unmarried).

- ◦ Damazy Lutkiewicz was born around 1848. On February 22, 1906, he died in Krakės (Lithuanian), or Kroki (Polish), from tuberculosis. He died a bachelor at age 58.

- ◦ Benedykt Lutkiewicz was born after 1845. He married Michalina Sipowicz, and they had the following children:

  - ◦ Józef Lutkiewicz was baptized on December 2, 1879 in Krakės (Lithuanian), or Kroki (Polish), Parish. Józef's godparents were Noble Jan Lutkiewicz (his uncle) and Antonina (probably his aunt), wife of Dominik Norwilo. On February 7, 1905, Józef married Helena Kuprewicz in Krakės (Lithuanian), or Kroki (Polish), Parish. The witnesses were Piotr Kuprewicz, Zygmunt Kimont, and Napoleon Dowgwillo.

  - ◦ Katarzyna Lutkiewicz was born on January 2, 1882 in Jaugiliai (Lithuanian), or Jawgiele (Polish) on January 2, 1882 and baptized the same day in Krakės (Lithuanian), or Kroki (Polish), Parish. Her godparents were Noble Józef Leszczyński and Katarzyna, wife of Jan Romaszkiewicz. She married Mateusz Bobinas on February 28, 1910 in Krakės (Lithuanian), or Kroki (Polish), Parish. The witnesses were Antoni Lutkiewicz, Piotr Kuprewicz, and Józef Lutkiewicz.

  - ◦ Michael Lutkiewicz was born around 1885. He married Katarzyna Sylwestrowicz on February 24, 1913 in Krakės (Lithuanian), or Kroki (Polish), Parish. The witnesses were Wincenty Karczus, Antoni Lutkiewicz, and Józef Lutkiewicz.

  - ◦ Bonifacy Lutkiewicz was born on May 18, 1890, in village Montwidowo. He was baptized in

Krakės (Lithuanian), or Kroki (Polish), Parish. His godparents were Józef Syrotowicz and Zofia, wife of Felicjan Kutkiewicz. He died on April 29, 1892 from measles.

- ○ Bogumila Lutkiewicz was born after 1845. She married Antoni Banio, and they had one son, Jan, in 1883. Unfortunately, he died on September 12, 1883, in the Jaugiliai (Lithuanian), or Jawgiele (Polish), from inflammation at the age of three weeks. (Note that "inflammation" could indicate pneumonia or meningitis.)

On June 12, 1885, Barbara Lutkiewicz, née Mieszkowski, died from old age in Jaugiliai (Lithuanian) Jawgiele (Polish). Stanisław died before her, but his death record has not been found.

Stefan Lutkiewicz, Samuel Jr.'s second son, married Helen Nieściukówna and bought Sviliai-Godvaisiskes-Neciukiskes Estate. Upon their deaths, they left the estate to their sons. This was documented in a division certificate dated December 3, 1792. Unfortunately, this certificate was no longer in the file and can't be found in Lithuania. Stefan and Helen had the following children:

- Wiktor Lutkiewicz was baptized on March 4, 1746 in Josvainiai Parish. His godparents were Władysław Macanowicz from Urniarze (Urneziai) in Datnów (Polish), or Dotnuva (Lithuanian), Parish and Anna Ugiańska from Betygoła Parish. The witnesses were Michał Rymkiewicz from Kraki Parish and Regina Butkiewicz, Kazimierz Witkowski, and Lutkiewiczówna from Urniarze.

  According to a note dated March 1, 1785, Wiktor was elected by noblemen to be the standard-bearer (cavalry master) of the Josvainiai Province. This note is no longer in the file and can't be found in Lithuania. He married Barbara Dowejko (born 1750), and they had six children:

o Dominik Lutkiewicz was born on June 30, 1776. He was baptized on July 2, 1776 in Jaswojnie (Josvainiai) Parish. His godparents were Noble Mateusz Korf and Barbara Białłozor. The witnesses were Noble Wincenty Dowgird and Babiańska—parishioners from Dotnuva (Lithuanian), or Datnów (Polish).

Dominik was the clerk of Raseiniai (Lithuanian), or Rosienie (Polish), Province and bought the Pakirsnovys-Rimgailai Estate from Wictorin Wojtkiewicz, the Marshal of the Noblemen of Šiauliai (Lithuanian), or Szawle (Polish), on December 19, 1805. This document was not in the file, and it is no longer in Lithuania. He was elected to be the judge of land in Raseiniai (Lithuanian), or Rosienie (Polish). Later he was elected the judge of the boundaries of land, according to a decree of August 24, 1820.

o Rozalia Lutkiewicz was born in 1781 and baptized in Josvainiai (Lithuanian) or Jaswojnie (Polish) Parish.
o Józef Lutkiewicz was born around 1783 and died around 1785.
o Marcin Lutkiewicz was born around 1787 and baptized in Josvainiai (Lithuanian) or Jaswojnie (Polish) Parish. He became a priest.
o Karol Lutkiewicz was baptized on November 3, 1794 in Josvainiai (Lithuanian) or Jaswojnie (Polish) Parish. His godparents were Judge of the Kaunas County Michał Kozakowski and the wife of the colonel of the army of the Grand Duchy of Lithuania, Krystyna Hołuba. The witnesses were Ignacy Mrokowski and Noble Anna Lutkiewicz from the noble settlement Swile. Karol's noble status was MD, and he married Marianne Koterla.

Karol partly inherited, and partly purchased, Pasusvys-Sviliai Estate with some peasants. This was documented on a certificate of the introduction of Karol and Marianne Lutkiewicz in the ruling of the estate on the December 14, 1826. This document was no longer in the file and can no longer be found in Lithuania. Karol and Marianne had two sons:

- Zygmunt Jan Lutkiewicz was baptized on May 7, 1825 by Vicar Jan Woronowicz of Josvainiai (Lithuanian) or Jaswojnie (Polish) Parish. He was born in Swile Territory. His godparents were Nobles Józef Juna and Tekla Witniewicz. The assistants were Andreas Farnowski, Eleanora Kreyska, Michale Krapski, and Ewas Farnoska.

- Mieczslaw Albin Lutkiewicz was baptized in Josvainiai (Lithuanian) or Jaswojnie (Polish) Parish on March 7, 1832. His godparents were Heronim Koterla and Antonina, wife of Onufry Lutkiewicz, a Marshal of Šiauliai (Lithuanian), or Szawle (Polish), County. The assistants were Józefata (wife of Hieronim Koterla), Stanisław Daniłowicz, Jan Prokopowicz, Regina Daniłowicz, and Olimpia Lutkiewicz, maiden.

  ○ Tekla Lutkiewicz was born around 1789.

- Michal Samuel Lutkiewicz was baptized on September 3, 1752 in Josvainiai (Lithuanian) or Jaswojnie (Polish) Parish. His godparents were Administrator of the Jaswojnie district office Felicjan Terpiłowski and Marianna Ongirska, maiden from Ongiry. He married Anna Wierzychowska and had two children.

Michal Lutkiewicz owned the Duogiai Estate, which he left to his two sons—Mateusz and Adam. This was documented on the division certificate of the estate between these two brothers dated February 13, 1820:

  ○ Mateusz Lutkiewicz was born September 11, 1782 in either Ejragola (Polish) or Ariogala (Lithuanian) Parish or Josvainiai (Lithuanian) or Jaswojnie (Polish) Parish.

  ○ Adam Lutkiewicz was baptized on January 16 (unknown year, but before 1782) in Ejragola (Polish) or Ariogala (Lithuanian) Parish. His godparents were Noble Antoni Dowgiałło and Łucja Rochdziewicz from Jankuny. Adam married twice. His first wife was Apolonia Florianowicz, and they had one son:

- Wincenty Jan Lutkiewicz was baptized on January 25, 1823 in Josvainiai (Lithuanian) or Jaswojnie (Polish) Parish. His godparents were Ludwik Wolszkiewicz and Aniela Lutkiewicz.

His second wife was Aniela Juchniewicz and they had five sons:

- Adam Dominik Lutkiewicz was baptized on December 30, 1827 in Josvainiai (Lithuanian) or Jaswojnie (Polish) Parish. He was a well-known landlord. He married Anna Lapinska, and they had five children:
    - Michael Lutkiewicz was born and baptized on February 5, 1864 in Krakės (Lithuanian), or Kroki (Polish), Parish. His godparents were Aleksander Lutkiewicz and Juzefata, wife of Józef. Michal married Aleksandra Dychavicz (Dichavičiūtė) on November 9, 1910. Michal died on March 7, 1941 and was buried in Lesciai Cemetery.
    - Sylvester Lutkiewicz was baptized on January 9, 1867 in Krakės (Lithuanian), or Kroki (Polish), Parish. His godparents were Stefan Gorbaczewki and Tekla Kisičniova. He immigrated to the United States and married Rosie (Francis) Travinski on June 30, 1897 in Cumberland Pennsylvania. They had one son, Stephen, on December 2, 1897. Sylvester worked as a miner when he arrived in Pennsylvania, but eventually owned and operated his own grocery store. Francis died in 1916, and Sylvester died from a stroke on August 16, 1934 in Mount Carmel Pennsylvania. They are buried in Mother of Consolation Cemetery in Mount Carmel.

- o Weronica Lutkiewicz was born on May 4, 1869 and baptized on May 11, 1869 in Krakės (Lithuanian), or Kroki (Polish), Parish. Her godparents were landlord Osip Waitkewicz and Weronika, wife of Gabriel Lutkiewicz (Gabriel was her uncle).
- o Elżbieta Lutkiewicz was baptized in Krakės (Lithuanian), or Kroki (Polish), Parish on November 17, 1870. Her godparents were landlord Ignas Sirvidas and Franciska Mackevičiūtė.
- Karol Lutkiewicz was baptized on February 3, 1830 in Josvainiai Parish.
- Zygmunt Lutkiewicz was baptized on October 3, 1832 in Josvainiai (Lithuanian) or Jaswojnie (Polish) Parish. His godparents were Józef Juchniewicz and Franciszka Butkiewiczówna (unmarried).
- Gabriel-Bronislaw Lutkiewicz was born on June 28, 1836 in Ongiry. He was baptized on June 29, 1836 in Josvainiai (Lithuanian) or Jaswojnie (Polish) Parish. His godparents were nobels Karol Spandowicz and Franciszka Wabikiewicz, maiden. Gabriel-Bronislaw Lutkiewicz married twice. His first wife was a 22-year-old widow, Leokadia Mikulski (Piotrowska). They married on July 28, 1864 in Krakės (Lithuanian), or Kroki (Polish), Parish. They had three children:
  - o Kazimiera Lutkiewicz was was born on May 8 in Malinówka and baptized on May 9, 1865 in Krakės (Lithuanian), or Kroki (Polish), Parish by Priest Józef Urbanowicz. Her godparents were Noble Aleksander Lutkiewicz and Barbara Mikulski, maiden.
  - o Adela Waleria Lutkiewicz was was born on January 10, 1867 in Malinówka. She was baptized five days later in Krakės (Lithuanian), or Kroki (Polish), Parish by Priest I. Jankowski

She. Her godparents were Noble Ludwik
Dowejko and Michalina Kimontówna, maiden.
- Adolf Lutkiewicz (birth date unknown).

On October 24, 1867, Leokadia Mikulski Lutkiewicz died
from fever in Malinówka. Gabriel married for a second time.
His second wife was Weronika Ciechanowicz, and they had
the following children:

- Jan Lutkiewicz—unknown when he was born.
- Antoni Lutkiewicz—unknown when he was
  born.
- Michalina Lutkiewicz—unknown when she
  was born.
- Katarzyna Lutkiewicz—unknown when she
  was born.
- Paulina Lutkiewicz was born around 1880. She
  married Teofil Rymkiewicz on February 19,
  1902 in Krakės (Lithuanian), or Kroki (Polish),
  Parish. They had at least one child—Weronika
  Rymkiewicz who was born on October 1, 1910
  in Rosczce, Lithuania. Weronika married
  Zymunt Świlczewski on December 26, 1939
  in Dotnuva (Lithuanian), or Datnów (Polish),
  Parish.
- Józef Lutkiewicz was born on March 14, 1883
  in Zwalany. He was baptized in Baisogala
  on March 20, 1883. His godparents were
  nobes Cyprian Janczewski and Franciszka
  Dobkiewicz, maiden. He came to Philadelphia,
  Pennsylvania and married Jadwiga (Ida)
  Stefanowicz. Joseph died on February 10, 1931
  in Philadelphia, and Ida died in November of
  1970.
- Ludwika Lutkiewicz was born around 1884.
  She married Kazimierz Dowgwillo on February
  7, 1906. They had nine children—Bronislaw
  (1906-1986), Otton (b. 1908), Antoni (b. 1909),

Stefan (1911-1911), Katarzyna (1913-1991), Jan (1914-1914), Weronika (1917-?), Kazimierz (1923-1978), and Donat (1926-1989). Ludwika died in 1978 in Lithuania. Kazimierz died on January 2, 1954 in Ingarka, Russia.

On May 30, 1904, Weronika Ciechanowicz Lutkiewicz died in the Poskierdumie Estate from pneumonia. She was 62 years old and left behind her husband, Gabriel Lutkiewicz, her sons—Jan, Antoni, and Józef—and her daughters—Michalina, Katarzyna, Paulina, and Ludwika. She was buried on July 1, 1904 by Priest Zoris in Urniaż cemetery.

- Aleksander Lutkiewicz was born on February 19, 1840 to Adam Lutkiewicz and Aniela Juchniewicz. He was baptized in Josvainiai (Lithuanian) or Jaswojnie (Polish) Parish on February 20, 1840. His godparents were Nobles Aleksander Juchniewicz and Konstancja Lutkiewicz, maiden. Aleksander was known as a landlord. He married 20-year-old Barbara Witkiewicz on February 20, 1870 in Krakės (Lithuanian), or Kroki (Polish), Parish. They had the following children:
  - Wincenta Lutkiewicz was born on February 24, 1871. She was baptized in Krakės (Lithuanian) or Kroki (Polish), Parish. Her godparents were Adam Lutkiewicz and Weronika, wife of Gabriel Lutkiewicz. Wincenta married twice. First, she married Jonas Girštautas and had five children- Romanas (1900-1901), Albinas (1901-1978), Michilina (before 1902-?), Ivona (before 1902-?), and Elena (1902-1903). Jonas died on December 6 1902 at the age of 30. Then, Wincenta married Adomas Galginas and had two children - Boleslaw (1912-?) and Stefania (1914-200). Adomas died before 1918. It is unknown when Wincenta died. Their daughter, Stefania Galginas married Antanas Damaševičius (1915-1994) and had at least five children: Mečislovas (1937-2018),

Edvardas (1939-1998), Vitalija (1941-2017), Alfonsas (1944-1984), and Julija (1948-2006). Some of their descendents live in England.

o   Józef Lutkiewicz was born on January 9, 1878, in Jankuny. He was baptized in Krakės (Lithuanian), or Kroki (Polish) Parish. His godparents were Noble Józef Wojnowski and Helena, wife of Marcin Wołłowicz.

o   Kazimiera Lutkiewicz was born on January 23, 1880 in Estate Antoszów. She was baptized in Krakės (Lithuanian) or Kroki (Polish), Parish. Her godparents were Noble Józef Kmito and Karolina, wife of Benedykt Bujnowski.

o   Stefan Lutkiewicz was born on September 18, 1882 and baptized in Krakės (Lithuanian) or Kroki (Polish), Parish two days later.

o   Aleksander Lutkiewicz was born on February 17, 1884 in Stuki and was baptized two days later in Krakės (Lithuanian), or Kroki (Polish) Parish. His godparents were Józef Niekrasz and Urszula, wife of Maciej Girsztowt. Aleksander died January 8, 1892 from a lesion.

o   Bolesław Lutkiewicz was born on January 3, 1886 in Stuki. On January 5, 1886, he was baptized in Krakės (Lithuanian), or Kroki (Polish) Parish. His godparents were Adolf Girsztowt and Antonina Bublewski, maiden. Bolesław died on July 11, 1892 from measles. This was only six months after two of his brothers'—Alesksander and Jan—deaths.

o   Jan Lutkiewicz was born around 1890. He died from diphtheria on January 14, 1892. This was a week after his brother Aleksander's death and about six months before his brother, Boleslaw's, death.

•   Tomasz Lutkiewicz was baptized on December 24, 1754 in Josvainiai (Lithuanian) or Jaswojnie (Polish) Parish. He was the son of Stefan Lutkiewicz and Helena Nieściukówna. His godparents were Jan Bacewicz from Ongiry and Helena Witkowska from

Świle. Tomasz married Anna Nowliki, and they had the following children:

- ○ Jan Stefan Lutkiewicz was baptized on December 14, 1788 in Josvainiai (Lithuanian) or Jaswojnie (Polish) Parish. He married Konstancja Butkiewicz, and they had the following children:
  - • Tomasz Dawid Lutkiewicz was baptized on December 13, 1817 in Josvainiai (Lithuanian) or Jaswojnie (Polish) Parish. His godparents were Nobles Nicodemus Butkiewicz and Ludwika Ibianska from Ongiry.
  - • Józef Anicety Lutkiewicz was baptized on April 4, 1824 in Josvainiai (Lithuanian) or Jaswojnie (Polish) Parish. His godparents were Nobles Józef Lukom and Zofia Ibiańska from Ongiry. He probably died before 1835, since he wasn't mentioned in the 1835 nobility confirmation documents.
- ○ Jan Lutkiewicz was born about 1790.
- ○ Mateusz Franciszek Lutkiewicz was baptized on September 17, 1792 in Josvainiai (Lithuanian) or Jaswojnie (Polish) Parish. His godparents were Marcin Lutkiewicz and Justyna Rowińska. The witnesses were Wincenty Mackiewicz and Bogumiła Lutkiewiczówna.

Mateusz married Tekla Rydgier, and they had five sons:

- • Leon Damazy Lutkiewicz was baptized on December 11, 1827 in Josvainiai (Lithuanian) or Jaswojnie (Polish) Parish. His godparents were Franciszek Ongirski and Apolinia Kozłowska.
- • Wincenty Policarp Lutkiewicz was baptized on January 26, 1830 in Josvainiai (Lithuanian) or Jaswojnie (Polish) Parish. His godparents were Jan Ongirski and Petronela, wife of Józef Brodowski.
- • Karol Theofil Lutkiewicz was baptized on November 4, 1831 in Josvainiai (Lithuanian) or Jaswojnie (Polish) Parish. Karol's godparents were Wincenty Kozłowski and Anna, wife of Benedykt Wołodkowicz.

- Leopold-Leonard Lutkiewicz was born on November 3, 1837 in Świle (Polish) or Sviliai (Lithuanian) and baptized on November 24, 1837 in Josvainiai (Lithuanian) or Jaswojnie (Polish) Parish. His godparents were Nobles Zachariasz Giniejto and Urszula, wife of Adam Tczontkowski.
- Emeryk Lutkiewicz was born on December 14, 1840 in Świle and baptized on January 12, 1841 in Josvainiai (Lithuanian) or Jaswojnie (Polish) Parish. Emeryk's godparents were Nobles Karol Lutkiewicz and Teresa Ibiańska, maiden.

  ○ Zofia Lutkiewicz was born about 1794.
  ○ Aleksander Ignacy Lutkiewicz was baptized on March 27, 1805 in Josvainiai (Lithuanian) or Jaswojnie (Polish) Parish. His godparents were Zachariusz Agirski and Marianna Agirska. He married Teresa Jagiełłowicz, and they had the following children:
    - Jan-Wincenty Lutkiewicz was baptized on October 25, 1831 in Josvainiai (Lithuanian) or Jaswojnie (Polish) Parish. His godparents were Józef Jagiełowicz and Natalia Arszówna (unmarried).
    - Julian-Wiktor Lutkiewicz was baptized on December 24, 1833 in Josvainiai (Lithuanian) or Jaswojnie (Polish) Parish. He died before 1835.
    - Norberta Aleksandra Lutkiewicz was born on August 4, 1841 in the morning and was baptized on August 17, 1841 in Jaswojnie (Josvainiai) Parish. Her godparents were Tomasz Lutkiewicz and Kolleta Lutkiewicz.
    - Julian Lutkiewicz was baptized on March 25, 1847 in Josvainiai (Lithuanian) or Jaswojnie (Polish) Parish. His godparents were Karol Lutkiewicz and Franciszka Przyiatkowska (unmarried).

- Marcin Lutkiewicz was born to Stefan Lutkiewicz and Helena Nieściukówna, but his birthdate is unknown. According to the 1820 nobility confirmation documents, he had one son—Francisek Lutkiewicz.

The last son of Samuel Sr. and his second wife, Marianna Bortkiewicz, was Kazmierz Lutkiewicz. He was born in 1689 in Kedaniai. He left his estate in Ruosciai, to his only son, Jerzy Lutkiewicz. Jerzy left his estate to his two sons, Antoni and Adam Lutkiewicz, and they divided it in accordance with the will dated July 6, 1758. This document is no longer in the file and can no longer be found in Lithuania. Jerzy's sons were:

- Antoni Lutkiewicz (unknown birth and death dates) married Marcjanna Witkiewicz and had two sons:
    - ○ Joachim Józef Lutkiewicz was baptized August 29, 1779. He married Katarzyna Utkiewicz. They had two sons:
        - Aleksander Lutkiewicz was baptized on January 23, 1824 in Datnów (Polish), or Dotnuva (Lithuanian), church. His godparents were Nobles Adam Sypowicz and Konstancja Parakiewicz.
        - Ludwik Lutkiewicz was born on September 8, 1828 in Raseiniai (Lithuanian), or Rosienie (Polish). He was baptized on September 19, 1828 in Datnów (Polish), or Dotnuva (Lithuanian), Church. His godparents were Nobles Józef Paszkiewicz and Apolonia Witkiewicz, maiden.
- Adam Lutkiewicz married Petronela Witkiewicz (probably the sister of Marcjanna, the wife of his brother, Antoni). It is unknown when he was born, but he died in 1801. He left a will dated November 11, 1801 and left his estate in Ruosciai to his two children, Franciszek and Faustina Lutkiewicz.
    - ○ Franciszek-Wawryzyniec Lutkiewicz was baptized in Dotnuva (Lithuanian), or Datnów (Polish), Church on July 10, 1796. His godparents were Jacob Rymkiewicz and Maryanna Lutkiewicz.
    - ○ Faustina Lutkiewicz – unfortunately, nothing is known about her.

Baltrejmus/Wojciech

Coming back to the branch of **Wojciech Lutkiewicz**—the son of **Baltremus** and grandson of **Jan Ludkievicz**—had three sons:

- Stanisław Lutkiewicz
- **Jerzy Lutkiewicz**
- Samuel Lutkiewicz

It is unknown if Stanislaus and Samuel had descendants. Jerzy Lutkiewicz, in addition to inherited estates, bought the Pauslovis Estate in Upytė territory from Songailai in 1667.

Jerzy Lutkiewicz had a son, **Balcer Kazimierz Lutkiewicz**, who inherited all the estates of the father. In addition, he was the clerk of Upytė Castle Court. He married **Anna Weronika Plater**, and they had two sons who inherited all of his assets—**Konstanty** and Karol Lutkiewicz. The family tree of Konstanty will be described first. This is my family line.

Konstanty had two wives—one is unknown and the other was Joanna Bartoszwicz. Konstanty Lutkiewicz's will, dated October 10, 1767, gives all his money and the part of Puslovis Estate that he and his brother Karol owned, as well as the Taujenai Estate, to his sons from his second marriage—Ignacy and Dominik Lutkiewicz. He noted that his sons from the first marriage—Antoni and **Andrzej Lutkiewicz**—had already received their parts of his assets.

- With the first unknown wife, he had the following children:
  - Antoni Lutkiewicz—unfortunately nothing is known about him.
  - **Andrzej Lutkiewicz** married **Rozalia Snarska**. He received Wołmontowicze (Polish), or Valmanciai (Lithuanian), Estate in Šiauliai (Lithuanian), or Szawle (Polish), County as a gift from his wife's parents, **Matthew Snarskiai** and **Anna Pergarowska**. There was a note dated January 25th, 1761, by which **Matthew** and **Anna Pergarowska Snarskiai** gifted this estate to their son-in-law, **Andrzej,** and to their daughter Rozalia Lutkiewicz. This note is not in the file and no longer exists in Lithuania.
- Tadeusz Lutkiewicz—Unfortunately, nothing more is known about him.
- Wincenty Lutkiewicz—Unfortunately, nothing more is known about him.
- **Szymon Lutkiewicz** was born about 1755. He married **Elżbieta Zacharzewska** (born about 1761). (Note that this is my family

line—I will continue a more detailed family tree for Szymon and Elżbieta in the next section.)

Rozalia Snarska Lutkiewicz must have died around 1771. She left a will dated January 2, 1771, leaving the Wołmontowicze (Polish), or Valmanciai (Lithuanian), Estate to her sons— **Szymon**, Tadeusz, and Wincenty Lutkiewicz.

On May 21, 1783, however a document was prepared by **Andrzej Lutkiewicz** (**Szymon**, Tadeusz and Wincenty's father) about this property. He made his brother Bartlomiej's son, Konstanty-Ferdynand (listed in the next section under his father, Bartlomiej), regent of this property. It is unknown why **Andrzej** did this. Konstanty had the title of Regent of Land and Court Secretary. There are six court documents from 1804-1815 denoting Konstanty as regent. Those properties were supposed to go to the sons of Andrzej, but all documents were given to Konstanty.

- ○ Bartlomiej Lutkiewicz married Helen Stejgwillo and had seven children:
  - • Antoni Lutkiewicz married twice. He married Bogumila Szulc on February 5, 1793 in Krakės (Lithuanian), or Kroki (Polish) Parish. His second marriage was to Anna Rymkiewicz. It is unclear who the mother of Konstanty Lutkiewicz was—documents refer to them as children of Antoni but don't refer to their mother. Marianna, Tekla, Yosefata, Dionizy, and Dominik Ignacy are the children of Anna Rymkiewicz, according to their baptism records and 1816 Revision Records (kind of a tax record in the Russian Empire).
    - ○ Konstanty Lutkiewicz was born in 1795 and died in 1816.
    - ○ Marianna Lutkiewicz was born in 1805.
    - ○ Tekla Lutkiewicz was baptized on August 24, 1807 in Pociūnėliai (Lithuanian), or Pacunele (Polish,) Parish. She was born in Kirkiły. Her

godparents were Nobles Paweł Ruczkowski and Bogumiła Dombrowskaborn.

- ° Yosefata Lutkiewicz was born around 1811.
- ° Dionizy Lutkiewicz was baptized on October 11, 1811 in Krakės (Lithuanian), or Kroki (Polish). His godparents were Józef Ryszkiewicz (treasurer) and Antonina Tomaszewska. He married Anna Downarwicz on May 4, 1843 in Basiogala (Lithuanian), or Bejsagoła (Polish), Parish, and they had the following children:
  - Jan Lutkiewicz—unknown when he was born.
  - Antoni Lutkiewicz was born March 5, 1851. He married Joanna Żongołowicz in 1877, and they had two children:
    - ° Jan Lutkiewicz was born on July 4, 1887 and baptized on July 12 in Pociūnėliai (Lithuanian), or Pacunele (Polish), Parish.
    - ° Maria Lutkiewicz was born on July 20, 1892 and baptized in Krakės (Lithuanian) Kroki (Polish) Parish on July 26.
      - Aniela Lutkiewicz was born on October 11, 1853 in Poniekielpie and baptized on the same day in Pociūnėliai (Lithuanian), or Pacunele (Polish), parish. Her godparents were Noble Ambroży Pacewicz and Tekla Pietkiewicz, widow.
      - Petronela Lutkiewicz was born on June 28, 1857 in village Poniekielpie. She was baptized in Pociūnėliai (Lithuanian), or Pacunele (Polish), Parish on June 29. Her godparents were Franciszek Samulewicz and Aniela, wife of Franciszek Mieczyński. On June 6, 1907, Petronela married Benedykt Martiszus, a 75-year-old widower from village Gudajcie. She was 45 years old. The witnesses were

       Franciszek Zinkus, Michał Zinkus, and Kazimierz Jodejko.

- o Dominik-Ignacy Lutkiewicz was baptized on September 1, 1813 in Krakės (Lithuanian), or Kroki (Polish), Parish. His godparents were Adam Jawgiel and Anna Milejkowa. He married Roza Kozlwoska on January 10, 1846 in Tytuvenai. They had one son, Adam Boleslaw Lutkiewicz, in 1851.

- Dominik Lutkiewicz was born around 1766 and was gifted the Kirkilai-Bartasiunai Estate by his mother on a document dated September 27, 1792. This is no longer in the file and can't be found in Lithuania. He had two wives. The first wife was Felicjanna Zaborski, and they had the following children:

  - o Onufry Stefan Lutkiewicz was baptized on September 25, 1807 in Kurtowiany (Kurtuvėnai) Parish. His godparents were Konstanty Lutkiewicz and Agata Mokrzecka. He was the clerk in the Court of Boundaries for Raisiniai. He married Julia Stankiewicz, and they had:

    - Julian-Gabriel-Onufry Lutkiewicz was baptized on April 28, 1846 in Siaulenai.

    - Konstanty-Izydor Lutkiewicz was born in Manor Sutkiszki on August 8, 1847. He was baptized on September 12, 1847 in Siaulenai. His godparents were Augustyn Kibort and Elżbieta, wife of Julian Stankiewicz

    - Dominik Jan Napoleon Lutkiewicz was born on May 24, 1849 in Manor Sutkiszki. His godparents were Noble Jacek Kownarski, the former judge of Šiauliai (Lithuanian), or Szawle (Polish), County, and Teresa, the wife of Mr. Butkiewicz (the former judge of Rosienie County).

- Stanisława-Katarzyna Lutkiewicz was born on January 19, 1851 in Manor Suliki. Her godparents were Noble Wincenty Stankiewicz (a former land judge) and Barbara, the wife of Kalikst Dowiat (the Marshal of Šiauliai (Lithuanian), or Szawle (Polish), County. Assistants were Noble Kajetan Dowiat and Hipolita, the wife of Grizdzi Włodwiło.
- Elżbieta Anna Lutkiewicz was born on September 17, 1853 in Manor Suliki. Her godparents were Noble Wiktor Stankiewicz, the Provincial Secretary, and Anna Wojtkiewicz.

Dominik's second wife was Katarzyna Iwazkiewicz, and they had one son:

- ○ Marcjan-Konstanty Lutkiewicz was baptized on May 26, 1819 in Okmiana (Akmene) Church. His godparents were Antoni Gurczyn and Urszula Grużewska. The witnesses were Job Gużewski, Elwira Gyżewska, Ignacy Koplewski, Anna Progulbicka, Leon Gurczyn, and Marianna Morzanska.

He had one son:

- Ignacy Lutkiewicz was born in 1840. He married Francishka Umiaz.

Going back to Bartlomiej and Helen Lutkiewicz's other children:

- Katarzyna Lutkiewicz was baptized on February 28, 1776 in Baisogala. Her godparents were Kazimierz Tangiel and Katarzyna Ruczkovska from Kirkily Manor.
- Konstanty Franciszek Lutkiewicz was baptized on December 6, 1778 in Baisogala Church. His godparents were Andrzej Lutkiewicz and Anna Rajunc.
- Mathias Utkievicz Lutkiewicz was born on July 9, 1781 in Kirkilai. His godparents were Adam Lutkiewicz and Anna Ruczkovska from Kirklily.
- Konstanty-Ferdynand Lutkiewicz was born around 1785 or 1786, according to 1816 tax documents. He was a forensic journeyman and Land Court Judge in Raseiniai (Lithuanian), or Rosienie (Polish). He is mentioned in the books *Kuryer litewski: 1829, Ner 51-100* and *Kuryer Litewski. Za dozwoleniem naywyzszego Rzadu Nayiasnicyszego, Volume 16.* The first book has series of newspaper articles, one of which includes a public disclosure signed by Konstanty Lutkiewicz that the debt proceedings against some landowners would be delayed until June of the next year. The second book has a series of newspaper articles published from 1833 that had a list of people whose lands were being confiscated, including an Aleksander Lutkiewicz, an announcement of court decision signed by Konstanty Lutkiewicz and the assessor, and another court announcement signed by assessor Konstanty Lutkiewicz.

Konstanty owned the Geišiai-Jaugiliai and Pousowie Estates in the Upita Province. He inherited this property from his parents and grandparents. He received estates in Puslovis, Taujėnai, and Paežeriai on April 5, 1797 in the Ukmergė Province from his Uncle Dominik Lutkiewicz. He also received other property from his brothers Antoni and Dominik Lutkiewicz which was recorded in a document on February 5, 1805. Unfortunately, this is no longer in the file or available in Lithuania.

Konstanty Lutkiewicz renounced his rights to these properties and gave them to Michal Lutkiewicz, the son of Karol Lutkiewicz, where Karol was his father's—Konstanty—uncle.

Konstanty Lutkiewicz purchased property (Kowiany, Jaugiliai (Lithuanian), or Jawgiele (Polish), and Zapolszczyzna Estates) from Rozalia Albert Bonicki. These three estates were in Raseiniai (Lithuanian), or Rosienie (Polish), Province. His ownership was confirmed in a document from 1816 that has been lost. He owned property with villages and people in them. It's important to note that this was before serfdom was eliminated by the Czarist Russian Empire. To confirm noble status, one had to have documentation that one had inherited both the property and the serfs on the property.

Konstanty Lutkiewicz married Karolina Strawińska, and they had:
- Telesfor-Ferdynand Lutkiewicz was born in Raseiniai (Lithuanian), or Rosienie (Polish), on January 4, 1815.
- Adolf Wincenty Karol Lutkiewicz was baptized on April 17, 1818 in Krakės (Lithuanian) Kroki (Polish) Parish. His godparents were Michał Nowicki (the deputy from the manor Lewkojnie in Poszuszwojnie Parish) and Barbara Olechnowicz, the wife of the administrator from Raseiniai (Lithuanian), or Rosienie (Polish), County and Milwidy Manor.

o Zygmunt Kalesanta Józef Lutkiewicz was baptized on July 12, 1821 in Krakės (Lithuanian), or Kroki (Polish), Parish. His godparents were Maciej Jacewicz and Józefa Mikucka. The witnesses were Dominik Mikucki and Ludwika Sapińska. He married Agata Kordzikowska on April 15, 1859 in Krakės (Lithuanian), or Kroki (Polish), Parish.

o Władysław-Walenty Lutkiewicz was born on February 9, 1825. He was baptized on February 20, 1825 with water and with oil on September 28, 1825 in Krakės (Lithuanian), or Kroki (Polish), Parish. His godparents were Onufry Towgin and Aurelia Lutkiewicz (unmarried) from Jaugiliai (Lithuanian), or Jawgiele (Polish). He married Józefa Barbara Korewa, and they had a son when Władysław was 60 years old. He died on July 26, 1889 when his son was only two years old. Józefa married again to Jan Witold Rychter on May 27, 1896 in Krakės (Lithuanian), or Kroki (Polish), Parish. Jan must have helped to raise Władysław's son:

  • Konstanty Piotr Lutkiewicz was born on September 11, 1886.

o Wiktor Edmund Lutkiewicz was baptized on November 16, 1826 in Krakės (Lithuanian), or Kroki (Polish), Parish. He married Kamila Zawadzki, and they had the following children:

  • Ryszard Franciszek Lutkiewicz was born in 1851.

  • Kazimiera Wanda Lutkiewicz was born in 1853. She married Stanisław-Ignacy-Stefan Gejsztor in 1888.

Going back to Konstanty, he and his second wife, Marianna Jutniewicz, had:

- o Dominik Lutkiewicz was born about 1745 in Dotnuva (Lithuanian), or Datnów (Polish). He bought the Peckai estate in Ruosciai on November 4, 1776. He married Ewa Gabrijallowicz (born 1853), and they had:
    - Anna Lutkiewicz was born around 1776 in Dotnuva (Lithuanian), or Datnów (Polish), Parish.
    - Antoni-Piotr Lutkiewicz was baptized on June 22, 1778 in Dotnuva (Lithuanian), or Datnów (Polish), Parish. His godparents were Adam Witkiewicz and Anna Syrwiatowiczówna. He had one son:
        - o Bonawentura Lutkiewicz was baptized April 9, 1805 in Dotnuva (Lithuanian), or Datnów (Polish), Parish.
    - Katarzyna Lutkiewicz was baptized around 1791 in Dotnuva (Lithuanian), or Datnów (Polish), Parish.
- o Ignacy Lutkiewicz was a Josvainiai Colonel in 1789. From 1789-1793, he was the Žemaičiai Castle Governor. This was an honorific title.

Going back to Karol Kazimierz Lutkiewicz, son of Balcer and brother of Konstanty, he married Constancia Wajdot. They had the following children:

- o An unknown daughter
- o Jerzy Lutkiewicz—Unfortunately, nothing more is known about him.
- o Michal Lutkiewicz had two sons:
    - Michal Tadeuz Adam Lutkiewicz was baptized on September 5, 1803 in Šiaulėnai or Szawlany (Polish) Parish.
    - Jakub-Gaudenty-Julian Lutkiewicz was baptized on February 14, 1808 in Šiaulėnai (Lithuanian) or Szawlany (Polish) Parish.

Szymon Lutkiewicz and Elżbieta Zacharzewska

Szymon Lutkieiwcz was the third son of **Andrzej Lutkiewicz** and **Rozalia Snarska** and grew up on the family estate, Valmanciai (Lithuanian), or Wołmontowicze (Polish). The estate was a gift from his mother's parents, Matthew Snarskiai and Anna Pergarowska.

Wołmontowicze (Polish), or Valmanciai (Lithuanian), was featured in Henryk Sienkiewicz' historical novel *The Deluge*, which was published in 1886 as the second book in a trilogy. The novel tells a story of a fictional Polish-Lithuanian Commonwealth soldier and Noble Andrzej Kmicic when the Northern Wars were being fought. The Northern Wars were a series of wars fought in northeastern Europe in the 16th and 17th centuries. Because of this historical event, tours are given in this area up to this day.

Szymon was born about 1755. He married **Elżbieta Zacharzewska** (born about 1761). She was also from a noble family, but it is unclear who her parents were. They lived in an estate in Wołmontowicze (Polish), or Valmanciai (Lithuanian).

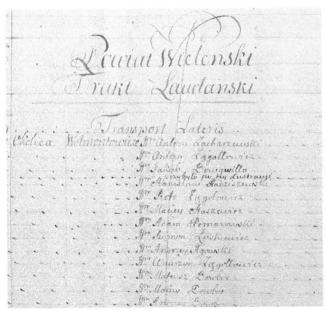

1790 Document Listing Families in the in Wołmontowicze (Polish), or Valmanciai (Lithuanian) Okolica (Neighborhood)

Szymon Lutkiewicz died on Oct 8, 1815 at the age of 60. He was given the sacraments: repentance, Eucharist, and extreme unction. He was buried at Pociūnėliai (Lithuanian), or Pacunele (Polish), cemetery.

His wife, **Elżbieta Zacharzewska**, died on January 25, 1839 on the Valmanciai (Lithuanian), or Wołmontowicze (Polish), Estate of old age and received holy sacraments. She left behind her children—Kazimierz, Felicjan, **Tomasz**, Petronela, Karolina, and Wiktoria. She was also buried Pociūnėliai (Lithuanian), or Pacunele (Polish), cemetery.

They had the following children:

- Lucia Lutkiewicz was a twin to Kazimierz and was baptized on April 13, 1787 in Pociūnėliai (Lithuanian), or Pacunele (Polish), Parish. She did not survive.
- Andrzej Kazimierz Lutkiewicz (Andrzej was added on a separate baptismal record after his sister, Lucia, died) was baptized on April 13, 1787 in Pociūnėliai (Lithuanian), or Pacunele (Polish), Parish. His godparents were Lawrence Zagolowicz and Elżbieta Zacharzewska. Andrzej married Bogumiła Andruszkiewicz (born 1767) and had the following children:
  - Ambrozy-Józef Lutkiewicz was baptized on June 6, 1815 in ciūnėliai (Lithuanian), or Pacunele (Polish), Parish. His godparents were Antoni Lutkiewicz from Jaugiliai (Lithuanian), or Jawgiele (Polish), and Elżbieta Gościewiczowa from Wołmontowicze. The witnesses were Jan Lachowski and Marcjanna Gujlewiczówna. Ambrozy-Józef Lutkiewicz married Józefa Januszkiewicz, and they had the following children:
    - Edward Lutkiewicz was baptized on March 19, 1840 in Kurszany (Kuršėnai) Parish. He was born on March 17, 1840 in Szekście. His godparents were Konstanty Taraszkiewicz and Antonina, the wife of Antoni Januszkiewicz.
    - Zenon Lutkiewicz was baptized on March 31, 1842 in Szekście. His godparents were Michał Gutkiewicz and Elżbieta, the wife of Piotr Wambut.
    - Wawrzyniec Lutkiewicz was baptized on August 16, 1844 in Kurszany (Kuršėnai) Parish. He was born in Szekście. His godparents were Józef Warpuciański and Aurelia Lutkiewicz.

○ Stefan-Andrzej Lutkiewicz was baptized on December 1, 1830 in Pociūnėliai (Lithuanian), or Pacunele (Polish), Parish. His godparents were Jakub Januszkiewicz and Konstancja Lastowska (unmarried).

○ Aurelia Lutkiewicz was baptized on July 10, 1818 in Pociūnėliai (Lithuanian), or Pacunele (Polish), Parish. Her godparents were Nobles Wincenty Snarski and Julianna Stasiewicz, both from Valmanciai (Lithuanian), or Wołmontowicze (Polish).

Andrzej Kazimierz died on April 25, 1847 in the noble settlement of Valmanciai (Lithuanian), or Wołmontowicze (Polish), from "overstrain". He received the holy sacraments. He left behind his wife, Bogumiła Andruszkiewicz, and children—Ambroży, Stefan, and Aurelia. He was buried on April 28 in Pacunele (Pociūnėliai) cemetery.

On April 6, 1854, Bogumiła Andruszkiewicz Lutkiewicz died at age 67 in Valmanciai (Lithuanian), or Wołmontowicze (Polish), from swelling. She was the widow of Kazimierz Lutkiewicz. She left behind three children— Ambroży, Stefan, and Aurelia. She was buried in the Pociūnėliai (Lithuanian), or Pacunele (Polish), cemetery.

• Felicjan Lutkiewicz was baptized on November 18, 1795 in Bejsagoła Parish. His godparents were Nobles Józef Stasiewicz and Anna Gościewiczówna. He married Konstancja Dowgwillo on April 25, 1833 in Bejsagoła Parish. She was also from a noble family. They had the following children:

○ Praxeda Lutkiewicz was baptized July 30, 1833 in Pociūnėliai (Lithuanian), or Pacunele (Polish), Parish. The godparents were Nobles Nikodem Domaszewicz and Tekla, the wife of Noble Feliks Dowgwiłło. She married Józef Dauksza and had at least one child: Józef Dauksza, who was born in 1865.

○ Michalina Franciszka Lutkiewicz was baptized on October 1, 1835 in Pociūnėliai (Lithuanian), or Pacunele (Polish), Parish. Her godparents were Nobles Mateusz Paszkiewicz and Benedykta, the wife of Nikodem Domaszewicz. She died January 27, 1836 at three months old from "weakness".

- o Kazimiera Wiktoryna Lutkiewicz was baptized on March 6, 1837 in Pociūnėliai (Lithuanian), or Pacunele (Polish), Parish. Her godparents were Mateusz Dowgwiłło and Antonina Rymkiewicz (widow). She died April 28, 1838, in the noble settlement of Valmanciai (Lithuanian), or Wołmontowicze (Polish), from measles and is buried in Pociūnėliai (Lithuanian), or Pacunele (Polish), Cemetery.
- o Marianna was baptized on July 11, 1839 in Pociūnėliai (Lithuanian), or Pacunele (Polish), Church. Her godparents were Antoni Dowgwiłło and Angela Rajuncówna (unmarried). Marianna married Jan Dowgiałło and had one child: Julianna, who was born in 1861.

Konstancja (Dowgwiłło) Lutkiewicz died on August 11, 1841 in the village of Szwintupie in childbirth at the age of 30 years old. She left behind two daughters—Prakseda and Marianna. She was buried in the local Pociūnėliai (Lithuanian), or Pacunele (Polish) Cemetery on August 13, 1841.

On January 4, 1864, Felicjan Ludkiewicz died from old age in Wołmontowicze. He never remarried after Konstancja died. He was 73. He left behind daughters Marianna and Prakseda and was a parishioner of Bejsagoła Parish. He was buried on January 7, 1864 in Pociūnėliai (Lithuanian), or Pacunele (Polish) Cemetery.

- Petronela Lutkiewicz was born around 1796. She married Ignacy Lastowski before 1828. They had the following children:
  - o Elżbieta Lastowski was born around 1812 and died on December 9, 1813.
  - o Marianna Magdalene Lastowska was born on November 28, 1814 in Goszczuny Territory and baptized in Pociūnėliai (Lithuanian) or Pacunele (Polish) Parish. Her godparents were Kazimierz Lutkiewicz, Barbara Downorwicz, Deorota Audroska, Marianna Lastowska, and Katarina Lutkiewicz.

- o Petronela Lastowski was born was born on May 15, 1815 in Goszczuny Territory and baptized on April 8, 1821 in Pociūnėliai (Lithuanian), or Pacunele (Polish), Parish. She married Noble Nikodem Borowski on September 28, 1841. Her sister, Wincenta, would marry Nikodem's brother, Józef, in 1848. Petronela and Nikodem had the following children: Wladislaw (1846-?), Ewa (1849-?), Adam (1852-?), and Zofia (1855-?). Nikodem died on March 10, 1886, leaving behind his wife, Petronela and his daughter, Zofia. It's not clear when Petronela died.
- o Konstancia Lastowski was born around 1818. She married Dionizy Gosztowt (1811-1868). Konstancia and Dionizy had the following children:
  - • Hiacenta Gosztowt (1836-1846)
  - • Konstanty Gosztowt (1839-1927) married Emilia Paszkiewicz/ Paškevičiūtė (1846-?), and they had the following children:
    - o Adolf Gosztowt (1865-)
    - o Kswera Gosztowt (1868-)
    - o Teodor Gosztowt (1871-?)
    - o Aleksander Gosztowt (1874-1927) married Maksimilijona (Amelia) Juchniewicz (1878-1936) who had a daughter, Regina Gosztowt, in Tiblisi, Georgia. They immigrated to Kenosha, Wisconsin and had two more children there—Emilia and Alfred.
    - o Zofia Gosztowt (1878-1880)
    - o Michilina Gosztowt (1880-?)
    - o Józef Gosztowt (1884-1885)
    - o Stanisława Gosztowt (1886-?)
  - • Julia Gosztowt (1847-?)
  - • Kazimiera Gosztowt (1848-1898)
  - • Ignacy Gosztowt (1848-1908)
  - • Michal Gosztowt (1850-?)
  - • Paulina Gosztowt (1853-?) married Jan/Jonas Kulikauskas.
  - • Józef Gosztowt (1858-?)

She died on August 13, 1868 in Poniekompie from the common cold at the age of 50. She left behind her husband, Dionizy Gosztowt, four sons—Konstanty, Ignacy, Michał, and Józef—and three daughters—Kazimiera, Julia, and Paulina. She was buried on August 15, 1868 in Pociūnėliai (Lithuanian), or Pacunele (Polish), cemetery.

On September 5, 1868 in village Poniekielpie, Dionizy Gosztowt died from a tumor. He received Holy Sacrament. He left behind four sons—Konstanty, Ignacy, Michał, and Józef—and three daughters—Kazimiera, Julia, and Paulina. His body was buried on September 8 by priest Leon Smilgiewicz in the Pociūnėliai (Lithuanian), or Pacunele (Polish), cemetery.

o   Nikolaj Lastowski was born in Goszczuny Territory in Krekenava (Lithuanian), or Krakinów (Polish), Parish and baptized on April 8, 1821 in Pociūnėliai (Lithuanian), or Pacunele (Polish), Parish. His godparents were Józef Jodkiewicz and [?]osina Gosciewicz. This record was torn, so the second named godparent's name was not clear.

o   Jerzy Wincenty Lastowski was born in Goszczuny Territory in Krekenava (Lithuanian), or Krakinów (Polish), Parish on April 22, 1825. He was baptized in Pociūnėliai (Lithuanian), or Pacunele (Polish) Parish. His godparents were Jacob Januszkiewicz and Gloria Nawlika.

o   Wincenta Agata Lastowki was born in Goszczuny Territory in Krekenava (Lithuanian), or Krakinów (Polish), Parish and baptized on January 21, 1828 in Pociūnėliai (Lithuanian), or Pacunele (Polish), Parish. She married Józef Borowski (1823-1886) on January 27, 1848 in Krekenava (Lithuanian), or Krakinów (Polish) Parish. Her sister, Petronela, married his brother, Nikodem, in 1841. Wincenta and Józef had the following children: Wladslaw (1849-?), Adam (1857-?), Ksaverij (1859-1862), and Ewa (1865-?).

Władysław married Aniela Raiciwicz on February 21, 1878. They had the following children: Waclaw (1880-1961), Bronislaw/Bruno (1882-?), Helena (1886-1947), Mary (1887-1975), Jan/John (1888-1954), Wincenta (1891-bef. 1919),

Agota/Agatha (1893-1988), Teodora (1896-1965), Anna (1897-1951), and Veronica (1897-1984). All of their children, except for Teodora and Wincenta, immigrated to the United States between 1902-1913, first settling in the Philadelphia, Pennsylvania area. Many have descendants alive today.

Józef Borowski died on April 27, 1886 at the age of 60, about one month after the death of his brother, Nikodem. Wincenta died in Pogorduwie at the age of 67 on December 28, 1893 from old age. She left behind two children—Władysław and Ewa Borowski. She was buried in Pacunele (Pociūnėliai) cemetery on December 30, 1893.

- Karolina Lutkiewicz was born June 25, 1798 in Wołmontowicze (Polish), or Valmanciai (Lithuanian), in Basiogala (Lithuanian), or Bejsagoła (Polish), Parish. She married Karol Mieczyński (he was the brother of Barbara who married Karolina's brother, Tomasz) and had the following children:
  - Faustina Mieczyńska was baptized on Febraury 15, 1828 at Pociūnėliai (Lithuanian), or Pacunele (Polish), Parish. Faustina's godparents were Noble Felicjan Lutkiewicz and Tekla Dawnarowicz (unmarried).
  - Zygmunt-Michal Mieczyński was born on the morning of September 27, 1830 in Bejmajnie. He was baptized at Pociūnėliai (Lithuanian), or Pacunele (Polish), Parish. His godparents were Ignacy Lastowski and Marianna, the wife of Stanisław Bojnowski.
  - Ignacy Florian Mieczyński was born on May 4, 1832 in Bejmajnie. He was baptized in (Lithuanian), or Pacunele (Polish), Parish. His godparents were Nobles Jakub Januszkiewicz and Petronela, the wife of Noble Wincenty Lutkiewicz.
  - Stefan Mieczyński was born on February 26, 1834 in Bejmajnie. He was baptized at Pociūnėliai (Lithuanian), or Pacunele (Polish), Church. His godparents were Tomasz Bujnowski and Petronela Lastowska (unmarried).
  - Karolina Mieczyńska was born in Bejmajnie on February 15, 1837. She was baptized at Pociūnėliai (Lithuanian), or

Pacunele (Polish), Parish. Her godparents were Marcin Zaleski and Anna Dowgwiłło (widow).

- ○ Elżbieta Zofia Mieczyńska was baptized on March 25, 1839 at Pociūnėliai (Lithuanian), or Pacunele (Polish), Church. She was born in Wołmontowicze (Polish), or Valmanciai (Lithuanian). Her godparents were Bonifacy Tarczyński and Benedykta, the wife of Nikodem Tomaszewicz.
- ○ Anna Mieczyńska was born in the morning of April 7, 1841 in Wołmontowicze (Polish), or Valmanciai (Lithuanian). She was baptized at Pociūnėliai (Lithuanian), or Pacunele (Polish), Church. Her godparents were Dionizy Lutkiewicz and Marianna Snarska (unmarried).

Karolina Lutkiewicz Mieczyńska died on August 23, 1886 at the age of 86 in the Manor Korejwiszki. She was a widow after her husband, Karol, died in 1866. She left behind her son, Ignacy, and two daughters—Katarzyna and Elżbieta. Karolina was buried on August 25, 1886 in Pociūnėliai (Lithuanian), or Pacunele (Polish), Cemetery.

- • Wiktoria Rajna Lutkiewicz was baptized on September 10, 1805 in Pociūnėliai (Lithuanian), or Pacunele (Polish), Parish. Her godparents were Michał Stasewicz and Wiktoria Jurewicz. The assistants were Mateusz Downarowicz and Petronela Dowgwiłło.

Tomasz Lutkiewicz Baptismal Record in Latin

- • **Tomasz Lutkiewicz** was baptized on August 15, 1801 in Bejsagoła. His godparents were Jospeh Pacewicz from Beinaiciai Manor in Krekenava (Lithuanian), or Krakinów (Polish), and Marianna

Dowgwillo from Wołmontowicze (Polish), or Valmanciai (Lithuanian), Manor. Tomasz Lutkiewicz married Barbara Mieczyńska, who was born November 8, 1801. Her parents were Nobles Antoni and Petronella Dowgwillo Mieczyńska (Petronella will be discussed in the Dowgwillo family tree section). They had the following children:

- o Konstanty-Aleksander Lutkiewicz was baptized on November 24, 1824 in Pociūnėliai (Lithuanian), or Pacunele (Polish), Parish. His godparents were Stanisław Bujnowski and Magdalena Snarski. He married Anna Markiewicz, and they had four daughters—Joanna, Salomea, Stefania, and Zofia (1860-1861). Konstanty died before 1899.

- o Agnieshka Lutkiewicz was born on April 20, 1828 in Wołmontowicze (Polish) or Valmanciai (Lithuanian), and was baptized on April 20, 1828, in Pociūnėliai (Lithuanian), or Pacunele (Polish), Parish. Her godparents were Nobles Joseph Zagollowicz and Petronella, the wife of Noble Ignacy Lastowski. She had three children out of wedlock:

  - Kazimiera Lutkiewicz was born in 1850. She died in Kirkiły from tuberculosis on May 5, 1852 at the age of two and was buried in Pociūnėliai (Lithuanian), or Pacunele (Polish), cemetery.
  - Franciszka Lutkiewicz was born on September 1, 1856 in the village Kuszlejkowicze. She was baptized in Pociūnėliai (Lithuanian), or Pacunele (Polish). Her godparents were Noble Konstanty Mieczyński and Eufrozyna Piatkiewicz, maiden.
  - Adam Lutkiewicz was born in 1861. He died in Wiertimy on September 20, 1861 from tuberculosis at the age of seven weeks and was buried in Pociūnėliai (Lithuanian), or Pacunele (Polish), cemetery.

- o Katarzyna Lutkiewicz was baptized on August 15, 1826 in Pociūnėliai (Lithuanian), or Pacunele (Polish), Parish. Her godparents were Józef Mieczyński and Rosa (Rozalia) Iłgowszczanka.

Adolf Mateusz Lutkiewicz Baptismal Record in Polish

○ **Adolf Mateusz Lutkiewicz** was baptized on September 21, 1830 in Pociūnėliai (Lithuanian), or Pacunele (Polish), Parish. His godparents were Nobles Jan Dowgwillo and Wictoria, a spouse of the Nobleman Józef Mieczyński. He married Barbara Dowgwillo (born on November 29, 1830 in Kaceniskiai Parish) on October 26, 1854 in Krekenava (Lithuanian), or Krakinów (Polish), Parish. She was also from a noble family. They had the following children:

- **Antoni Lutkiewicz** was born on June 25, 1857 in Bobiniškiai Manor and baptized the same day in Krekenava (Lithuanian), or Krakinów (Polish), Church. His godparents were Casimir Carženowicz and Mrs. Eufrozina Mieczyńska. He married twice. He first married 28-year-old **Barbara Stankiewicz** on February 23, 1886 in Krakės (Lithuanian), or Kroki (Polish), Parish. Barbara brought a six-year-old daughter, Teresa, to the marriage.

Antoni and Barbara had the following children:

○ Jan Lutkiewicz was born on June 20, 1887 in Naujas Kaimas. He was baptized by Rev. Kupriewicz in Krakės (Lithuanian), or Kroki (Polish), Parish on June 21, 1887. His godparents were Kalikst Witort and Helena, the spouse of Wincenty Wojshwilo. On January 4, 1889, Jan died in the village of Noworzeczka at the age of two from a whooping cough. He was buried in Pilanskie cemetery.

○ Valeria Lutkiewicz was born on March 2, 1889 and was baptized in Krakės (Lithuanian), or Kroki (Polish), Parish. She died in Canada on November 25, 1985 due to complications of surgery.

Kazmieriz Lutkiewicz Baptism Record in Russian

o **Kazimierz Lutkiewicz/Charles Lucas** was born on March 25, 1891 in Naujoji Veja village and was baptized three days later in Krakės (Lithuanian), or Kroki (Polish), Parish by Rev. Malinowski. His godparents were Rev. Kazimierz Malinowski and Mrs. Christina Gruzewska. He died on October 6, 1967 in Kankakee, Illinois from a massive GI hemorrhage.

o Stanisław Lutkiewicz was born on October 25, 1895 in Nova Recka. He was baptized on October 29, 1895 in Krakės (Lithuanian), or Kroki (Polish), Parish by Rev. Greffel. His godparents were Simon Stankiewicz and Wictoria, a spouse of Tadeusz Czyzewski. He died April 16, 1900 from scarlet fever.

o Michalina Lutkiewicz was born in 1897. Her death record said, "on May 8, 1919 Noblewoman Michalina Lutkiewicz died from ship fever (typhoid)." She was buried in Mantviliskis on May 9. However, she really died of complications after beating by Russians and exposure to cold night air.

o Romuald Lutkiewicz was born on August 1, 1899 in Montvidavas, and he was baptized by Rev. Puidokas in Krakės (Lithuanian), or Kroki (Polish), Parish. His godparents were Michael Wolodko and Barbara, a spouse of Bonawentury

Jagiellowicz. He died November 27, 1899 from atrophy.

Barbara Stankiewicz Lutkiewicz died in 1933 or 1934 from a massive stroke. Antoni married a second time to Viktorija Grigytė and they married on February 12, 1934 in Krakės (Lithuanian), or Kroki (Polish), Parish. They had one child:

○ Marijona Michilina (or Marytė) was born on May 10, 1936 in Mantvisliskis.

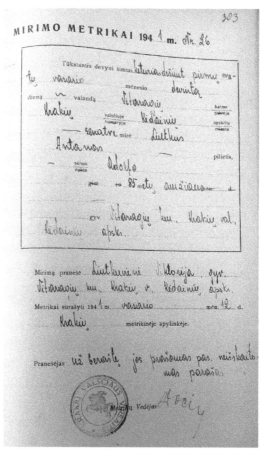

Antoni Lutkiewicz Death Record in Lithuanian

Antoni died on February 9, 1941 in Mantvisliskis, and Viktorija died in 1978. Antoni, Barbara, and Viktorija are buried in a family plot in Mantvisliskis.

- Iewa or Eva (born around 1861) married 31-year-old Mateusz Lutkiewicz (son of Mateusz Lutkiewicz and Franciszka Rymszewicz) on February 12, 1891 at Krakės (Lithuanian), or Kroki (Polish), Parish. It's unclear how they were related. They had two children:
    - Wilhelmina was born on March 2, 1892 in Nowa Wieś but baptized on May 25, 1892 in Krakės (Lithuanian), Kroki (Polish), Parish. Her godparents were her Uncle Antoni Lutkiewicz and Noble Michalina, the wife of Adam Jagiełowicz.
    - Kazimierz was born on July 22, 1894 in Nowa Wieś. His godparents were Bonawentura Jagiełłowicz and Aniela, the wife of Wincenty Wojszwiłło.
- Scholastyka (born around 1855) was 22 when she married a 64-year-old widowed noble from Kaunas named Wincenty Adam Kruszynski on January 24, 1877 in Krekenava (Lithuanian), or Krakinów (Polish), Parish. They had one child less than two months after they married:
    - Leontyna was born on March 15, 1877 in Poskidumie, Lithuania. She was baptized two days later in Krakės (Lithuanian), or Kroki (Polish), Parish. Her godparents were peasants Ignacy Szarow and Barbara, her grandmother. When she was 32 years old, Leontyna married Antoni Orłowski on September 5, 1910 in Szady. Antoni was a 45-year-old bachelor from Biała and the son of Karol Orłowski and Rozalia Juchniewicz. The witnesses were Jerzy Malej and Otto Klin.

Before 1886, Wincenty Adam Kruszynski died and Scholastyka remarried to a noble widower named Józef Wojszwiłło in Krakės (Lithuanian), or Kroki (Polish), Parish on February 23, 1886. He was 67 years old and Scholastyka was 31 years old. They had one child together, seven months later. Józef died on February 7, 1892, six years after his son was born:

- Tomasz Wojszwiłło was born on September 18, 1886 in Nowa Wieś. He was baptized in Pociūnėliai (Lithuanian), or Pacunele (Polish), Parish two days later. His godparents were Noble Kalikst Witort and Emilia Rymkiewicz, maiden.
  - Ona or Anna (1865-1939) married 38-year-old Alfonsas Valiuškevičius on June 16, 1885 in Krekenava (Lithuanian), or Krakinów (Polish), Parish. He was a soldier for Czar Alexander II in the Russo-Turkish War (1877–78). He was still a soldier when he came home for his wedding. Witnesses to their marriage were her brother, Antanas Lutkiewicz, Józef Wojtkiewicz, and Szymon Stankiewicz, the brother of Antanas' wife, Barbara Stankiewicz. They had seven children:
    - Antanas Valiuškevičius born in 1887 and died in 1953.
    - Jan (John) Valiuškevičius (Waleszkiewicz) was born on May 20, 1889 in Dotnuva (Lithuanian), or Datnów (Polish), Lithuania. He came to the United States around 1912 and settled in Grand Rapids, Michigan where he married Anna Budnek on October 19, 1914. John died on January 25, 1980.
    - Anelina Valčkevičiute born in 1892. She married Jeonimas Balandis on February 12, 1924 in Dotnuva Parish. Anelina died on December 10, 1960.
    - Juozpas Valiuškevičius born on March 7, 1894 at Kirkily, a parish of Baisogala, and was baptized in Pociūnėliai (Lithuanian), or Pacunele (Polish), Parish. His godparents were Antanas Dambrauskas and Paulina, the wife of Bogdanas Čeliu. He married Ona Zukauskaite on January 23, 1923. Juozpas died on December 18, 1960 at the Kaunas State Hospital from kidney cancer. He was buried in Gelainiai cemetery, close to his parents. Ona died in 1966 in an automobile accident.
    - Pranciskus Valiuškevičius was born on April 17, 1899 and was baptized in Dotnuva (Lithuanian), or Datnów (Polish), Parish. Although he intended

to join his brother Jan in Michigan, he got on the wrong ship and arrived in Buenos Aires, Argentina on April 8, 1930. He sailed on the Lloyd Sabaudo. He married and had at least one son born before World War II.

- Aleksandra Valčkevičiute was born on June 4, 1902. She married Vladislovas Gorodeckas on September 30, 1930 in Dotnuva (Lithuanian), or Datnów (Polish), Parish.
- Stanislovas Valiuškevičius was born in 1905 and died on July 20, 1974 in Lithuania.

o Józefa was born around 1872. She married 22-year-old Józef Lubin on January 21, 1892 at Krakės (Lithuanian), or Kroki (Polish), Parish. They had nine children:

- Marijona was was born on December 10, 1892 in Huta and was baptized three days later in Krakės (Lithuanian), or Kroki (Polish), Parish. Her godparents were her Uncle Alfonsas Valiuškevičius and her Aunt Eva, the wife of Mateusz Lutkiewicz. Marijona married a peasant from the Kroki district named Władysław Szwiegżda on October 28, 1916. He was a 24-year-old bachelor and the son of Aleksander Szwiegżda and Franciszka, née Kowalewski. The witnesses were Kazimierz Wojnowski and Onufry Jurewicz.
- Antonina was born June 14, 1894 in Huta. Her godparents were Antoni Masilewski and Elżbieta, the wife of Kazimierz Uss.
- Michalina was born September 1, 1896 in Huta. Her godparents were her Uncle Alfonsas Valiuškevičius and Michalina, the wife of Adam Snyszko.
- Stanislaw Lubin was born around 1913. He died at the age of nine from kidney inflammation on February 27 1912.
- Krystyna was born around 1904. She died at the age of two from tuberculosis on February 14, 1906 in the village Milwidy.

- Marcin Lubin was born around 1908. He died at the age of three from tuberculosis on November 7, 1911.
- Kazimierz was born around 1912. He died at the age of one year from "weakness" on January 11, 1913.
- Anna was born around 1915. She died at the age three from "weakness" on September 13, 1918.
- Helena Teresa was born around 1916. She died at the age of two from "weakness" on January 30, 1918.

On December 15, 1898, 69-year-old Noblewoman Barbara Lutkiewicz (Dowgwillo) died in Guta from a tumor. She was a parishioner of Krakės (Lithuanian), or Kroki (Polish), Parish. She left behind her husband, Adolf Lutkiewicz; her son, Antoni; and her daughters, Scholastyka, Ewa, Anna, and Juzefa. She was buried on December 17, 1898 in a local cemetery in Piliuona.

On April 14, 1916 in Montvidavas Village, 96-year-old town-dweller Adolf Lutkiewicz, from Surviliskis, died in Montvidavas Village. He was a widower and parisioner of Krakės (Lithuanian), or Kroki (Polish), church. He was buried on April 18, 1916 in a local cemetery in Montvidavas.

Continuing with the other children of Tomasz Lutkiewicz and Barbara Barbara Mieczyńska:

○ Szymon Lutkiewicz was baptized on October 17, 1832 in Pociūnėliai (Lithuanian), or Pacunele (Polish), Parish. His godparents were Nobles Tadeusz (Tomasz) Paszkiewicz and Karolina Lutkiewiecz, the spouse of Karol Mieczyński. Symon Lutkiewicz married 23-year-old maiden Paulina Mackiewicz (the daughter of Aleksander and Carolina, née Grovska, Mackiewicz) on January 29, 1861 in Krekenava (Lithuanian), or Krakinów (Polish), Church. They were residents of the Bobinski Hamlet. The witnesses were Nobles Kazimierz Solohub, Nicodem Ejdrigiewicz, Joseph Mackiewicz, and Adolf Lutkiewicz.

Symon and Paulina had four children:

○ Ewa Lutkiewicz was born on December 27, 1861 in the noble settlement Babiniszki. She was baptized in Vadaktai on January 1, 1862. Her godparents were Noble Józef Mackiewicz and Antonina Jurewicz, maiden. Ewa had four children out of wedlock, and three immigrated with her to Minnesota around 1914. Their descendants are still living in the United States today.

- Franciszka Lutkiewicz was born in 1884. She died on October 15, 1888 at the age of four from whooping cough in the village Noworeczka.
- Witold Lutkiewicz was born on June 15, 1887 and baptized in Wodokty (Polish) or Vadaktai (Lithuanian) Parish and immigrated to the United States in 1910 where he married Magdalena Zaltowski in Minnesota in 1915. Witold died in 1975 in Duluth, Minnesota, and Magdalena died on March 16, 1965.
- John Lutkiewicz was born on February 16, 1891 in Lithuania, and he died on December 16, 1971 in Virginia, Minnesota.
- Michalina Anna Lutkiewicz was born on July 9, 1894. She married Kazimierz (Charles) Grigal in Lithuania around 1912 and immigrated to Virginia, Minnesota around 1914. They had four children: Stanisława/Stache, Charles, Valentine, and Stanley. Michalina died on February 25, 1969 in Virginia, Minnesota, and Charles died on November 30, 1970.

○ Anna Lutkiewicz was born on January 4, 1864 and baptized the next day in Wodokty (Polish) or Vadaktai (Lithuanian) Parish. Her godparents were nobles Augustyn Żyliński and Aniela, wife of Antoni Bogdanowicz. She probably died as a child.

○ Józef Lutkiewicz was born on August 12, 1868 in village Ciołki in Bejsagoła parish and baptized in Pociūnėliai (Lithuanian), or Pacunele (Polish), Parish. His godparents were: Noble Jerzy Markiewicz and Anna, the wife of Konstanty Lutkiewicz. Józef married Stefania Chodorowicz on February 12, 1890 in Krakės (Lithuanian), or Kroki (Polish), Parish. They had the following children: Scholastyka (1891-1961), Zofia 91895-1985), Jadwiga or Ida (1898-?), Veronica (1902-1982), and Michal (1905). The entire family immigrated to the United States in the early 1900s and settled in Cedarville, Michigan. They have descendants living in the United States today.

o   Wincenta/Vincenta Lutkiewicz was born around September 1876 in Lithuania. She married John Wutkevicz around 1898, and they immigrated to Cedarville, Michigan around 1908 and lived next door to her brother, Józef. Vincenta and John had one child—John Leo Wutkevicz who was born on April 24, 1907. John Wutkevicz Sr. died on November 3, 1945 and Wincenta died in 1960. They are all buried Stephenson Township Cemetery in Menominee County, Michigan.

Paulina died on October 13, 1918 in Wołmontowicz from old age. She was 80 years old and received the Holy Sacrament. She was a widow when she died, and she left behind her son Józef, and her daughters, Wincenta and Ewa.

o   Elżbieta Lutkiewicz was baptized on December 11, 1834 at the Pociūnėliai (Lithuanian), or Pacunele (Polish), Parish. She was born in Wołmontowicze (Polish), or Valmanciai (Lithuanian) Hamlet of Baisogala Parish. Her godparents were Nobles Michal Gosciewicz and Pranciszka, the spouse of Noble Joseph Mieczyński. Elżbieta died on June 4, 1840, from fever at the age of five years old.

o   Anna Lutkiewicz was was born around 1836. She died on September 29, 1845 in Kirkiły from whopping cough at the age of nine years old. She was buried in Pociūnėliai (Lithuanian), or Pacunele (Polish), cemetery.

Barbara Lutkiewicz, née Mieczyńska, died on March 21, 1837 in childbirth. She was 35 years old. She left behind her husband, Noble Tomasz Lutkiewicz, sons—Syzmon, Konstanty, Adolph—and daughters—Agnieszka, Elżbieta, and Anna. On March 23, 1837, she was buried in Pociūnėliai (Lithuanian), or Pacunele (Polish) cemetery.

Tomasz remarried to Pranciszka Piesunko. They had three children:

- o Rozalia Lutkiewicz was born on July 30, 1841 in the Uzpurviai Hamlet of the Basiogala (Lithuanian), or Bejsagoła (Polish), Parish. She was baptized the same day in Pociūnėliai (Lithuanian), or Pacunele (Polish), Parish. Her godparents were Nobles Tadeusz Gosztowt and Marianna, the spouse of Noble Wincenty Rymkiewicz. She married a 25-year-old bachelor of peasant status, Jan Styczkobier, on June 27, 1865 in Krakės (Lithuanian), or Kroki (Polish), Parish. They had at least one child, Antoni Styczkobier, who died on May 23, 1868 from whooping cough at the age of one.

- o Jerzy Lutkiewicz was born on April 10, 1844 in Wołmontowicze. He was baptized in in Pociūnėliai (Lithuanian), or Pacunele (Polish), Parish. His godparents were Nobles Aleksander Pornarowski and Konstancja Piepielówna (unmarried). He died at age two in Kirkily on October 15, 1845 from whooping cough. He was buried two days later in Pociūnėliai (Lithuanian), or Pacunele (Polish), cemetery.

- o Julian Lutkiewicz was born on April 14, 1847 in Kirkiły. He was baptized in Pociūnėliai (Lithuanian), or Pacunele (Polish), Parish. His godparents were Noble Mateusz Dowgwiłło and Scholastyka Pernerewska, a widow. On February 20, 1857, at the age of nine, he died in Kirkiły from diarrhea.

- o Aniela Lutkiewicz was born on August 5, 1850 in Kirkiły. She was baptized in Pociūnėliai (Lithuanian), or Pacunele (Polish), Parish. Her godparents were Nobles Józef Dawksza and Tekla, the wife of Szymon Lawdański.

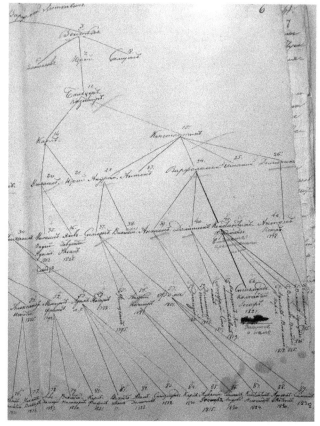

Fragment of Lutkiewicz Family Tree in St. Petersburg File Translated from Russian for Szymon Lutkiewicz's Family Line: Bartłomiej, 3 Wojciech, 7 Jerzy, 11 Balcer-Kazimierz, 15 Konstanty, 22 Andrzej, 37 Szymon, 57 Tomasz, 88 Adolf Mateusz

CHAPTER NINE

Dowgwillo Extended Family Tree

In the Nobility Confirmation documents from the archives in St. Petersburg, there is documentation provided about the Dowgwillo family tree going back to 1639 that refers to many villages that no longer exist. They can be found on maps made prior to World War I that are in Russian or Polish. Most of these extinct villages were near churches that the Dowgwillos were baptized or married in.

The earliest Dowgwillo documented was Józef, the son of Bartlomiej. He had four sons—Jan, Gabriel, Stanisław, and Mikołaj—and two daughters— Konstancia and Anna. Unfortunately, nothing is known about Józef's daughters, so I will break the family tree down in four lines by each son, in four sections.

Most information will be focused on Stanisław's line; this is my direct line in two ways: firstly, Stanisław's fourth great-granddaughter was Barbara Dowgwillo, the mother of Antoni/Antanas Lutkiewicz, my 2nd great grandfather; secondly, Stanisław's second great-granddaughter was Petronela Dowgwillo, the great-grandmother of Antanas Lutkiewicz on his father's, Adolf, side.

Starting with Józef, there was a document gifting property in Towginajcie (Polish, which is how it is written in the document), or Tauginaičiai (Lithuanian), in a subdivision known as Gienie in Veliuona County from Józef to his sons—Jan, Gabriel, Stanisław, and Mikloj— dated May 23,1639. It was recorded in the official Vilnius Town Court

Registry in 1703. This land was originally given to Józef by his wife, Magdalena.

Józef's First Son Jan Family Tree

Jan's first son was Mikołaj Dowgwillo. He was married Anna Towgin, and they had one son:

- Gregory Dowgwillo was born November 21, 1697. He had two sons:
    - Francis Dowgwillo was born April 30, 1727. He had one son:
        - Stanisław Dowgwillo was born August 9, 1754. He married Krystyna Aluszewska.
    - Antoni Dowgwillo was born on May 20, 1831 and died on April 21, 1897. He had two sons:
        - Jan Dowgwillo was born on January 18, 1771 and married Magdalena Szurkówna.
        - Dominik Dowgwillo was born on August 4, 1773. He married Katarzyna Serafinowicz. They had a son, Ferdynand on January 13, 1816.

Ferdynand Dowgwillo married Petronela Michałowska and they had a son, Aleksander. Aleksander Dowgwillo (1844-?) married Pawlina Wojtkiewicz (1854-1923) and they had a son, Józef, born on August 19, 1879. Józef Dowgwillo immigrated to the United States in the early 1900s, became a farmer, and married Barbara Milauskas. They changed their last name to Dougwell and had three children – Marie, Bernice and Frances. Barbara died on December 7, 1948 in Tucson, Arizona. Józef died in San Jose California on August 24, 1966 from cancer.

According to a document presented in Raseiniai (Lithuanian), or Rosienie (Polish), Town Court (Extract #567, page 437) on June 28, 1713, Mikolaj and his wife, Anna Towgin, sold Mikolaj's inheritance from his father, Jan Dowgwillo, to his brother Gabriel Dowgwillo for 6800 grosze (Polish gold coins: 100 grosze = 1 złoty). This included land, house, farming implements, vegetable garden, forests, meadows, and local peasants with their families. The document specifically said that Gabriel's son, Gregory, would have no claim to this property.

Jan's second son was Gabriel Dowgwillo, and he must have died in February 1731 in Lithuania. His will was presented in Raseiniai (Lithuanian), or Rosienie (Polish), Town Court (recorded in court book #264, page 470) on February 8, 1731. According to his will prepared on January 4, 1731, he was suffering a "severe illness" at the time but was of "sound mind and thoughts." He gave his "immortal soul to the Almighty God and his sinful body to the dirt." He requested that his sons—Antoni and Józef—bury him in the local parish cemetery with sacraments.

Gabriel left his land holdings in Gienie and Towginajcie-Poszwentopie (Polish, which is in the document), or Tauginaičiai (Lithuanian), in Veliuona County, and the portion of land that used to belong to his brother, Mikolaj, to his sons—Antoni and Józef. He received the holdings in Veliuona County from his father Jan, the son of Józef Dowgwillo. The land holdings included arable land, farming implements, meadows, forests, brooks, rivers, and peasants with their families.

He left his daughter, Helena, 8000 złoty (Polish coins) which were to be kept by Noble Andrew Budgin. He also requested that his sons should add 400 złoty (Polish coins).

Gabriel's wife must have died before him. Unfortunately, her name has not been found. Gabriel had two sons:

o   Antoni Dowgwillo—his birthdate is unknown. He married Ewa Rajuniec.
o   Józef Dowgwillo was born around 1715 in Lawda. He married Barbara Lutkiewicz (1717- January 14, 1778) on November 11, 1742 in Krekenava (Lithuanian), or Krakinów (Polish), Parish. It's unknown how Barbara is related to our Lutkiewicz branch of the family.

Józef died on May 1, 1785. His wife, Barbara prepared a gifting document on March 12, 1786 that was presented in Raseiniai (Lithuanian), or Rosienie (Polish), Town Court in 1787 giving Józef's property in Towginajcie-Gienie to his son Andrzej, providing that Andrzej pay his brothers—Mateusz and Jan—1000 zlotys (Polish coins) each.

Józef and Barbara had five children:

- Bogumiła Dowgwillo was born on October 23, 1744. She married Bartłomiej (Guszewicz) on October 25, 1767 in Krakinów (Polish) or Krekenava (Lithuanian) Parish.
- Maria Dowgwillo was born on January 5, 1749.
- Mateusz Dowgwillo was born on September 15, 1754.
- Jan Dowgwillo—his birthdate is unknown.
- Andrzej Dowgwillo was born around 1743. He married Antonina Łostowska on February 28, 1791 in Krekenava (Lithuanian), or Krakinów (Polish) Parish. They had the following children:
  ○ Anna Dowgwillo was born September 5, 1795.
  ○ Ignacy Dowgwillo was born November 25, 1798.
  ○ Barnabus Bartłomiej was born August 25, 1801. He appears in 1835 on the list of subscribers in the fourth volume of the *Encyclopedic Lexicon*, with the note that he is the secretary of the heraldry. In the *Address Calendar of the Russian Empire from 1836-1842*, he is listed as an attorney at the Land Court in Wilejce. He performed the same function according to these calendars from the years 1843-1849 in Bobruisk.
  ○ Wincenta Dowgwillo was born around 1806 and married Jan Bogdanowicz (1805?) on February 5, 1839 in Krakinów (Polish) or Krekenava (Lithuanian) Parish. They had three children – Franciszek (1841-?), Barnaba (1850-?), and Fabian (1850-?).
  ○ Wiktoria Dowgwillo was born around 1808 and married Józef Downarowicz (1790-?) on February 5, 1828 in Krakinów (Polish) or Krekenava (Lithuanian) Parish.
  ○ Petronela Dowgwillo was born March 5, 1812.
  ○ Adam Antoni Dowgwillo was born June 17, 1792. He married Kunegunda Stankiewicz, and they had four children. Adam Antoni died at age 57 in Kuszlejsowicze from internal disease on October 6, 1850. He left behind his wife, his son—Cezar (1822-?) and daughters—Józefa, Leona, and Feliksa.

Adam Antoni and Kunegunda had the following children:

- Feliska Dowgwillo—her birthdate is unknown.
- Leona Dowgwillo—her birthdate is unknown.
- Józefa Dowgwillo—her birthdate is unknown.
- Cesar Adolf Paulin Dowgwillo born in 1822. He married Stanislava Nawlicka on August 22, 1848 in Krekenava (Lithuanian), or Krakinów (Polish), Parish. Cesar's property was confiscated twice by resolutions of the Russian Senate in the library of Tsarskoye Selo in 1849 and 1851. Cesar and Stanislava had the following children:
    - Antoni Witold Dowgwillo was born November 19, 1850. He married Anna Szaszewicz (1851-?) on November 22, 1877 in Krekenava (Lithuanian), or Krakinów (Polish) Parish.
    - Jan Dowgwillo was born April 15, 1852. He married Julia Matusewicz on November 23, 1902 in Kurszany. They lived in their own house at Zydkapiu Street in Šiauliai (Lithuanian), or Szawle (Polish). They had no offspring. After her husband's death, Julia lived in Gurogi with her mother until she died in 1937 at the age of 72.
    - Aurelia Marcella was born January 24, 1855.
    - Boleslaw Apolinary Dowgwillo was born July 23, 1849. He attended the Polotsk Miliary Junior High School and the Second Constantine Military College in St. Petersburg, graduating on July 21, 1870 as a second lieutenant. He was appointed as a prosecutor by ordinance of June 7, 1872 and Staff Captain on April 10, 1876. He is mentioned in Russian-Turkish War of 1877-78 memorial books. The Russo-Turkish War of 1877–78 was a conflict fought in the Balkans and Caucasus between the Ottoman Empire and the Eastern Orthodox coalition led by the Russian Empire and composed of Bulgaria, Romania, Serbia, and Montenegro. The Russian-led coalition won the war, pushing

the Turks back all the way to the gates of
Constantinople. As a result, Russia succeeded
in claiming provinces in the Caucasus, and
the principalities of Romania, Serbia, and
Montenegro formally proclaimed independence
from the Ottoman Empire. After almost five
centuries of Ottoman domination (1396–1878),
a Bulgarian state re-emerged.

Boleslaw was in the 63rd Uglicki Infantry
Regiment. He was wounded in the leg on
August 30, 1877 during the Battle of Plewna
(currently in Bulgaria). This was one of the
fiercest battles in the second half of the 19th
century. He is also mentioned as a commander
of the 3rd battalion of this regiment (1887-1889)
in the memorial books of Grodno Province.
He was stationed in Sokółka, which is now in
Belarus. He was decorated with the Order of
Saint Anna 4th class and the Order of Saint
Stanisława, 3rd class in 1877, Saint Anna, 3rd
class in 1880, and Saint Stanisława, 2nd class
in 1888.

In 1896, Boleslaw was awarded the Saint
Włodzimierz in for 25 years of impeccable
service as an officer. Boleslaw was then
transferred to the Caucasus, where in 1891 he
was exchanged as an officer in the 2nd Caucasus
Infantry Reserve Battalion (personnel), and in
the years 1898-1900 he was mentioned in the
officers of the 155 Cuban Infantry Regiment.
Under provisions laid out on June 4, 1901, he
was appointed a colonel and dismissed from
service in this regiment for health reasons,
maintaining his "uniform and salary." He
died at the age of 56 in the province of Orzeł.

Boleslaw married Ludwika Dąbrowska, and they had the following children:

- Ludwika Dowgwillo was born around 1877. Nothing more is known about her.
- Aleksander was born September 16, 1878 and began his military career after a six-class high school education for cadets in Nizhny Novgorod. He was assigned to the 155 Cuban Infantry Regiment (Order of July 31899.) He started his education at the Tiflis [Tbilisi] Infantry School. In 1903, he took officer exams and received the rank of second lieutenant on May 20, 1905. Starting June 19, 1906, he was assigned to the 3rd Battalion Regiment. On July 8, 1907, he was assigned to the 158 Kutajski Infantry Regiment. By February 14, 1908, he was a senior adjutant in the staff of the 40th infantry division, and in the same year, he was stationed in Suwałki for several months. By an order of September 20, 1910, he became a lieutenant, and by an order of October 25, 1914, he was promoted to the staff captain of this unit. Nothing more is known about him after January 1917, when the Menshevicks called for nationwide revolution in Russia which resulted in the Czar being overthrown.
- Helena Dowgwillo was born around 1888. Nothing more is known about her.
- Stanisław Dowgwillo was born in 1886. He graduated from the Cadet School Bachtina in Orle (1905) and the Military College in Kiev. During World War I, he was a lieutenant in the 302 Suraż Infantry Regiment. He was captured by the Germans on August 27, 1914 near the village of Possesern.

Stanisław, a captain at the time, was transferred

to Poland between May 13 and May 20, 1919 by order L992/IV in the ranks of the 11th Polish Rifle Regiment of the Polish Army in France. This regiment was established on April 15, 1919 and was part of the 6th Polish Rifle Division of General Champeaux. This regiment was renamed the 53rd Infantry Regiment of Borderland Infantry in September of 1919. According to the Polish Officer's Yearbook of 1923 and 1924, he was a reserve officer of the 44th Infantry Regiment of the Borderlands. In the Personnel Journel (R.13, No.4 February 22, 1932), it states that Reserve Captain Stanisław Dowgwillo died in Lutsk on February 22, 1931.

Józef's Second Son Gabriel and His Family Tree

Gabriel Dowgwillo married a woman named Dorota, and they had two children:

- Jerzy was born on April 7, 1686 in Towginajcie (Polish) or Tauginaičiai (Lithuanian). He was baptized in Krekenava (Lithuanian), or Krakinów (Polish), Parish. No further information is known about him.
- Jan was born on September 2, 1691 in Towginajcie (Polish) or Tauginaičiai (Lithuanian). He was baptized in Krekenava (Lithuanian), or Krakinów (Polish), Parish. His godparents were Jan Towgin and Eva Rymkiewicz. No further information is known about him.

Józef's Third Son Stanisław and His Family Tree

Stanisław Dowgwillo had two sons—Lukasz and Michal Dowgwillo. Lukasz was my eighth great grandfather.

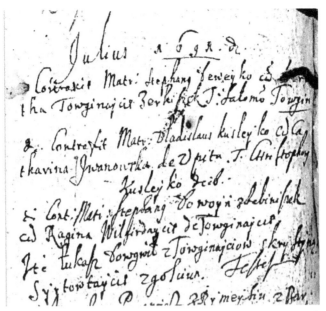

Marriage Record of Łukasz Dowgwillo and Krystyna Syrtowt in Latin

○ **Łukasz Dowgwillo** married **Krystyna Syrtowt** on July 8, 1691 in Krekenava (Lithuanian), or Krakinów (Polish), Parish. They had one son:

   • **Józef Dowgwillo** died around 1723. This is an approximate date deduced by a will he prepared on November 6, 1723, which was presented in Raseiniai (Lithuanian), or Rosienie (Polish), Town Court in 1724. **Józef** left his property in Towginajcie (or Uszpurwie) to his sons **Marcin** and Jan.

      ○ **Marcin Dowgwillo** married **Marija Žongolowicz** (1706-1786). **Marcin** probably died around 1785, and Marija died at the age of 80 on March 2, 1786 in Towginajcie.

      On December 21, 1785, **Marcin** and his brother, Jan Dowgwillo, prepared a gifting document that was presented in 1787 in Raseiniai (Lithuanian), or Rosienie (Polish), Town Court. Marcin and Jan gave their property in Towginajcie (or Uszpurwie) that they inherited from their father, Józef, to their sons—Andrezj and Laurenty (sons of Marcin) and Jan (son of Jan).

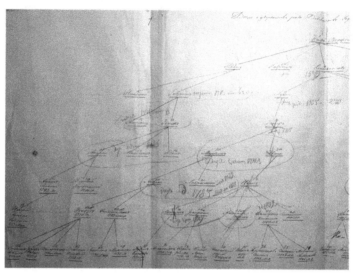

Fragment of Dowgwillo Family Tree in St. Petersburg File Translated from Russian for Stanisław Dowgwillo's Family Line: 1 Józef, 4 Stanisław, 8 Łukasz, 14 Józef, 20 Marcin, 30 Andrzej, 43 Izydor, 44 Ezachiel Leon, 64 Stefan Albin, 65 Józef Paweł, 66 Benedykt, 67 Dionizy Ignacy, 68 Antoni, 69 Michał

Marcin and Marija had the following children:

- Laurenty Dowgwillo was born in August of 1741. He died on January 9, 1807 in Towginajcie.

  Laurenty and his brother **Andrzej** filed a document that was prepared on January 27, 1788 and presented in Raseinai Town Court on February 3, 1788 to establish they were the owners of Towginajcie (or Uszpurwie), along with the peasants on the land.

  Then on June 14, 1789, they prepared a document that was presented in Szawle (Polish), or Šiauliai (Lithuanian), Land Court on June 20, 1789. **Andrzej** gave his part of Towginajcie (or Uszpurwie) to his brother Laurenty and renounced all claims to the property.

- Jan Dowgwillo was born May 31, 1744.
- Marianna Dowgwillo was born December 4, 1746.
- Helena Dowgwillo was born October 13, 1749.
- Anna Dowgwillo was born July 1, 1753.
- **Andrzej Dowgwillo** was November 18, 1756. He married **Katarzyna Rojcewicz** on January 3, 1789 in Krekenava (Lithuanian), or Krakinów (Polish), Parish. They had the following children:
  - Izydor Dowgwillo was born May 12, 1790. He was baptized by Priest Thad Merchilewicz. Witnesses were Nobles Laurenty Dowgwillo and Sophia Roykiewicz. He married Zofia Brygida Buharewicz, and they had the following children:
    - Stefan Albin Dowgwillo was baptized on April 7, 1814 at Krekenava (Lithuanian), or Krakinów (Polish), Parish. His godparents were Nobles Józef Downawicz and Viktoria Downawicz from Glitany. He married Francizka Bortkiewicz and died March 7, 1870.
    - Aniela Dowgwillo was born around 1816. She married Jan Babinski on June 2, 1836 in Krakės (Lithuanian), or Kroki (Polish), Parish. They had two children—Ludwika (1836-1836) and Aleksander (1840-1840) before Aniela died of tuberculosis on June 14, 1840 at the age of 21.
    - Agnes Dowgwillo was born January 25, 1818 and was baptized in Krekenava (Lithuanian), or Krakinów (Polish), Parish. Her godparents were Ignacy Olinski and Rozalia Paskiewicz from Glitany, Krekenava (Lithuanian), or Krakinów (Polish), Parish.
    - Karolina Anna Dowgwillo was baptized on January 19, 1819 by Priest Nicholas Dramontt. Her godparents were Antoni Prosewicz and Catherine Jamontowna from Glitany, Krakės (Lithuanian), or Kroki

(Polish), Parish. She died on January 31, 1819.

- Józef Paweł Dowgwillo was born March 21, 1820. He was baptized in Krekenava (Lithuanian), or Krakinów (Polish), Parish. His godparents were Józef Giedroyi and Roza Gosztowttoswa. Witnesses to the marriage were Tomasz and Karolina Dowgwillo from Glitany.

- Anna Kunegunda Dowgwillo was born on July 30, 1822 and was baptized in Krekenava (Lithuanian), or Krakinów (Polish), Parish. Her godparents were Andrezj Gudnin and Anna Mutusewicz from Glitany, Krekenava (Lithuanian), or Krakinów (Polish), Parish.

- Benedykt Dowgwillo was baptized by priest Thad Merchilewicz of Senkany Parish, on March 17, 1824. His godparents were Nobles Marcil Gurnicki and Elżbieta Kupuprinska. He married Teofila Syryjatowicz (born around 1830) on November 16, 1849 in Krakės (Lithuanian), or Kroki (Polish), Parish. They had the following children:
  ○ Jan Dowgwillo was born on December 29, 1850. He married Stanisława Romaszkiewicz (1870-1938) on January 17, 1895 in Krakės (Lithuanian), or Kroki (Polish), Parish. They came to Cedar River, Michigan had the following children:
    ○ Kazimierz Dougovito (1895-1966)
    ○ Katarzyna Dougovito (1896-1916)
    ○ Anna Dougovito (1902-1939) married Anton Atkocunis (1891-1963).
    ○ Carl Dougovito (1904-1973) married Mary Scaritski (1914-2007).

- ○ Walter Dougovito (1908-1969) married Monica Payant (1914-2001).
- ○ Bronis Dougovito (1910-1910)
- ○ Joseph Dougovito (1912-1975) married Olga Jaunsen (1909-1996).
- ○ Kazimierz Dowgwillo born in 1853 in Nawryczki Village. Kazimierz participated in the 1863 Uprising against Russia. He married Kazimiera Dolongowska on February 27, 1878 in Krakės (Lithuanian), or Kroki (Polish), Parish. They had one son:
  - • Józef Dowgwillo was born in Pilnów on November 17, 1892. He became a priest. He died on September 8, 1964 in Suraż and is buried at the Suras Parish cemetery.
- ○ Katarzyna Dowgwillo was born in Puljany, Lithuania and was baptized on March 13, 1855. She married Kalikst Witort (1850-1925) on February 22, 1881 in Krakės (Lithuanian), or Kroki (Polish), Parish. They had eight children—Zofia, John, Edward, Władysław/Walter, Stefania/Stella, Anna, and Władysława/Charlotte. They came through Canada in 1907 on their way to Illinois. Katarzyna died on November 22, 1925 in Melrose Park, Illinois.
- ○ Wiktoria Dowgwillo was born on December 8, 1857. She married twice: the first marriage was to Julian Lipniewicz (1862-1891), and they were married on May 28, 1891 in Krakės (Lithuanian), or Kroki (Polish), Parish.

Unfortunately, Julian died about seven months later. Wiktoria married for a second time to Michal Tarasewicz on February 7, 1893 in Krakės (Lithuanian), or Kroki (Polish), Parish.

- ○ Maria Dowgwillo was born around 1860. Unfortunately, she died on March 14, 1862 under the age of two at Nowarzeczka.

- ○ Wincenta Dowgwillo was born on October 7, 1862 in Nowa Wies. She married Franciszek Piotrowicz on January 19, 1886 in Montwidow, Lithuania.

- ○ Bronislaw Dowgwillo was baptized on January 27, 1865 in Noworeczki.

- ○ Teofil Dowgwillo was baptized on April 27, 1867 in Nowa Wies. He married Jadwiga Pawlik on July 10,1901 in Lipawa, Latvia. He died on November 20, 1923 in Lipawa, Latvia.

- ○ Anna Dowgwillo was born around 1870. She died on January 24, 1939 in Lublin, Poland. Anna married Józef Dubiński on May 6, 1892 in Krakės (Lithuanian), or Kroki (Polish), Church, and they had two children:
  - ○ Jan Dubiński was born around 1901 in Lublin, Poland. He married Halina Agata Pliszczyńska on April 2, 1929 in Lublin, Poland. They had one child, Jan Dublinski, who died as an infant on April 26, 1930 in Lublin.
  - ○ Boleslaw Dubiński was born around 1909 in Lublin, and he died on December 20, 1945, also in Lublin.

- Dionizy Ignacy Dowgwillo was born July 26, 1826. He married Irena Iwaszkiewicz zd. Łukowicz on June 28, 1877. He later married Irena Michałowska, and they had one son:
  - Bronisław Dowgwillo was born January 25, 1883 in Rymkiszki.
- Józef Dowgwillo was born around 1830. He married twice, first to Teofila Chodorowicz (1837-1873) around 1855. They had the following children:
  - Anna Dowgwillo (1855-?)
  - Aleksander Dowgwillo (1861-1878)
  - Zygmunt Dowgwillo (1868-1868)
  - Stefan Dowgwillo (1870-1919)
  - Elwira Dowgwillo (?-?)
  - Felicjanna Dowgwillo (?-?)
  - Benedykt Dowgwillo (?-?)
  - Józef Dowgwillo (?-?)

  After Teofila's death on April 18, 1873 from "weakness," Józef married Ewa Gosztowt on May 5, 1873. They had the following children:

  - Feliks Dowgwillo (1874-?)
  - Hipolit Dowgwillo (1877-1959) immigrated to Philadelphia, Pennsylvania where he married Marjonna Zaworska (1892-1953).
  - Katarzyna Dowgwillo (1880-1917) immigrated to Philadelphia and married Władysław/Walter Staniewicz (1877-1915).
  - Teresa Dowgwillo (1883-1884)
  - Teresa Katherine Dowgwillo (1890-1961) immigrated to Philadelphia and married Michael Szwagżdis (1883-1947).
  - Ezachiel Leon Dowgwillo was born April 10, 1792 in Pacuny. He married Anna Malkiewicz on January 28, 1819 in Krekenava (Lithuanian), or Krakinów (Polish), Parish.

However, on his marriage record, he used the name Józef Ezachiel Dowgwillo. Witnesses to this marriage were Antoni Prosciewicz, Jan Zongullowicz, Piotr Malkiewicz, and Jan Malkiewicz. Ezachiel and Anna had the following children:

- Antoni Dowgwillo was baptized on May 11, 1820 by Priest Nicholas Dramontt in Krekenava (Lithuanian), or Krakinów (Polish), Parish. His godparents were Jacob Szysnkowicz and Catherine Grygayiowa, and the witnesses were Izydor Dowgwillo and Petronella Malkiewicz from Winele, Krekenava (Lithuanian), or Krakinów (Polish), Parish. He married Konstancja Łopatto on January 21, 1862 in Krekenava (Lithuanian), or Krakinów (Polish), Parish.

- Michal Dowgwillo was baptized on September 28, 1825 by Priest Nicholas Dramontt, the vicar of Krekenava (Lithuanian), or Krakinów (Polish), Parish. His godparents were Antoni Domaszewicz and Angela Gralewska from Posadele.

- Stefania Dowgwillo was baptized on May 23, 1826 in Krekenava (Lithuanian), or Krakinów (Polish), Parish. Her godparents were Michal Wutkiewicz and Apolonia, the wife of Jakub Dowgwillo.

- Roza Dowgwillo was baptized on July 21, 1832 in Krekenava (Lithuanian), or Krakinów (Polish), Parish. Her godparents were Karol Guinbrewicz and Brygyta, the wife of Michal Lipskiego.

o Bonacela Dowgwillo was born in Glitany and was baptized by Priest Jan Maszkiewicz on August 21, 1794 in Krekenava (Lithuanian), or Krakinów (Polish), Parish. Her godparents were Michal Budrewicz and Rosalia (last was name illegible).

o Jakub Sebastian was born in Glitany and was baptized by Priest Thad Merchilewicz in Krekenava (Lithuanian), or Krakinów (Polish), Parish on July 11, 1797. His godparents were MD Nobles Jakob Tomakewicz and Joanna Royieszricz.

o **Antoni Dowgwillo** was born in Glitany and was baptized by Priest Adam Umiaz in Krekenava (Lithuanian), or Krakinów (Polish), Parish on June 6, 1800. His godparents were Antoni Josztowott and Sophia Reydwicz. Priest Nicholas Dramontt of Krakinow Parish married Antoni Dowgwillo, a bachelor from Goszcsuny, to **Ewa Rukuizaite**, a maiden from Posadele Village, on September 21, 1820 in Krekenava (Lithuanian), or Krakinów (Polish), Parish. The record indicated that after three banns were announced in Krakinow Parish, no obstacles were detected. Their record stated, "We the undersigned declare by God's calling and mutual attraction, not coerced by anyone, but of our own free will we took this sacrament and swore to each other mutual matrimonial commitment which is confirmed by our signatures." The witnesses were Izydor Dowgwillo, Ezekiel Dowgwillo, Jan Zagulowicz, and Kaietan Wienzychowski. All signatures were xxx, indicating they were illiterate. **Antoni's** property was confiscated in 1830 by Senate Decree #14000 for taking part in the 1830 Uprisings against Russian occupation in Lithuania. **Antoni** was not included on any nobility confirmation documents as a result. **Antoni** and **Ewa** had the following children:

- **Barbara Dowgwillo** was born on November 29, 1820 in Kacenisikiai Manor and was baptized a day later by Priest Mykolos Budziz in Šėta Parish. Her godparents were Jakub Dowgwillo and Tekla, the spouse of Kazimierz Petravicius. She married Adolf Lutkiewicz on October 26, 1854 in Krekenava (Lithuanian), or Krakinów (Polish), Parish. The witnesses to their marriage were Heronim Markiewicz, Jan Wonsowicz, Antoni Dowgwillo— her father—and Kaeten Wolski. Barbara and Adolf went on to have **Antoni**, Ewa, Scholastyka, Anna, and Józefa Lutkiewicz. **Barbara** died of a tumor in Guta on December 15, 1898, and she was buried in Piliuona Cemetery.

- Ignancy Lukasz Dowgwillo was born on October 20, 1822 in Girelė. His godparents were Ignacy Mieczyński and Józefa Jurewicz. He married 25-year-old maiden Juzefa Nowicka on July 27, 1858 in Pagiriai Parish. She was the daughter of Kazimierz and Ursula Wolowicz Nowicki. Witnesses to the wedding were Michal Klimkiewicz, Tomasz Dowgwillo, and Michal Nowicki.

  ○ Anna Dowgwillo born July 17, 1804.
  ○ Karolina Dowgwillo was born on January 16, 1806. She married Antoni Stankiewicz (b. 1792) on May 9, 1835. They were both from Montwidowo village and had two children—Józef (1839-1841) died as a toddler from diarrhea and Hipolit (1842-1845) died at the age of three from an unknown disease. Karolina died on January 26, 1845 from tuberculosis.
  ○ Józef Dowgwillo's second son, Jan Dowgwillo, was born on May 21, 1718 in Goszczuny. He married Eufrozyna Żongołowicz (1724-1789). They had the following children:
    - Jan Dowgwillo was born in 1754 in Tauginaičių.

      On January 17, 1829 Jan prepared and presented a Gifting Document to the Szawle (Polish), or Šiauliai (Lithuanian), Land Court that gave his property in Towginajcie to Felicjan Dowgwillo, his youngest son from his second wife. He included a provision that Felicjan provide compensation to his brothers— Wincenty, Mateusz, Józefat, and Antoni.

      On June 24, 1784, Vicar Antoni Dowgwillo from Kirkiły Parish married Jan Dowgwillo, a bachelor from Towginajcie, to Clara Downorwicz (1763-1798), maiden, from Goszczuny. There were no impediments to this marriage in Krekenava (Lithuanian), or Krakinów (Polish), Parish. They had the following children:

- ○ Mateusz Dowgwillo was born on September 17, 1784 in Pociuneliai. On October 26, 1820, Vicar Nicolas Drammont of Krakės (Lithuanian), or Kroki (Polish), Parish married Nobles Mateusz Dowgwillo and Elżbieta Satkowska of Towginajcie territory in Krekenava (Lithuanian), or Krakinów (Polish), Parish. There were no impediments to this marriage, and the three banns were read in the church. The document was signed with an "x" for Mateusz Dowgwillo and Elżbieta Satkowska. Witnesses were Felix Juchniewicz, Felicjan Dowgwillo, Benedyct Domaprewicz, and Jerzy Satkowski. They had two sons:
  - Paweł Bernard Dowgwillo was born in 1821.
  - Tomasz Dowgwillo was born on December 13, 1824 and died six days later on December 19, 1824.
- ○ Ferdynand Dowgwillo was born May 15, 1788. He died on October 16, 1804.
- ○ Antoni Dowgwillo was born June 14, 1796. He married Anna Bujnowski (1795-1855), and they had the following children:
  - Wincenty Jerzy Dowgwillo was baptized on January 10, 1819 by Priest Stanisław Perkowski from (Lithuanian), or Pacunele (Polish), Parish. His parents were Antoni Dowgwillo and Anna Bujnowski, and his godparents were Łopata Syzling and Tekla Jukniewicz from Towginajcie. It's important to note that the Nobility Confirmation documents in St. Petersburg claim he was born on April 22, 1819.
  - Jan Dowgwillo was born on 1822.

- ○ Józefat Dowgwillo married Cecylia Bujnowski (1788-1858), and they had the following children:
  - Aleksander Dowgwillo was born April 21, 1815. He married Petronella Pernerowski, and they had four children:
    - ○ Anna Dowgwillo (1854-1855)
    - ○ Anna (1857-?) married Mikolaj Babiański (1849-?)
    - ○ Józef Dowgwillo (1863-?) married Antonina Urniaz and had four children: Feliks (1890-1956), Michal (1892-1930), Adolf (1895-1987), and Stefania (1899-?). Feliks, Michal, and Adolf immigrated to the United States.
    - ○ Aleksandra Dowgwillo was born on January 18, 1871 and baptized on January 27 in Krakės (Lithuanian), or Kroki (Polish), Parish. Her godparents were Landlord Benedykt Dowgwillo and Valeria Petrauskaitė.
  - Karol Józef Dowgwillo was born March 8, 1820.
  - Tomasz Łukasz Dowgwillo was baptized on October 8, 1826 at Pociūnėliai (Lithuanian), or Pacunele (Polish), Parish. His parents were Nobles Józefat Dowgwillo and Cecilia Bujnowska from Towginajcie. His godparents were Nobles Wincenty Downarwicz and Kataryna Bujnowska. He married Milewska Grażyna and they had four children:
    - ○ Jan Dowgwillo born June 18, 1860. He married Petronela Łukjańska. They had eight children: Józef (1887-?), Jerzy/George (1890-?), Marianna (1891-?), Stanislaw/Stanley (1894-1958), Zofia/Sophia (1896-1976),

Aleksansdra (1898-?), Władysław (1903-1908), and Wacław (1908-?).

Jerzy/George, Stanislaw/Stanley, and Zofia/Sophia immigrated to the United States in the early 1900s. George married Cecilia Akstin (1894-1928) in Massachusetts and had three children- George, John and Annie. Sophia married Antoni Beresniewicz (1888-1944) in Šėta Parish on September 23, 1923. Antoni traveled from Oyster Bay New York to Lithuania to marry Sopia. They settled in Oyster Bay, New York and had four children-Helen, Evelyn, Alice and Elizabeth. Stanley never married but lived in Massachusetts. George and Sophia have descendants living in the United States today.

- o Anna Dowgwillo was born around 1862.
- o Antonina Dowgwillo was born around 1870.
- o Wiktoria Dowgwillo was born around 1872.
- Anna Dowgwillo was born on November 9, 1830 in Towginajcie. She married Jan Lopata.

Jan Dowgwillo remarried to Barbara Kontowt (1768-1834) after Clara died in 1798. They had the following children:

- o Wincenty Dowgwillo was born in 1805.
- o Felicjan Stefan Dowgwillo was born December 18, 1799. He first married Elżbieta Owsianow (?-1848) on February 15, 1827 in Krekenava (Lithuanian), or Krakinów (Polish), Parish.

- Bronislaw Higinus Dowgwillo was born January 19, 1832 in Towginajcie (Polish) or Tauginaičiai (Lithuanian). He worked as a dentist before dying in Warsaw, Poland on March 24, 1897.
- Wanda Dowgwillo was born in 1832. She died on November 22, 1837.
- Zacharjasz Dowgwillo was born on February 25, 1833.
- Mawrycy Władysław Dowgwillo was born on September 13, 1838 in Towginajcie (Polish) or Tauginaičiai (Lithuanian). He died on May 22, 1840 in Towginajcie (Polish) or Tauginaičiai (Lithuanian).
- Mawrycy Dowgwillo was born on September 9, 1840 in Towginajcie (Polish) or Tauginaičiai (Lithuanian). He married Olga Dementowicz on February 3, 1881 in Janiszki.
- Wanda Felicjan Dowgwillo was born on June 10, 1842.

Felicjan Stefan remarried to Paulina Gasztowt (1812-1857), and they had two children:

- Ryszard Dowgwillo was born in 1851. He died at age four in Towginajcie (Polish) or Tauginaičiai (Lithuanian) from internal disease on June 13, 1855.
- Elwira Dowgwillo was born January 30, 1854 in Towginajcie (Polish) or Tauginaičiai (Lithuanian).

On January 20, 1854, Felicjan Stefan died at age 55 in Towginajcie (Polish) or Tauginaičiai (Lithuanian) from meningitis or brain inflammation. He left behind his wife, Paulina, his sons—Bronislaw,

Zachariasz, Maurycy and Ryszard—and a daughter—Wanda.

Coming back to the other son of **Stanisław, Michal Dowgwillo** had one son:

- **Stanisław Dowgwillo** was born January 2, 1715. According to a sales document that was prepared on May 14, 1724 and presented in Raseiniai (Lithuanian), or Rosienie (Polish), Town Court, Stanisław sold the peasants and property in Towninajcie (or Uszpurwie) he received from his father, Michal, to Gabriel (Unfortunately, the last name of Gabriel is not provided by the document). As part of the sale, his sons Jakub and Kazimierz had no rights to it.

  Stanisław married **Anna Łostowska,** and they had two children:

  - Kazimierz Dowgwillo-no further information is known.
  - **Jakub Dowgwillo's** birthdate is unknown. **Jakub's** clear documentation began when he married **Franciszka Iłgowska** on June 24, 1770. His farm was located in Wołmontowicze in Bejsagoła Parish. His father, Stanisław, bought it in 1741 from Antoni Borkowski. I have been unable to find a baptism or death record for Jakub but was able to find out, based upon an extract of his will that was prepared on June 4, 1788 and presented in Raseiniai (Lithuanian), or Rosienie (Polish), Town Court on June 13, 1788, that he left his property Wołmontowicze-Marwojszyszki to his sons, Filip, Jan, Piotr, and Jerzy. I assume, based on the will, that he died in approximately 1788.

The last piece of documentation, a sales document, mentioning Jakub was from June 2, 1795. It was presented in 1796 in Telšiai Land Court. Filip, Jan, Piotr, and Jerzy (sons of Jakub who will be listed after this section) sold their part of their property in Wołmontowicze-Marwojszyszki to Jan Momtwillo.

Jakub and Franciszka had at least seven children:

- Filip Dowgwillo was born on April 27, 1768 in Wołmontowicze (Polish), or Valmanciai (Lithuanian). Filip was born before his parents were married. There is a note on his baptism record that he was born as an illegitimate child of a couple of nobles, which would have made ineligible for claiming nobility status. There is a note on the margin that states that his birth was "legitimized" by the subsequent marriage of his parents on June 24, 1770, per page 44 of the *Krakinów/Krekenava Marriages Book 1730-1812*. It is difficult to know if the Russian authorities realized this when reviewing his nobility status. Typically, this would have made Filip and his children not eligible for nobility status.

Filip married Petronela Downarowicz, and they had the following children:

- ° Feliks Dowgwillo was born in 1795. He married Tekla Jankiewicz, and they had the following children:
    - Szymon Dowgwillo was baptized on October 21, 1826 at Pociūnėliai (Lithuanian), or Pacunele (Polish), Parish. His godparents were Martin Turezynski and Tekla Downorwicz from Wołmontowicze in Bejsagoła Parish.
    - Kazimiera Dowgwillo was born in 1828. She died on November 6, 1830.
    - Kazimierz Dowgwillo was born on March 4, 1829 in Wołmontowicze.
    - Eufemia Eufrazyna was born on September 13, 1831 in Wołmontowicze. She died on February 16, 1832.
    - Roza Dowgwillo was born on April 5, 1833 in Wołmontowicze.
    - Ludwik Dowgwillo was born on September 1, 1835 in Wołmontowicze. He married Roza Domaszewicz on February 12, 1856 in Krekenava (Lithuanian), or Krakinów (Polish), Parish, and they had the following children:
        - ° Aniela Dowgwillo (1857-1859)

- o Tekla Dowgwillo (1858-1922) married Albin Rymkiewicz. (1834-1909), and they had one son, Antoni Rymkiewicz (1888-1951).
- o Józefa Dowgwillo (1860-?) married Adolf Rozewicz.
- o Feliks Dowgwillo (1863-?)
- o Kazimierz Dowgwillo (1865-1866)
- Aniela Dowgwillo was born August 5, 1837. She died on May 21, 1838.
- Nikodem Dowgwillo was born on September 16, 1839 in Wołmontowicze. He married Petronella Proscewicz on February 9, 1860 in Bejsagoła Parish.
- Anna Dowgwillo was born on July 18, 1842 in Wołmontowicze. She married Justyn Paszkiewicz on November 11, 1861 in Szczodrobów.

Feliks died in 1853 at age 58 in Noworeczki from tuberculosis. He left behind his wife, Tekla, sons— Szymon, Ludwik, and Mikołaj—and daughters —Róża and Anna.

- o Barbara Dowgwillo was born on December 12, 1787 to Filip Dowgwillo and Petronela Downarowicz.
- o Mateusz Dowgwillo was born on September 22 1799. He married Petronella Wojtkiewicz (1805-1855), and they had the following children:
  - Ewa Dowgwillo was born on December 24, 1832 in Pociūnėliai (Lithuanian), or Pacunele (Polish).
  - Józef Benedykt Dowgwillo was born on May 25, 1835. He married Aleksandra Kazimiera Jurewicz on November 7, 1861 in Sękany, and they had the following children:
    - o Ignacy Kleofas (Klemens) Dowgwillo was born on September 9, 1862 in Sękany. He married Apolonia Konopińska on November 5, 1891 in Surwiliszki (Polish) or Surviliškis (Lithuanian).
    - o Olimpia Dowgwillo was born on December 17, 1864 and died on April 29, 1878.
    - o Jarosław Dowgwillo was born around 1866. He married Anna Downarowicz (1878-1941) on

    January 21, 1897 in Smigle, Lithuania. He died
    on November 12, 1948.

- Anna Dowgwillo was born on August 1, 1837 in Pociūnėliai (Lithuanian), or Pacunele (Polish). She married Felicjan Bankowski on February 3, 1858.
- Longin Mateusz Dowgwillo was born on September 9, 1840 and died on October 7, 1840 in Pociūnėliai (Lithuanian), or Pacunele (Polish).
- Leonard Dowgwillo was born on November 6, 1841 in Pociūnėliai (Lithuanian), or Pacunele (Polish). He married Aleksandra Szwenkiewicz on February 5, 1863 in Surwiliszki (Polish) or Surviliškis (Lithuanian).
- Anton Longin Dowgwillo was born in 1842. He married twice. His first wife was Aleksandra Szykszniewicz. They married on February 5, 1863 in Surwiliszki (Polish) or Surviliškis (Lithuanian) and had one child, Anna (1863-?). Aleksandra died before 1874.

Anton's second wife was Eleanora Rajuniec. They married on October 27, 1874 in Krekenava (Lithuanian), or Krakinów (Polish), Parish. They had ten children: Ksawery (1875-1877), Bronislawa (1878-?), Edward (1880-1881), Michael (1882-1923), Franciszek (1884-1884), Antonina (1886-1937), Wincenty (1888-?), Anna (1890-?), Aleksandra (1891-1934), Olga (?-?) and Ludwik (1894-1962).

Anton and Elenora's sons, Wincenty and Michael immigrated to the United States in 1907 and settled in Kenosha Wisconsin. Their daughters, Antonina and Aleksandra, joined their brothers in 1909. Eleanora immigrated to Kenosha Wisconsin with Ludwik in 1912, as a widow. It's unknown when or where Anton died. Olga joined her mother and sisters before 1926. Eleanora died on February 25, 1926 in Kenosha Wisconsin.

- Julia Dowgwillo was born on February 29, 1844 in Pociūnėliai (Lithuanian), or Pacunele (Polish). She married Wincenty Skinder on January 31, 1861. They had eight children: Ewa Gartruda (1861-?), Wincenta (1864-?), Anna (1868-?), Bolesław (1869-1924), Juliusz (1873-1957), Jadwiga (1875-?), Wiktoria (1880-?), Jan (1883-1969).

  Julia and Wincenty's sons, Juliusz and Jan, immigrated to Chicago Illinois in the late 1890s. Juliusz married Elżbieta Mosiej in 1903 and had three children: Cezary (1903-1919), Harriet (1905-1988) and Edward (1906-?). Jan married Władysława (Lottie) Bielska in 1912 and had three children: William (1913-1971), Leonard (1916-1964) and Vladislava (1919-1919). Both Juliusz and Jan were buried in St. Casimir's Cemetery in Chicago.

- Jan Dowgwillo was born on June 19, 1847 in Pociūnėliai (Lithuanian), or Pacunele (Polish).

  Mateusz Dowgwiłło, age 60, died in Kuszlejkowicz from fever on December 6, 1857. He was a widower but left behind sons—Longin, Jan, and Józef—and daughters— Ewa, Anna, and Julia.

  o Józefata Dowgwillo was born on March 13, 1802 to Filip Dowgwillo and Petronela Downarowicz. She married Ignacy Rymkiewicz on January 28, 1830 in Bejsagoła Parish.
  o Jan Alozy Dowgwillo was born on June 24, 1804. He married Bogumiła Borodzka, and they had the following children:
    - Marcella Dowgwillo was born November 11, 1840.
    - Michal Dowgwillo was born on August 16, 1842. He married Stefania Jagmin on

August 14, 1886 in Krekenava Parish. They had one child, Antoni Dowgwillo, in 1890.

- Kazimierz Dowgwillo was born on August 14, 1844 and died on April 17, 1912.
- Józef Dowgwillo was born on September 29, 1846.
- Konstanty Dowgwillo was born on February 18, 1849. He married Roza Paskiewicz and they had five children:
  - Aniela Dowgwillo was born in 1887. She was thirteen years old when she died on October 31,1900.
  - Jan Dowgwillo was born on May 20, 1892 in Glitany and was baptized in Krakės (Lithuanian), or Kroki (Polish), Parish. He immigrated to Kenosha Wisconsin around 1910. He was a machinist at American Motors Corporation. He married Stefania Atkuczunas on July 5, 1913. They had three children- Irvin, Richard and Irene. Jan died in June 1982 and Stefania died on October 10, 1991.
  - Piotr Dowgwillo was born in 1894 and died on April 4,1895. He was about 6 months old.
  - Antoni Dowgwillo was born on April 24, 1896 and died on March 10, 1897.
  - Stefan Dowgwillo was born on September 1, 1898. He married Stanisława Narbut on August 15, 1925 in Bejsagoła Parish.
  - Konstancja Dowgwillo was born on February 7, 1809 to Filip Dowgwillo and Petronela Downarowicz. She married Felicjan Lutkiewicz (1797-1863) on April 25, 1833 in Bejsagoła Parish. They had four daughters—Prakseda, Michalina Franciska, Kazimiera Wiktoria, and Marjanna Lutkiewicz before Konstancja died

on August 11, 1841 in Szwintupiein during childbirth.

o Antoni Dowgwillo was baptized on June 4, 1811 by Priest Francisek Penutoi. He was the son of Nobles Filip Dowgwillo and Petronela Downarowicz from Beymaymie Territory. His godparents were Nobles Stanisław Buynowski and Petronella Mieczyńska from Pociūnėliai (Lithuanian), or Pacunele (Polish), Parish.

From 1860-1865, Antoni was connected to the Onikszty Parish. In 1881, he lived in Malinówka (or the Małachówka Folwork) Siesicki Parish in Wilkomirski district. "Folwork" is a Polish word for a serfdom-based farm. These were large agricultural enterprises.

He married Józefa Nowicka, and they had the following children:

- Stanisław Dowgwillo was born on May 11, 1860 in Troupie, Lithuania.
- Joanna Dowgwillo was born on April 1, 1862 in Onikszty, Lithuania.
- Wincenty Dowgwillo was born on April 3, 1865 in the village of Szlawiany (Slavenai) near Onikszt and was baptized in Oniksztach Parish in Viłkomirski district. He married twice—first to Konstancja Plesmowicz (1870-1890), and second to Bronislawa Mackiewicz (1876-1927) in Kaunas.
  o Wincenty and Bronislawa had the following children:
    - Stanisław Dowgwillo was born on March 31, 1900 in Vilnius. He married Helena Buchowska and they had two children. Their daughter,

Irena, was born on January 1, 1922 in Vilnius and died on April 11, 2018 in Olsztynek. Their son, Zbigniew Ryszard, was born on July 12, 1923 in Vilinius and died on July 27, 1945 in the former Zeithain Prison. He was buried a day later at the camp cemetery in grave number 44 before his remains were transferred to Neuburxdorf Cemetery in 2004.

- Helena Dowgwillo was born October 30, 1901 in Vilnius. She married Stefan Iwanowski. Helena died on September 14, 1960 in Świebodzin, Poland and Stefan died on July 27, 1975.

- Jadwiga Dowgwillo was born on June 15, 1903 in Vilnius. She died on July 1, 1903 and was buried in Rossa Cemetery.

- Maria Dowgwillo was born on August 1, 1904 in Vilnius. She married Bazyli (Ogiejczyk) Puszkin on December 22, 1922 in Vilnius. He died tragically on November 19, 1958 during work when he was hit by a closing wagon door. Maria died on May 21, 1976. Maria and Bazyli are both buried at the "Srebrzysko" Central Cemetery in Gdańsk, Poland.

- Stefania Dowgwillo was born on August 8, 1906 in Vilnius. She married Mieczysław Niedźwiedzki on August 8, 1928 in the Church of Jacob and Philip. They moved to Szczecin Zdrojów. Stefania died in Poland on December 16, 1985, and Mieczysław died on July 7, 1983.

- Jan Dowgwillo was born on February 10, 1908. He married Katarzyna Żołnier on July 17, 1934 in Vilnius. They had three children—Arkadiusz Zenon, Mirosław Bronisław, and Bożena Anna. Jan died in 1971, and Katarzyna died in 1977 in Poland.
- Teodor Dowgillo was born November 9, 1909 in Vilnius. He died on February 24, 1914.
- Regina Dowgwillo was born on September 12, 1914 in Vilnius. She died on June 24, 1916.

Antoni died on November 2, 1887 at the Posada Folwork from tuberculosis. He was buried at the church in Siesiki, Wilkomirski district. Józefa died sometime after 1890.

- Teofila Dowgwillo was born on June 2, 1771 to Jakub Dowgwillo and Franciszka Iłgowska.
- Jan Dowgwillo was born on June 26, 1773. He married Barbara Gonkiewicz on October 13, 1794 and they had the following children:
  - Isabella Barbara Dowgwillo was baptized on February 25, 1797 by Priest Antoni Waluszwiez. Her godparents were Ignancy Laslawski and Rozalia Gonkiewicz.
  - Barbara Katarzyna was baptized on April 14, 1797 by Priest Antoni Waluszwicz. Her godparents were Nobles Ignacy Turynzynski and Barbara Pernowska, and witnesses to the baptism were MD Nobles Karol Karyzno and Anna Bowgonowa.
  - Dionizy Jerzy Dowgwillo was baptized on April 14, 1801 by Priest August of Krekenava (Lithuanian), or Krakinów (Polish), Parish. His godparents were Mateusz Ozynski and Brig Domazemiez.

○ Bartłomiej Kajetan Dowgwillo was born on August 24, 1803. He married Marianna Wojtkiewicz on January 28, 1835 in Krekenava (Lithuanian), or Krakinów (Polish) Parish. Bartłomiej died on July 27, 1848. They had the following children:

- Katarzyna Dowgwillo was born on May 2, 1836 in Kirkily.
- Konstanty Dowgwillo was born on July 23, 1838 in Kirkily. He married Bernarda Szulc. They had the following children:
    ○ Wladyslaw Dowgwillo (?-?) married Elżbieta Jocas (1888-?) on July 25, 1907 in Kurtowiany. They had four children: Zofia (1908-?), Waclaw (1910-?), Julia (?-?) and Elżbieta (1913-2000). Their daughter, Elżbieta Dowgwillo married Bronius Jonušas (1899-1976), a well-known Lithuanian composer. Elżbieta and Bronius fled Lithuania when the Soviets took over at the end of WWII. They became "displaced persons" or refugees in Germany before immigrating to the United States in 1949. They have descendants living in the United States today.
    ○ Maria Dowgwillo was born around 1883. She married Kazimierz Adolf Mackiewicz (1866-?) on October 14, 1907 in Poniewież.
- Barbara Dowgwillo was born on November 25, 1840.
- Franciszka Dowgwillo was born on October 2, 1843. She married Antoni Mozejko (1842-1889) on May 20, 1868. She died on July 22, 1886.

○ Karol Bartłomiej Antoni Dowgwillo was baptized on January 6, 1808 by Priest Stefan Sadowski in

Bejsagoła Parish. The godparents were Petrus Dowgwillo and Zofia Gonkiewicz.

- o Ignacy Dowgwillo born in 1812. He married Roza Domaszewicz on January 23, 1834 in Bejsagoła Parish, and they had the following three children:
  - Adam Dionizy Dowgwillo was born on May 25, 1836. He was sent to Siberia for his participation in the January Uprising but ended up in Kashgar. A well-known Swedish explorer, Sven Anders Hedin (1865-1952), traveled through the area and spent time with Adam. Sven wrote a book, *From Pole to Pole*, about his experience that included a story about how much alcohol Adam could consume and not become intoxicated. Adam died between 1895 and 1899 in Kashgar.
  - Józef Dowgwillo was born in 1841.
  - Konstanty Dowgwillo was born in 1848.
- **Petronella Dowgwillo** was born on June 24, 1775 to Jakub Dowgwillo and Franciszka Iłgowska. She married Antoni Mieczyński in Żagunie, and they had six children:
  - o Karol Mieczyński was born in 1784, and he married Karolina Lutkiewicz, the sister of Tomasz Lutkiewicz. Karol died on June 14, 1866 at the age of 80 from old age. He left behind his wife, Karolina, sons—Zygmunt, Ignacy, and Stefan— and daughters—Katarzyna and Elżbieta. He was buried on June 16, 1866 in Pacunele/Pociūnėliai Cemetery.
  - o **Barbara Mieczyńska** was born on November 8, 1801 and baptized in Krekenava (Lithuanian), or Krakinów (Polish), Parish. Her godparents were Józefat Narkiewicz and Marianna Dryziewicz. She married **Tomasz Lutkiewicz**, the brother of Karolina Lutkiewicz on November 3, 1825, and they had seven children—Konstanty Aleksander, Katarzyna, Agnieszka, **Adolf Mateusz**, Szymon,

Elżbieta, and Anna Lutkiewicz—before her death on March 21, 1837 while in childbirth.

- ○ Marianna Mieczyńska was born January 24, 1804 and baptized in Pociūnėliai (Lithuanian), or Pacunele (Polish), Parish. Her godparents were Jerzy Dowgwillo and Barbara Dowgwillo.
- ○ Józefa Mieczyńska was born on March 15, 1806 and baptized in Pociūnėliai (Lithuanian), or Pacunele (Polish), Parish. Her godparents were Mathias Ilgawski and Katarzyna Dowgwillo.
- ○ Franciska Mieczyńska was born on March 10, 1808 and baptized in Pociūnėliai (Lithuanian), or Pacunele (Polish), Parish. Her godparents were Wincenty Mieczyński and Magdalena Dyrzewicz.
- ○ Johanna Mieczyńska was born July 25, 1810 and baptized in in Pociūnėliai (Lithuanian), or Pacunele (Polish), Parish. Her godparents were Antoni Domapewicz and Franciska Towginowa.
- • Marianna Dowgwillo was born on March 10, 1777 to Jakub Dowgwillo and Franciszka Iłgowska.
- • Antonina Dowgwillo was born June 6, 1779.
- • Piotr Dowgwillo was born on June 27, 1780. He married Anna Wilgard (1778-1848) and they had at least seven children:
  - ○ Katarzyna Dowgwillo was born April 21, 1806 and died on October 28, 1816.
  - ○ Bonifacy Dowgwillo was born January 6, 1808.
  - ○ Marianna Dowgwillo was born on August 18, 1809. She married Stanislaw Rymkiewicz on April 14, 1828 in Bejsagoła Parish.
  - ○ Michal Tomasz Dowgwillo was born on December 20, 1813 and died on January 22, 1814.
  - ○ Barbara Dowgwillo was born on December 13, 1815.
  - ○ Wincenty Dowgwillo was born on January 10, 1819.
  - ○ Józefata Dowgwillo was born on March 27, 1822.

- Marianna Dowgwillo was born on August 4, 1782 to Jakub Dowgwillo and Franciszka Iłgowska.
- Jerzy Dowgwillo was born on April 13, 1784. He married Anna Rozwin, and they had at least two sons:
  - Florjan-Sebastian Dowgwillo was baptized on May 26, 1810 by Priest Francisek from Wołmontowicze in Bejsagoła Parish. His parents were Nobles Jerzy Dowgwillo and Anna Rożwin. His godparents were Ignacy Turnzyski and Flevia Stejgwillo, and witnesses to the baptism were Antoni Lushunewski and Anna Dowgwillo, all from Wołmontowicze in Bejsagoła Parish.
  - Ludwik Justin Dowgwillo was born in 1819.
- Józef Dowgwillo was born on March 15, 1786 Jakub Dowgwillo and Franciszka Iłgowska.

Józef's Fourth Son Mikołaj and His Family Tree

Mikołaj Dowgwillo was married to Magdalena, last name unknown. They had one son:

- Jan Dowgwillo was born on March 24, 1702. His godparents were Władysław Gowian and Joanna Żongołowicz.

On February 8, 1724 Jan Dowgwillo prepared and presented a purchase document in September of 1724 to the Raseiniai (Lithuanian), or Rosienie (Polish), Town Court of a property called Bierze (Polish), or Birzai (Lithuanian), located in Wielona (Polish), or Veliuona (Lithuanian), region. He acquired this property from Mackiewicz (first name unknown).

On March 23, 1768 Jan Dowgwillo prepared a will. Later that same year, it was presented in Raseiniai (Lithuanian), or Rosienie (Polish), Land Court. Jan gave his property to his son, Maciej Dowgwillo.

Jan Dowgwillo married Anna and had the following children:

• Maciej Dowgwillo was born on February 16, 1742 in Dotnuva (Lithuanian), or Datnów (Polish), Parish. His godparents were Jan Bobianowicz and Katarzyna Galewicz, and Jerzy Kasiunas and Krystyna Lencka.

On November 4, 1788, Maciej Dowgwillo prepared a gifting document for presentation in Raseiniai (Lithuanian), or Rosienie (Polish), Town Court in December of 1788. Maciej Dowgwillo inherited the land known as Bierze (Polish), or Birzai (Lithuanian), and one peasant from his father. He gave this land and peasant to his son, Jan, and made a provision that his other sons (Mateusz, Antoni, and Stanisław) were to receive money.

Maciej Dowgwillo married Dorota, née Mickiewicz. They had the following children:

 ◦ Jan Dowgwiłło was born June 22, 1765. His godparents were Franciszek Babiański and Anna Łowgiłowa, and the witnesses were Jakub Suchodolski and Katarzyna Mickiewicz. Jan married Helena Kontowt, and they had the following children:

  • Józef Jerzy Dowgwillo was born in 1798. He married Anna Radyk. He died on March 25, 1881 in Girże. Józef and Anna had the following children:

   ◦ Szczepan Klemens Dowgwillo was born in 1834. He married Eugenia Chomentowska on February 5, 1867 in Krekenava (Lithuanian), or Krakinów (Polish), Parish. They had the following children:

    • Stanisław Józef Dowgwillo was born November 11, 1865. He married Maria Rakowicz on February 7, 1895 in Surwiliszki. They had eight children – Piotr (1896-1920), Zofia

(1898-1973), Bronisława (1900-1958), Witold (1902-1988), Antonina (1904-1969), Jadwiga (1906-1986), Maria (1909-1979), Wanda (1913-2003).

Stanisław served in the Polish Soviet War. In 1919, he returned from German captivity and disappeared. His spouse placed announcements in the *Kurier Warszaw* on May 25,1922 in an attempt to find him, and Stanisław eventually returned. It seems he became an auditor in the income department of the State Railways in Radom. He died on February 16, 1924 in Warsaw, Poland and Maria died on November 29, 1951.

- Jan Dowgwillo was born around 1867. He married Barbara Pawlowicz on January 23, 1896 in Truskow.
- Stefania Dowgwillo was born around 1871. She married Stanisław Towiański (1861-?) on November 25, 1890 in Trusków. They had the following ten children:
  - Jaroslaw Towiański was born on September 5, 1891 in Szczukiszki, Lithuania. He married Karolina Senonis on February 7, 1910.
  - Helena Towianska was born on May 12, 1893. She went to the United States around 1910. Helena married Józef Bilida on March 6, 1916 in Detroit, Michigan, and they had eight children: John, Stephanie, Julia, Sophia, Joan, Helen, Frances, and Florence.

Helena died on February 19, 1967 in Detroit, and Joseph died in 1975. Their descendants are still living in the United States.

- ○ Józef Towiański was born around 1894. He died on June 26, 1898 in Szczukiszki, Lithuania.
- ○ Emeryk Towiański was born on April 13, 1898. He died on June 30, 1898 in Szczukiszki.
- ○ Ksawery Towiański was born in March of 1897. He died on March 20, 1897 in Szczukiszki.
- ○ Aniela Towiańska was born on September 6, 1899 in Szczukiszki.
- ○ Faustyn Towiański was born February 15, 1901 in Szczukiszki.
- ○ Michal Towiański was born on October 1, 1902 in Szczukiszki. He married Zofia Jukniewicz on July 8, 1924.
- ○ Zofia Towiańska was born on May 13, 1904 in Szczukiszki.
- ○ Władysław Towiański was born on June 19, 1905 in Szczukiszki. He married Genowefa Narwillo on October 25, 1932 in Vadaktai (Lithuanian), or Wodokty (Polish), Lithuania. He died on September 7, 1949.
- • Józefa Dowgwillo was born on March 14, 1877 in Daszkańce (Polish) or Daškoniai (Lithuanian).
- • Stefan Dowgwillo was born on June 1, 1879 in Bortkuny (Polish) or Bartkūnai (Lithuanian).
- ○ Jan Piotr Dowgwillo was born on June 21, 1815 to Józef Dowgwillo and Anna Radyk.

He and Kazimiera Ibiańska (1851-1902) were married on February 11, 1868 in the Roman Catholic Parish of Kowno by Priest Augustyn Strzedziński, after three banns on January 28, February 2, and February 4 announced to the people gathered at the liturgy.

Noble Jan Piotr Dowgwiłło was a 25-year-old bachelor and parishioner of Łonie filial church. Kazimiera Ibiańska was a 17-year-old maiden and was a parishioner of Kowno parish. She was the daughter of Nobles Kazimierz Ibiański and Teofila, née Doliński. Witnesses were Władysław Ejmont, Aleksander Żelnio, Piotr Radyko, and many others gathered for this occasion.

They had the following children:

- Feliks Dowgwillo was born on September 5, 1869 and died on March 16, 1871 in Wędziagoła.
- Władysław Dowgwillo was born on November 2, 1871 in the noble settlement Boniszki of the Wendziagoła Parish. He was baptized on November 17, 1871 in Wendziagoła Parish by Priest A. Stankiewicz with all rites of the sacraments. His godparents were Władysław Skirgajło and Józefa wife of Piotr Wysokiński, and they were assisted by Stefan Dowgwiłło and Teodora Michałowska. He probably died before 1893 because another son was born and given this name in 1893.
- Kazimierz Dowgwillo born in 1874. He married Ludwika Lutkiewicz (1884-1978) on February 7, 1906 in

Krakės (Lithuanian), or Kroki (Polish),
Parish. Kazimierz and Ludwika had the
following children:

- ° Bronislaw Dowgwillo was born on
  December 3, 1906 in Lelanwiszki.
  He died on September 18, 1986 in
  Toronto, Canada.

- ° Otton Dowgwillo was born on
  February 6, 1908 and married Ona
  Ona Jaruskaite on August 11, 1934
  in Poland. He died around 1946.

- ° Antoni Dowgwillo was born August
  10, 1909 in Ekście Lithuania. He
  married Alina Martyna (born in
  1905) in Poland.

- ° Stefan Dowgwillo was born on
  April 30, 1911 and died on May 2,
  1911 in Ekście, Lithuania.

- ° Katarzyna Dowgwillo was born
  in 1913. She married Felicjan
  Romaszkiewicz (1902 - 1975) on
  February 3, 1931 in Czekiszki
  (Polish) or Čekiškė (Lithuanian).
  She died on February 22, 1991 in
  Kaunas, Lithuaunia.

- ° Jan Dowgwillo was born in May
  of 1914 and died on December 4,
  1914.

- ° Weronika Dowgwillo was born
  on October 1, 1917. She married
  Walenty Butkiewicz on February
  18, 1939 in Czekiszki (Polish) or
  Čekiškė (Lithuanian).

- ° Kazimierz Dowgwillo was born in
  1923 and died in 1978.

- ° Donat Dowgwillo was born in 1926
  and died in 1989.

- Emilia Dowgwillo was born on August 17, 1880. She married Stanisław Żotkiewicz (1887-1932). She died on November 22, 1921 in Kruwondy (Polish) or Krūvandai (Lithuanian), Lithuania.
- Stefan Dowgwillo born May 20, 1876. He married Elżbieta Paszkowska (1886-1959) in 1919 in Kaunas.
- Jan Dowgwillo was born around 1880 and died in 1941.
- Władysław Dowgwillo was born on March 28, 1893 in the Jasnopole Estate and was baptized three days later in Wilkija (Polish) or Vilkija (Lithuanian) Parish by Vicar Kazimierz Skrypko with all rites of the sacrament. His godparents were Wincenty Rodziewicz and Leokadia, the wife of Zenon Dubiński.
- Aleksandra Dowgwillo—unfortunately her birth date is not known, but it was after her brother's birth in 1869. She married Władysław Adam Boharewicz (1863-?).
- Jadwiga Dowgwillo—her birthdate is not known, but it was after her brother's birth in 1869. She married Edward Lutkiewicz whose parents are unknown. They had the following children:
  - Stefan Lutkiewicz married Sabina Motowt.
  - Otton Lutkiewicz married Genowefa Siratowiczowna around 1942. He died on February 15, 1985, and she died on May 13, 2007. Genowefa was well-known in Poland for writing about the Soviet displacement of

people during and after World War II.

- ○ Henryk Lutkiewicz (?-?)
- ○ Władysław Lutkiewicz (?-?)
- ○ Zygmunt Lutkiewicz (?-?)
- ○ Mamert Lutkiewicz (?-?)
- ○ Janina Lutkiewicz (?-?)
- ○ Rozalia Dowgwillo was born on May 30, 1845 in Gojlusze in Bobty (Polish) or Babtai (Lithuanian) Parish to Józef Dowgwillo and Anna Radyk. She died on June 8, 1883 in Telziai (Polish) or Telšiai (Lithuanian), Lithuania.
- Ignacy Mateusz Dowgwiłło was born on August 25, 1798 to Jan Dowgwillo and Helena née Kontowt. His godparents were Wincenty Lewgowd and Anna Ryszkiewicz. The witnesses were Jan Kontowt and Józefata Rogowska. He married Eleanora Pietraszewski (1803-1844), and they had the following children:
    - ○ Wincenty Dowgwillo was born on April 7, 1824. His godparents were Józef Piskorski and S. Kilnicka, and the witnesses were Józef Dowgwiłło and Teodora Jatowtówna. He married twice. His first marriage was to Tekla Czechowicz (1831-1856) on February 10, 1853 and his second marriage was to Franciszka Mojrzyrlówna (1834-?) on January 29, 1857. Wincenty died on March 19, 1887.
    - ○ Józef Dowgwillo was born on April 9, 1829 in Bierże. His godparents were Franciszek Konopinski and Eleonora Konopinska. He married twice. His first marriage was to Pelagia Milewicz (1830-1889) on February 5, 1852 and his second marriage was to Katarzyna Janajcew (1848-?) on September 20, 1892 in Krakes Parish.
    - ○ Wincenty Aleksander Dowgwillo was born around 1833. He married Aleksandra Tracewska on November 20, 1860. They had

five children – Mamert Antoni (1863-1926), Teodor (1865-1924), Karol (1868-1947), Konstancja (1870-1874), Józef Leopold (1873-1938), and Wincenta (1877-?).

Mamert and Karol immigrated to Baltimore Maryland in the late 1890s, changed their last name to Deugwillo, married other Lithuanian immigrants and had children. Mamert married Jadwiga (last name unknown) and Karol married Maria Anna Jędruszkiewicz (1873-1959). They are all buried in the Holy Rosary Cemetery in Maryland. Their descendants live in the United States today.

- Józefat Dowgwiłło was born April 4, 1801 1798 to Jan Dowgwillo and Helena née Kontowt. His godparents were Jan Babiański and Anna Rogowska.
o Mateusz Dowgwillo was born on September 22, 1776 to Maciej Dowgwillo and Dorota, née Mickiewicz. His godparents were Antoni Rogowski and Ewa Mickiewicz. He married Felicjanna Zdzitowiecki, and they had the following children:
  - Zygmunt-Mateusz Dowgwiłło was born on February 12, 1810. His godparents were Antoni Dowgwiłło and Klara Szalkowa, and the witnesses were Franciszek Zdzitowiecki and Katarzyna Dowgwilanka (unmarried variant of Dowgwiłło). He had the following children:
    o Ignacy Dowgwillo was born on February 2, 1835.
    o Francizek Dowgwillo was born on March 2, 1837.
    o Józef Dowgwillo was born on March 18, 1839.
  - Jan Piotr Dowgwiłło was born on June 24, 1815. He was the son of Mateusz and Felicjanna, née Zdzitowiecki. His godparents were Ignacy Jatowt and Rozalia Zdzitowiecka.
  - Florian Szymon Dowgwiłło was born on October 19, 1819. His godparents were Ludwik Jasubowicz and Teofila Dowgwiło.

- ○ Stanisław Dowgwillo was born on June 2, 1788 to Maciej Dowgwillo and Dorota, née Mickiewicz.
- ○ Antoni Dowgwillo was born to Maciej Dowgwillo and Dorota, née Mickiewicz.

EPILOGUE

There is always more to do in genealogy—another record to find, another connection to make. The struggle to compile my findings in a way that is interesting to my other family members not-so-interested in genealogy is a goal I find worthwhile to pursue, and hopefully, this is meaningful to them.

What prompted me to write this at this time was the loss of my cousin, Tom Lucas, to Covid-19 in December 2020. I knew Tom all my life as my Great-Uncle Tony's son. He was born in Gary, Indiana and moved to California with his parents, siblings, and my great-grandmother when he was eight. He graduated from Fresno State and worked at Valley Chrome, the business started by his dad and my grandfather. He was married and had children and grandchildren. He had a larger-than-life personality: he didn't know a stranger, was a master scuba diver (accomplished over 750 dives all over the world) and had the Lucas sense of humor.

Back Row: Cathy, Tom, Eileen, Eva Duoba, Ray, Claire
Massart, Tony, Fran Stone, George, Greg Lucas
Front Row: Christine and Matthew Lucas

What I didn't know was how he defended his sister, Christine, when they were young. Christine had gotten beaten up by a bully living on their block on Richert Street in Fresno, California. When she got home, Tom saw her crying, found out what happened, and went after the bully. Tom dragged the bully home, pounded on the front door and told the bully's dad to keep his son away from his sister, or he would come and pound the dad. I also didn't know how instrumental he was in redirecting the family business in 1990 to focus on the manufacturing end. These were some of the stories shared at his memorial service. I wanted to make sure that the stories I have about other family members get passed on sooner rather than later.

ENDNOTES

1   Geni Lithuanian Nobility. https://www.geni.com/projects/Lithuanian-Nobility/49949

2   Ibid.

3   Wikipedia. History of Lithuania. https://en.wikipedia.org/wiki/History_of_Lithuania

4   Ibid.

5   Ibid.

6   Ibid.

7   Wikipedia. Suwalki. https://en.wikipedia.org/wiki/Suwa%C5%82ki

8   Ibid.

9   Gaidis, Henry J. A Hundred Years Ago Lithuanians Americans Joined the Struggle For Lithuanian Independence, *Draugas News*. http://www.draugas.org/news/a-hundred-years-ago-lithuanian-americans-joined-the-struggle-for-lithuanian-independence/#:~:text=The%20Third%20National%20Congress%20of,the%20government%20formed%20under%20it.

10   Wikipedia, History of Lithuania. https://en.wikipedia.org/wiki/History_of_Lithuania

11   Ibid.

12   Ibid.

13   (2020 April 12) 1918 Flu Roared Through Steubenville Area, *Harold Star Online*, 1. https://www.heraldstaronline.com/news/local-news/2020/04/1918-flu-roared-through-steubenville-area/

14   Ibid.

15   Ibid.

16   Ibid.

17   Ibid.

18   (1949 July 29) Confessed Con Man, Pal Held to Jury $4600 Atomic Fraud, *Chicago Tribune*, 21. https://www.newspapers.com/clip/67295573/charles-lucas-court/?xid=637&_ga=2.4398517.727571245.161025

0739-1331647476.1601249408

[19] Wikipedia. Russon Turkis War. https://en.wikipedia.org/wiki/Russo-Turkish_War_(1877%E2%80%931878)

[20] Wikipedia. Collectivization in the Soviet Union. https://en.wikipedia.org/wiki/Collectivization_in_the_Soviet_Union

[21] Wikipedia. Population Transfer in the Soviet Union. https://en.wikipedia.org/wiki/Population_transfer_in_the_Soviet_Union

[22] (1963 October 31) Antone J. Atkoncunis, Of Cedar River, Dies, *The Menominee Journal*, 1.

[23] (1973 January 8) Lt. Col. Dougoveto Dies Suddenly, *The Menominee Journal*, 2.

[24] (1969 February 6) Walter Dougoveto Dies, *The Menominee Journal*, 1.

[25] (1975 May 1) Final Rites Wednesday for Joseph Dougveto, *The Menominee Journal*, 1.

[26] (1960 May 12) John Stravinski Drowning Victim, *The Menominee Journal*, 1.

[27] (1969 January 2) Mrs. Lawrence Hupy Dies in Marquette, *The Menominee Journal*, 1.

[28] (1917 April 8) Man Held For Murder of Woman, *The Philadelphia Inquirer*, 3. https://www.newspapers.com/image/169042790/?terms=%22walush%22&match=1

[29] (1947 November 19) Fairview Man Ends Life After Bludgeoning Wife, *Courier Post*, 1. https://www.newspapers.com/clip/66361389/suicide-of-anthony-gestite/?xid=637&_ga=2.44495521.461096804.1614041069-1331647476.1601249408

[30] Sea Service Record, Swadis, Michael, File Number 318198.

[31] Allen, Robert E., *The First Battalion of the 28th Marines On Iwo Jima: A Day-By-Day History*, McFarland and Company, ISBN 0-7864-0560-0, 1999, pp. 41-43, p. 414.

[32] (1956 April 23) Obituary Felix Dowgwillo. *The Bristol Daily Courier*, 3. https://www.newspapers.com/clip/62691213/obituary-for-catherine-mitchel/?xid=637&_ga=2.12802609.727571245.1610250739-1331647476.1601249408

[33] (1930 December 27) Farmer Kills Self in Barn. *The News-Palladium*, 3. https://www.newspapers.com/clip/67226273/michael-dongvilla-suicide/?xid=637&_ga=2.18118079.727571245.1610250739-1331647476.1601249408

[34] (1969 August 29) Mrs. Dongvillo 69 Drowns in Canal. *The South Bend Tribune*, 1.

[35] (1987 May 30) Adolf Dongvillo Retired Farmer Dies at 91. *The Hearald Palladium*, 12. https://www.newspapers.com/image/365976274/?article=46f2dcfd-8b79-4817-aaaa-1400e5a7139d&focus=0.03744453,0.07236921,0.19999738,0.3353404&xid=3355&_ga=2.101003783.727571

245.1610250739-1331647476.1601249408

36 (1993 March 18) Edward Vetort Jr., *The Menominee Journal*, 2.

37 Northern Michigan Wildcats Hall of Fame https://www.nmuwildcats.com/ SportsHOF

38 Ken Gunderman (1944 February 3) The Sports Parade. *The Escanaba Daily Press*, 10. https://www.newspapers.com/image/33909435/?terms=%22francis%20 Vetort%22&match=1#

39 (2009 April 22) Francis J Vetort, *The Peshtigo Times*. http://www.peshtigotimes. net/?id=11468

40 (1956 February 19) Watts and Polio Meet Today Handball Final, *The Courior Journal*, 33. https://www.newspapers.com/clip/67434486/ herman-vetort-and-handball/?xid=637&_ga=2.17635775.727571245.161 0250739-1331647476.1601249408

41 Record Group 338: Genearl Orders 3rd Infantry Division Boxes 129-131 – National Archives and Records Administration, College Park, Maryland. http://www.valerosos.com/1stLt.HermanJ.Vetort.html

42 (1974 March 15) Rotary Will Hear Unit Commander From Fort Hood, *Waco-Tribune Herald*, 36. https://www.newspapers.com/clip/67434910/ col-herman-vetort-ft-hood/?xid=637&_ga=2.8738483.727571245.16 10250739-1331647476.1601249408

43 Record Group 338: Genearl Orders 3rd Infantry Division Boxes 129-131 – National Archives and Records Administration, College Park, Maryland. http://www.valerosos.com/1stLt.HermanJ.Vetort.html

44 Prabook.com https://prabook.com/web/herman_joseph.vetort/507998

45 (1987 March 18) Obituaries Stanley Walter Grigal, *Mesabi Daily Times*, 13.

46 Ibid.

47 (1982 October 13) Obituary Raymond E Sanders. *Baxter Bulletin*, 6. https://www.newspapers.com/clip/67063203/obituary-for-raymond-e-sanders-aged/?xid=637&_ga=2.32194554.535522402.1609720569-1331647 476.1601249408

48 (2005 September 13) Obituary Mildred Gostow Sanders. *Baxter Bulletin*, 2.

49 (1964 April 24) Chrysler Plans Casting Plant Ground Breaking. *Indianapolis Star*, 35. https://www.newspapers.com/image/105284570/#

50 (2003 December 21) Obituary Driskell Evelyn Lousie. *Chicago Tribune*, Section 4 9. https://www.newspapers.com/image/232067967/?terms=EVELYN%20 L%20DRISKELL&match=1

51 Wikipedia. Second Battle of the Marne. https://en.wikipedia.org/wiki/ Second_Battle_of_the_Marne

52 Wikipedia. Argonne Offensive. https://en.wikipedia.org/wiki/Meuse%E2%8 0%93Argonne_offensive

Lightning Source UK Ltd.
Milton Keynes UK
UKHW010116300721
387973UK00001B/17